Letters from Windermere, 1912–1914

LETTERS
from
WINDERMERE

1912–1914

Edited by
R. Cole Harris
and
Elizabeth Phillips

University of British Columbia Press
Vancouver
1984

© UBC Press 1984
Reprinted 1991
Printed in Canada on acid-free paper ∞

This book has been published with the help of grants from the
Canada Council and the British Columbia Heritage Trust.

ISBN 0-7748-0214-6 (cloth)
ISBN 0-7748-0394-0 (paper)

Canadian Cataloguing in Publication Data

Philips, Daisy, d. 1960.
Letters from Windermere, 1912–1914

(The Pioneers of British Columbia ; 5)
Letters written chiefly by Daisy Phillips.
Includes index.
ISBN 0-7748-0394-0

1. Phillips, Daisy, d. 1960. 2. Frontier and
pioneer life – British Columbia – Windermere
Lake Region. 3. Windermere Lake Region (B.C.) –
Biography. I. Harris, R. Cole. II. Phillips,
Elizabeth, 1913-   III. Title. IV. Series.
FC3845.W5Z49 1984   971.1'45   C84-091554-3
F1089.W5P49 1984

UBC Press
University of British Columbia
6344 Memorial Rd
Vancouver, BC V6T 1Z2
(604) 822-3259

Printed and bound in Canada
by John Deyell Company

CONTENTS

ILLUSTRATIONS

MAPS

PLATES *following page 118*

The Owl and the Pussy-cat went to sea
In a beautiful pea green boat
They took some honey and plenty of money
Wrapped up in a five pound note. . . .
They sailed away for a year and a day
To the land where the Bong-tree grows,
And there in a wood a Piggy-wig stood
With a ring at the end of his nose.

EDWARD LEAR

Something of this is being heard, I am
not merely talking to myself, that is in the
wilderness, a thing I could never bear to do
for any length of time.

SAMUEL BECKETT
Happy Days

INTRODUCTION

These letters from the Windermere Valley of southeastern British Columbia, written just before the First World War, describe the establishment of a
short-lived English home in a Canadian wilderness. Most of them are by a
newly married Englishwoman, Margaret Ann Dionysia (Daisy) Phillips; a
few, by her husband, Captain John Noel (Jack) Phillips. All were to sent to
Daisy's mother or sister who lived in Windsor, England, when the letters
began.

The Phillipses were middle-class people trying to create a home in one
place out of values that came from another. Their letters, probably like
many others that have not survived, reveal this attempt from the inside and
with great clarity. Other immigrants brought other values, but all have
faced, with the Phillipses, the problem of adjusting the memories of old
circumstances to the realities of new ones. In this sense the meaning of these
simple letters is general as well as particular. They tell the story of the in-
tersection of an English dream with the Windermere Valley and also
something of the story of all immigrants to any new settlement in Western
Canada. Moreover, the Phillipses, who planted fruit trees where they could
not be grown and faced recall to an English regiment as the First World War
loomed, were far from the first or the last to turn their hopes and energies to
a project that by force of circumstances beyond their control could not suc-
ceed. Between the idea and the shadow in their case lay almost three years in
Windermere.

The Phillipses were part of an educated and increasingly mobile middle
class for whom emigration to the United States or the British colonies was a
possible solution to the problem of earning a living in England. Raised in
some comfort, often in large families, such people were accustomed to a
standard of living and social status that a divided, frequently belated inheritance could hardly sustain. Perhaps there was a position for one son in a

father's business, but probably not more at a time when business management was becoming less familial. The professions were also increasingly competitive as more people received good educations and family name began to count for less than examination results. Overall, there were more educated people than positions for them, and therefore many felt that their talents or social expectations had inadequate outlets. For middle-class women, who considerably outnumbered their male counterparts in England at the beginning of the twentieth century, long term prospects were particularly curtailed: marriage, tending an aging relative, teaching, perhaps nursing.

At the same time dislocation was becoming normal. Children were sent away to school, and adults, especially in the middle class, less commonly lived where they had been born. People moved in changing social circles defined increasingly by class and less by regional background. Almost everyone had friends or relatives in America or in one of the colonies. Army, government, and church sent many people abroad, where they often lived with inexpensive servants and exclusive clubs. When they returned, England may not have seemed quite the same and their place there less comfortable and secure. For middle-class people the idea of emigration was in the air, and in the three decades preceding the First World War, they comprised almost 30 per cent of all emigrants from the British Isles.

Most of them sought professional, clerical, or business opportunities in cities overseas—positions for which they were well trained and lacked sufficient English opportunity. Some turned to land and agriculture, a respectable outlet for people accustomed to status and perhaps ill-equipped for business or the professions. In England the countryside had long attracted middle-class nostalgia—and many a son with an urban inheritance. The images of village, yeoman, local gentry, and hunt were, as they still are, powerful English variants of the agrarian myth. An "estate," or a farm, in Hampshire, the Cotswolds, or Western Canada (or in Australia, New Zealand, or South Africa) was an appealing prospect, and agricultural labour on one's own land was socially acceptable. When advertising and comfortable steamship sailings made distant pastures appear the more accessible, many middle-class people emigrated, transplanting a retrospective English vision thousands of miles from England.

Such, generally, were Jack and Daisy Phillips. He came from a London family who had been grain and coal merchants in Knightsbridge for three generations. His father, Thomas Edward Phillips, largely dissipated a considerable fortune, much of it going to assemble and maintain a mounted company of the Volunteer Queen Victoria's Rifles. Thomas Edward had three sons, Francis, Jack, and Kenneth, and they spent much of their childhood in Heston, Middlesex (now part of greater London), on "the Vicarage Farm," where their father employed a dozen men and seven boys, kept an emu sent by a relative in Australia, and supplied the army barracks at nearby Hounslow and the family business. In 1887 the farm at Heston was given up, and two years later, when Jack was fourteen, his mother died. His father took to drink, married his housekeeper, and was considered a family disgrace. Neither his sons nor his sisters had much more to do with him, and when he died (while Jack and Daisy were in the Windermere), most of his little remaining money went to his second wife. Jack and his brothers had been sent to a small and, as it turned out, rather poor school in Brighton run by a family friend, George Oxley (Daisy's uncle). Jack wrote the entrance examination for the officers' college at Sandhurst, failed mathematics (perhaps because of his schooling), and in 1895 at nineteen years of age took the Queen's shilling, and, to what must have been the horror of his family, enlisted as an ordinary soldier in the Devonshire Regiment. In 1900 he was commissioned as a 2nd lieutenant, transferred to the Lincolnshire Regiment, and sent to South Africa, where the Lincolns were one of the regiments formed into the Mounted Infantry to cope with the fast-moving commandos of the Boer army. He was in several engagements, including the Battle of Spion Kop and the Relief of Ladysmith, and was wounded. After the war he served for three years in Uganda and the Sudan in the King's African Rifles, and he was then posted to Gibraltar, from where he made occasional visits to England. By 1912 he had not lived in England for a dozen years. He was estranged from his father, had no connection with a wealthy uncle who had gone into brewing and had sold out, very profitably, to Watneys, and faced a chorus of straight-laced paternal and maternal aunts who disapproved mightily of his father and remembered Jack's own inauspicious entry into the army.

Daisy was born and raised in Windsor, daughter of Frederick Oxley, owner and publisher of the *Windsor and Eton Express*. With her five brothers and sisters she grew up in a narrow, four-storey, early nineteenth-century house on High Street. Both she and her younger sister Freda were sent to a boarding school in London, and the boys (Stanley, Stewart, Arthur, and Gilbert) to the Brighton school run by their Uncle George. Stanley, the eldest son, took over the newspaper after his father's death in 1902. The other boys eventually left Windsor, Stewart for Malaya. The girls, unmarried, lived at home. Freda had attended the Slade School of Art in Bloomsbury and then studied landscape painting at the Newlyn School of Art at Penzance, Cornwall. She won prizes for her drawing, but her artistic career went no further. Both she and Daisy had travelled a little on the continent. Not wealthy, the Oxleys were a respected business family; Daisy, who was thirty-five when she married Jack, had lived almost all her life with the gossip, clothes, servants, and etiquette of Windsor's middle class.

Frederick Oxley and Thomas Edward Phillips had been friends at Oundle Public School in Northamptonshire; their sons knew each other at school in

Brighton. After Jack's mother died, Daisy's mother apparently took a special interest in him. He wrote to her several times from Africa, and when on leave in England he visited the Oxley family in Windsor. In 1912 he was thirty-seven and eager to marry, but having been abroad so long, he cannot have known many English women. Daisy was an obvious choice. There was not much money—a little capital from ivory obtained on East African hunts, a modest pension if he resigned from the army. At the Canadian Pacific Railway Company offices at Charing Cross in London, Jack saw an attractive pamphlet, based on an article in *The Field* magazine (February 1912), that described the Windermere Valley in the Kootenay District of southeastern British Columbia. There for about £1,000, which must have been approximately what Jack could raise, it claimed that a man could acquire land, build a house, establish an orchard, enjoy good hunting, and live peacefully amid beautiful surroundings. It was a vision of home for a homeless man, and he made up his mind quickly. He proposed to Daisy, and not wanting to tell his relatives that he had decided to resign his commission so that he could go to British Columbia to become a fruit farmer, persuaded her to keep the engagement secret from his family. He conceded reluctantly that her own family would have to know, and her mother, sister, and eldest brother attended their wedding in London at St. Gabriel's Pimlico. They spent their honeymoon in London shopping and saying good-bye to their friends and relatives before they sailed on the *Empress of Ireland* from Liverpool on 9 April 1912, bound for Windermere which, then, was not much more than a name on the map of British Columbia. It lay in the broad, deep trench between the Rocky and Purcell Mountains, not far from the headwaters of the Kootenay and Columbia rivers, ninety miles from a railway and about one hundred-fifty miles as the crow flies west of Calgary (Map 1).

In 1912 British Columbia was at the end of a decade of orchard land promotion and full of agricultural talk. In the southern interior commercial orchards had been planted on low land beside Okanagan Lake in the 1890's, and shortly after 1900 land companies began developing the benches above the lake and building irrigation works. Okanagan apples won prizes at major exhibitions, including each year from 1906 to 1909 the gold medal for apples awarded by the Royal Horticultural Society in London. Optimism was unqualified, and during the years from 1906 to 1908 development spread to the West Kootenays where promoters acquired land along Kootenay Lake and attracted settlers to prospective fruitlands that, rather than the mines that had launched the first Kootenay boom, were portrayed as the real wealth of the region. The fruit boom reached its extreme about 1910 when young graduates of Eton and Marlborough, many of them problem sons of titled families, began arriving at the Marquis of Anglesey's estate on the Thompson River near Kamloops; there Chinese workers built flumes and laid out orchards while young Englishmen played polo and drank ginger beer. The bottles were made for them in England. By 1911–12 when the fruit land promotions reached the Windermere Valley in the East Kootenays, there was abundant evidence that orcharding in British Columbia was not straightforward—frost damage, orchards dying inexplicably, serious blights where there had been none initially, inadequate irrigation. But at a time of general provincial optimism and rampant speculation, agricultural enthusiasm was undaunted. Participating in the boosterism of the day, the government published a *Handbook of British Columbia* (1913) which stated categorically: "It is now an established fact that apples of excellent quality will grow as far north as Hazelton on the Skeena River between 55 and 56 degrees north."

The pamphlet that had attracted the Phillipses was a clever example of the widespread, often fraudulent, orchard land promotions in British Columbia before the First World War. It was written by Robert Randolph Bruce, mining engineer, land promoter, and former C.P.R. land agent, who eventually became a lieutenant-governor of British Columbia. Bruce had come into the Windermere in 1897 as an employee of the C.P.R., and as the fruit boom developed elsewhere, he recognized that the Windermere benches, too, could be subdivided into farm lots and promoted as orchard land. To this end he organized the Columbia Valley Irrigated Fruit Lands Ltd., acquired land from the C.P.R., arranged to advertise it in England through the C.P.R.'s Land Department, and set out to attract people like the Phillipses.

Bruce's pamphlet and article worked only too well, bringing more settlers in the spring and summer of 1912 than the company had anticipated, some of them on the *Empress of Ireland* with the Phillipses. On the pamphlet's cover a pretty young mother and cherubic child, both in English fashions, were framed by boughs laden with apples. Inside, watercolours in an English style showed sailboats on a lake rimmed by mountains, bungalows with English cottage gardens, cattle grazing on newly cleared land—a roughened version of the sweeping English park—and a well-dressed lady under a laden apple tree on an "old-time Miner's Ranche." A panorama announcing "Windermere, British Columbia: Orchards, Sports, Homes" combined the best of two valleys: the mountain grandeur of the Windermere and the settled benches of the Okanagan two hundred miles to the west. No one in England would spot the deception.

In the text Bruce, describing himself as an old timer, told of the early mining excitement, the miners' inadvertent plantings, and their eventual realization that the valley's real wealth lay in agriculture. For years the Windermere was an idyll awaiting development:

We felt we were wasting time in the valley, but yet we could not tear ourselves away from it. We tried strawberries and found them luscious and plentiful. We tried hens and turkeys, pigs and sheep, to find a fuller purse and a better table. We gave up buying canned vegetables, and raised our own tomatoes, asparagus, celery, and green peas, and when we were not busy we would go off back into the hills and replenish the larders with deer or bear, blue grouse or partridge, or get a boat and go up the lakes hunting the wild duck and geese amongst the bulrushes at the southern end of Windermere Lake. When the cold weather began to set in in November, and just after we got the first fall of snow, that was when we went back after deer; and a glorious time we had when we would gather round the camp fire at night after a big day's hunt. Then on the Windermere Lake after the frost came, we had a beautiful sheet of ice for skating and ice-boating. We found that though the temperature would go down to 20 or 30 below zero, the air was dry, and kept the system tingling with life. We were full of energy and bustling over with health, and just had to be doing something. Then we would get a fall of a few inches of snow, and the jingle of sleigh bells would be heard all through the valley. Perhaps a week or two later the great Chinook wind would begin to blow, warm and soft, and would lick up the snow and leave all bare and open again. In the spring we would all be busy in our gardens and fields, and the open, parklike country would be carpeted with wild flowers.

But now, according to Bruce, the isolation was over. A railway connection to the C.P.R. mainline at Golden was virtually built, the "endless" prairie market for fruit was close at hand, and tourists would soon "leave behind dollars in the pockets of the thrifty poultry wife." Institutions and services were available, even scientific agricultural advice from a government experimental farm. There were settlers of the right type, men who had shot tigers in India and enjoyed a game of polo on the newly laid-out ground. The land company had built irrigation canals and opened up the benches for settlement at £10 to £30 an irrigated acre. The valley was in the making, bustling and growing, yet retaining its peaceful calm. "Yes, it is a beautiful valley . . . ," concluded Bruce, "its beautiful sun-lit glades shortly to be perfumed with cherry and apple blossom, and may those new to it find in it as much pleasure in the future as this 'Old timer' has experienced in the past."

The pamphlet implied — without being so ill-bred as to say so directly — that the ingredients for successful settlement by people of the right sort were all at hand. It made what was unfinished or uncertain, which was virtually everything in the valley, seem settled and accomplished. The railway to Golden, apparently all but completed, would not open until 1917; the irrigation canals, apparently built, were at least a year behind the Phillipses. The myriad problems of determining what varieties grew best, adjusting sen-

sitive crops to largely unknown environments, mastering benchland irrigation, and then of finding markets and developing institutions that would
enable individual growers to reach them profitably, lay ahead, unan-
ticipated. Although a few apple trees had survived on protected sites near
the lake, no one really knew whether commercial orcharding was feasible.

Farming in the Windermere Valley was an economic adventure for which
the Phillipses were even less prepared than the land company. Jack knew
nothing about farming; Daisy, nothing about housekeeping. Committed to
Windermere from the time he left England, Jack regretted not arriving a
week earlier, brushed aside criticism of the valley, and bought almost immediately. Four days after arrival they were camped on their own lot,
twenty-eight acres of forested, unwatered benchland at the edge of a steep
ravine above Toby Creek, a small tributary of the Columbia River (Map 2).
They understood that a flume would be built to provide irrigation and
domestic water and that the land was suitable for orcharding. In fact, at
3,200 feet above sea level, the winters were too long and severe and the
growing season too short for apples. They were camped in a place they did
not know, that required skills they did not have, and that was climatically
unsuited to the main crop they were trying to grow. They paid to have some
things done—a little clearing, some fencing and ploughing, a bungalow
built—but labour was scarce and expensive and much of the work had to be
their own. Somewhat obliquely the letters tell the story: books on farming;
water belatedly available; crops doing less well than expected; sales of a few
head of lettuce, a few dozen eggs (not enough to pay for chicken feed), and a
small crop of clover; growing disenchantment with the Columbia Valley
Irrigated Fruit Lands Company and, eventually, a Settlers' Association
formed to fight it; at the end, horticultural advice sent to England; but never
anything like a commercial farm. At most, although they had not realized it,
they were creating a small, subsistence holding.

Moreover, Jack was a soldier. He had told his wife on their wedding day
that a soldier's first duty was to his regiment. He knew, and she knew,
where his responsibility lay in the event of war, and they arrived in Windermere less than two-and-a-half years before the start of the First World War.
There was nothing they could do to affect the course of European events,
and for the most part the letters push off the prospect of war. When it came,
the only question was when they would leave.

Although the Phillipses' Windermere years were doubly fated, their lives
turned on other assumptions. They were creating a home. Until the last
months agricultural problems and war were far in the background, and
their letters revolve around the practical, psychological, and cultural problems of home in a strange place. This is their great interest. On the ship and

only hours from England, Daisy could feel that "me is gone"; later, on their land in Windermere, new surroundings only stiffened her resolve to be English. "I feel quite sure that I have not altered and never shall." Canadian locomotives, like Canadian mountains, "are magnificent and fill one with admiration," but they were not loved. Rather the sound of English parish bells lurked in new air, and memories returned to the privet hedges and "all the soft green" of "fair, dear England." Canada was "not England and Canadian ways and people are totally different in nearly every way." Daisy, especially, had to deal with this discordance. She was not a thinker about the world and would not do so analytically. But her chatty correspondence, full of impressions, ordinary details of daily doings, and shopping lists, revolves around her challenge of homemaking in British Columbia and enables us to understand it a good deal more clearly than she did herself.

Daisy did not want to change. She and Jack had come to Canada to live English lives, and she was full of the assumptions and prejudices of her background. Letters became her lifeline back to this familiar world. With a lag of two weeks, they connected Windermere and Windsor and the newly married Daisy to people she knew far better than her husband. She wrote avidly and was often exasperated when Jack imposed rest on scarce letter-writing time. English letters were devoured, especially for homey doings and at the beginning when there was not much else to hold on to. Her own correspondence was largely about the everyday details of her new life, written without pretention to close relatives. Less crafted and theatrical than Susanna Moodie's letters from pioneer Ontario and never intended for the public, Daisy's are probably even closer to the psychological bone. She loved to hear of everyday English doings because her own life had suddenly lost this context; she described her Windermere activities less to report novel experiences than to reassure her relatives, and herself, that familiar ways could be transplanted. In sum, although Daisy never thought quite this way, the letters describe her coping with the particular alienation born of migration to a new land and were themselves a large part of her unconscious strategy for survival.

Building and furnishing a house was another. If the larger environment did not conform to memories of England, a house could be built and furnished to do so, and Daisy threw her energies into this focussed, reproducible England. Their house, built during their first summer in Windermere, was a bungalow, a style from British India popularized before the First World War. The furnishings came, crated, from Windsor or from the Army and Navy Stores in London; the arrangement was to be "artistic," which to Daisy meant Arts and Craft and a dash of Art Nouveau. Material for curtains and covers would come from England, preferably from Liberty's, a fashionable London store in Regent Street. The letters are full of the details. Dress, too, could be controlled. Daisy enjoyed clothes, had no intention of conforming to "tasteless" Canadian standards, and dressed carefully on her limited budget. Shopping lists sent to her obliging sister Freda maintained the English supply.

The larger social environment also lent some English comfort. Most of the orchardists were English, drawn by the publicity that had attracted the Phillipses and from approximately their class. In the valley were public school and Oxbridge educations, retired generals and admirals, tons of English furniture, and wives used to servants and ready to commiserate about the problems of life without them. Some of these people were passing through, adventuring for a time in Windermere, and some others who intended to stay soon found pioneer orcharding more than they could handle and left. Yet most settled down, friendships formed, gossip circulated, and teas, the occasional dinner, and the even more occasional party maintained social conventions. As often elsewhere in Canada a considerable edge of European gentility had penetrated the wilderness. The Christmas party given by General and Mrs. Poett, to which Daisy walked terrified across a frozen lake, was finer than any she remembered in Windsor. But, especially for women, connections outside the house were difficult and sporadic. Rural telephones were not yet in the valley and nearest neighbours were long walks away; it was an event when someone dropped in. For the first year the Phillipses did not have a horse, and when Daisy became pregnant her movement was much curtailed by doctor's and husband's orders. In these circumstances, her defence of the England she knew rested principally on household and letters.

It was a difficult defence eight thousand miles from home. More than perhaps anything else, the cost of Canadian labour stood between the Phillipses and the life they would have liked to lead. For three hundred years in pioneer agricultural areas in North America, the high cost of labour had posed a problem for those not accustomed to using their own. Unlike European colonies in Africa or Asia, there were not ready supplies of native workers, while the relative accessibility of land raised the cost of immigrant labour, often to several times its European value. For people like the Phillipses who could not afford these labour costs, the alternative was to work themselves. This was Daisy's predicament. Caught between the cost of labour and a middle-class, Edwardian (and, with her husband, a military) standard of correctness on a pioneer farm before the advent of labour-saving appliances, her life was consumed by domestic work that in England a woman of her class would never have done. At first, while living in tent or barn, English standards could be relaxed. Life was almost a picnic. Later, in a house intended to be a permanent home and as English as possible, they had to be maintained. So Daisy worked—usually not unhappily—to uphold a symbol. Between her initial request for a pamphlet on the laundering of handkerchiefs and her departure less than three years later, she had learned to cook on a wood stove, sew, clean a house, and wash clothes without running water, electricity, or servants. As long as there were only the two of them, she could just manage (with some help from her husband on washdays and with the floors). In the evening they dressed for dinner, dined with silver and china, and then Daisy scrubbed the pots. There was no margin. Her life was filled with husband and house, and when a baby came either standards would decline or help had to be found. Resources were stretched to their limit and servants did come from England, first Molly Gleave, a nurse with hospital training who had spent some time on a farm in Alberta, and then Amelia Harris, the Phillips family's nurse. Neither worked out very well. The house was too small, its occupants too set in their ways and too inclined to bring English memories of service to bear on a small house in the wilderness where people were on top of each other and domestic standards were symbols of home. The long and short of it was that English service was hardly reproducible in the Windermere Valley and this alone put enormous pressure on middle-class English lives.

There were other problems, equally basic. In the Windermere Valley Englishness was suddenly an identifying characteristic in a society made up of people of different ethnic backgrounds. Daisy, herself, began defining people as much by ethnicity as by class. English and Canadians were her main social groups. The latter tended to come from Ontario or the Maritime provinces, to be of Irish or Scottish descent, and to be products of two or three Canadian generations of rural or small town life. Their experiences, and that of a middle-class English woman raised in the shadow of Eton, Ascot, and Windsor Castle were very different. In Canadian eyes many ways of people like the Phillipses were simply ridiculous, whereas Canadians, Daisy thought, had no taste or sense of deference. The two groups judged each other by different standards. There were others culturally even farther removed: "Chinks," native Indians, a few Swedes. Stray Austrian and Italian counts (who worked as carpenters) and especially the mannered, wealthy Poett family (with German relations) tended to be assimilated in an English definition of the better sort of people. Not in the Windermere was the range of English social classes, the people who knew their place. Hence, as Daisy remarked to her sister, being poor "does not make a bit of difference socially to us which is a great thing out here." Abstracted from England, Englishness itself became a badge; most of the fine gradations of English social stratification could not be reproduced because the society they defined was absent.

Nor were the institutions that, in England, supported middle-class life. The few stores in the valley did not have the right goods or goods of the right quality. The Eaton's catalogue served for a sewing machine, but not for anything fashionable. Even string had to come from England. Bruce's pamphlet had mentioned polo, but the letters do not. In the Windermere sport was an individual rather than a collective activity, and the English clubs were absent. In Daisy's eyes the minister of the Anglican church was a boring Canadian, certainly not one to encourage an English sense of belonging. And there was the problem of school: well brought up English children could not be sent to Canadian schools. If the Phillipses did not yet face this problem, some of their friends did. As in other things, there was one standard, and it was English.

But the Phillipses' setting was not English, least of all their physical environment. The birds did not sing with English voices or the grass grow with English green. The mountains were grand but foreign, and there was so much unused space. Daisy and Jack lived as would have been impossible in England: a good walk through virgin forest to nearest neighbours, three miles down a dusty road to a new village of wooden buildings of western North American style. Mountains and emptiness were all around. The lush, composed, picturesque, English landscape—the past that was impregnated in it and the aesthetic values that composed it—were gone. In the Windermere the Phillipses were surrounded by undigested nature interrupted by a few modern works including their own tiny patch of attempted Englishness. They were players without most of their props.

In short, the letters reveal some of the pressures for social and cultural change that would begin to reshape English lives in the Windermere Valley. Even in two-and-a-half years the changes were considerable. By the time she left Daisy probably coped almost as well in the kitchen as the Canadian wives whose practical skills she had initially admired. Both she and Jack were increasingly involved with Canadians, he in the Settlers' Association (formed as agricultural problems and the exaggerated claims and prices of the land company became more obvious), and she, at the end of their stay, in women's war work. However woeful Daisy considered Canadian button holes, the barriers between people of different cultures were beginning to break down as they lived with each other and coped with many of the same challenges. But the most striking changes followed from the Phillipses' very defence of their Englishness. In their new home behaviour that was implicit in England had become explicit; put another way, the Windermere Valley had tended to reduce the whole array of custom to a leaner selection of symbols.

This, in a sense, had happened to their marriage. When Daisy and Jack married and emigrated to Canada, they detached themselves—and their marriage—from a social context and, in so doing, threw themselves particularly together. Tucked away on a farm lot in Windermere without close neighbours and no old friends, and with extended families in England, their marriage virtually filled their daily social space and bore much of the brunt of the pressures for social change in their new environment.

Fortunately, their views of marital roles approximately coincided. Both assumed a patriarchal household, which Jack interpreted against military standards of spit-and-polish and punctuality. Daisy, who like her husband had no use for the suffragettes, brought a more homey vision—no doubt what she had known in Windsor—that placed her in charge of domestic arrangements within her husband's overall charge of the family. When Jack ordered, Daisy obeyed, usually happily enough. But their personalities were very different. Jack was shy, reserved, and formal, not a talker. After years in the army and a family life that had ended, to all intents and purposes, almost twenty-five years before when his mother died, he did not quite know how to deal with people. Daisy was far more ebullient, made friends easily, talked readily about the doings in her world, and enjoyed clothes and company. He reflected the ordered, male loneliness of army life overseas, and she the bustle and gossip of Windsor.

The two fitted very happily together. Daisy was ready to accommodate army standards—which as regards cleanliness and order were not too different from her own—and if an open window at 30° below was a little more than she could handle, indirect comments from her sister in a letter to Jack would eventually close it. By the end of their Windermere stay, he was beginning to accept the noise and disruption of a baby. But the whole Windermere undertaking imposed very differently on each of them. For Jack marriage made a home where there had been none. By transferring his marriage to British Columbia he perpetuated both the exile from England that had long been familiar to him and much of the hearty open air life that he had known in Africa. The weeks of tenting, so novel to Daisy, were familiar enough to him. Essentially Jack had added a wife and home to a robust, out-of-doors life where, or so he hoped, he could still hunt, ride, and enjoy some social standing. Farming was new, but it was an adventure full of fresh air and exercise. He and most of the men of his background loved the Windermere. Daisy and most other English wives were more ambivalent. She had left home, friends, and servants in Windsor. In Windermere the sexual division of labour placed her in a house, there to establish and maintain a home to English standards in pioneer conditions. Other wives were in the same boat. They worked, saw each other rarely, and when they did their talk was wont to drift away to a gentler England of servants and leisured ways. The Windermere Valley, they understood, was just fine for their husbands.

When the First World War was declared, the Phillipses knew that they would leave. Daisy loved her Windermere home and Jack had spent the happiest days of his adult life there, but duty was duty and they would go. They lived on edge, Jack chafing to get back to his regiment, hearing of friends called up and killed, and waiting for the telegram. When it came just before Christmas, 1914, they left quickly, packing the things they had so recently unpacked, opening parcels from England, dashing off a final letter, and leaving behind the empty shell of their New World home. Back in England Jack reported to his old regiment, the Lincolnshires, and was soon posted to France. Daisy smuggled herself on the troop train at Waterloo Station and rode with him to Southampton. In early April he was wounded at Hill 60 during the first battle of Yprès. A leg was amputated but gangrene set in, and he died in the army hospital in Boulogne on 18 April 1915. Daisy, who had managed to obtain permission to visit her wounded husband, was at his side. In the June dispatches he was cited for most gallant and distinguished service.

Daisy never returned to the Windermere, although until her death in 1960 she corresponded with friends she had made there. After the war the lot on Toby Creek was sold for far less than Jack had paid for it. Eventually the house was torn down. The fruit trees died, and apart from a garden, no one tried again to farm the land. Jack's capital had gone into Windermere, and Daisy was left with no money or occupational training and the paltry pension of an officer's widow. For a time she worked in a military hospital and eventually took charge of the cooking, employing some of the skills she had learned in Canada. She and her daughter Elizabeth lived in a succession of small apartments and for some years in a small house near Oxford. Elizabeth received a good education because one of her father's regimental friends paid the school bills that Daisy could not afford. Later Elizabeth, like her aunt Freda, was trained as an artist. Over the years she and her mother lived intermittently together in London, occasionally seeing Amelia Harris who, when in her eighties, was killed during the blitz of London in World War II. For Daisy the Windermere interlude, when she and her husband had tried to establish a farm where they could not, became the golden time of her life. Her retrospective vision of Windermere and Robert Randolph Bruce's clever promotion of it converged in the end.

The letters from Windermere were kept by Daisy's sister Freda and given to Elizabeth when Daisy died. In 1966 Elizabeth sent them to the Provincial Archives of British Columbia in Victoria. A dozen years later, while investigating one of the Kootenay mining booms, I encountered them there, felt they reflected a quality of our Western Canadian experience with unusual poignancy, and wrote to Elizabeth Phillips. We soon agreed that the letters should be edited and published. Elizabeth has furnished photographs and many long letters and commentaries filled with insight about her parents and their world. Patricia Startin, my secretary at the time in Vancouver, greatly assisted us both as we jointly edited and lightly footnoted the letters, and I have written this introduction. The letters are not quite as Daisy and Jack wrote them. We have corrected spellings, capitalized and punctuated more consistently, shortened the run-on sentences that Daisy was wont to write, and imposed paragraphs on pages of uninterrupted script. We have eliminated some repetitions and some references to people in Windsor who could not be identified — but not all lest Daisy herself be misunderstood. A few lines have been omitted for personal reasons at Elizabeth Phillips' request. All these deletions are marked with ellipses. Long before the letters were sent to the Archives in 1966, some details of family finance, early references to Daisy's pregnancy, and a block of letters from the six months surrounding Elizabeth's birth were removed. What remains, then, is not the complete correspondence from Windermere to Daisy's mother and sister in Windsor, but quite enough to take the reader well inside the expatriate minds of two English people who lived for a time in British Columbia.

In many ways these minds were very narrow. Dominated by the pretentions and mores of the English middle class and quick to assume that what was different was inferior, they were products of the England of their day, of the late years of an empire that sent English people around the world and then drew many of them back to fight. Yet the Phillipses' challenge of homemaking in a strange place has been the challenge of almost all immigrants to Western Canada. Daniel Harmon, a New Englander living with a Cree wife at Fort St. James shortly after Simon Fraser established it, also struggled with the conflicting realities of different homes and finally sent his half-breed son away to New England where the little boy soon died. Jack Hodgins' wild Irishman Keneally or Joy Kogawa's Obasan, indeed most of us when we think about it, have faced the same problem in a place that, apart from its indigenous few, is not much older than the Phillipses' coming to it. In Eastern Canada, too, where the generations have built up a little, the implications of coming to terms with here when what one really knows is there are only slightly more buried. It has been almost inevitable, as with Susanna Moodie in Margaret Atwood's interpretation of her, to deny the ground we stand on. Finally, and at yet another scale, there are placeless elements in the Phillips letters that lie somewhere between Edward Lear and Samuel Beckett and have to do with courage, fate, and the ironic joys of life. Daisy was Pussy-cat and also Winnie, buried in the sand, and the short Windermere years were her Happy Days.

Cole Harris
University of British Columbia
February, 1984

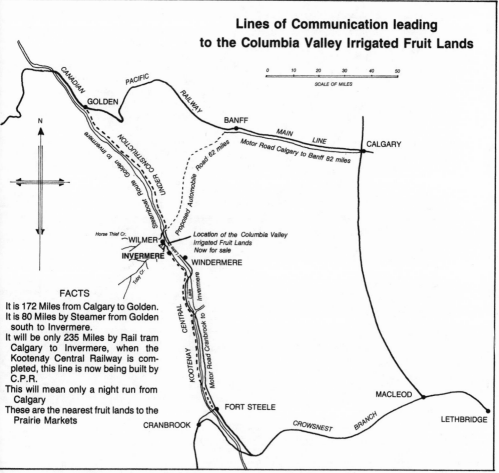

Lines of Communication leading to the Columbia Valley Irrigated Fruit Lands

0   10   20   30   40   50
SCALE OF MILES

N

CANADIAN PACIFIC RAILWAY

GOLDEN

BANFF

MAIN LINE

CALGARY

Motor Road Calgary to Banff 82 miles

Proposed Automobile Road 62 miles

Steamboat Route Golden to Invermere

UNDER CONSTRUCTION

Horse Thief Cr.

WILMER

INVERMERE

Location of the Columbia Valley Irrigated Fruit Lands Now for sale

WINDERMERE

Toby Cr.

River

Lake Invermere

KOOTENAY CENTRAL

Motor Road Cranbrook to Invermere

FORT STEELE

CRANBROOK

CROWSNEST BRANCH

MACLEOD

LETHBRIDGE

FACTS

It is 172 Miles from Calgary to Golden.
It is 80 Miles by Steamer from Golden south to Invermere.
It will be only 235 Miles by Rail tram Calgary to Invermere, when the Kootenay Central Railway is completed, this line is now being built by C.P.R.
This will mean only a night run from Calgary
These are the nearest fruit lands to the Prairie Markets

Redrawn from a 1910 CVIFL Co. map in the Provincial Archives of British Columbia

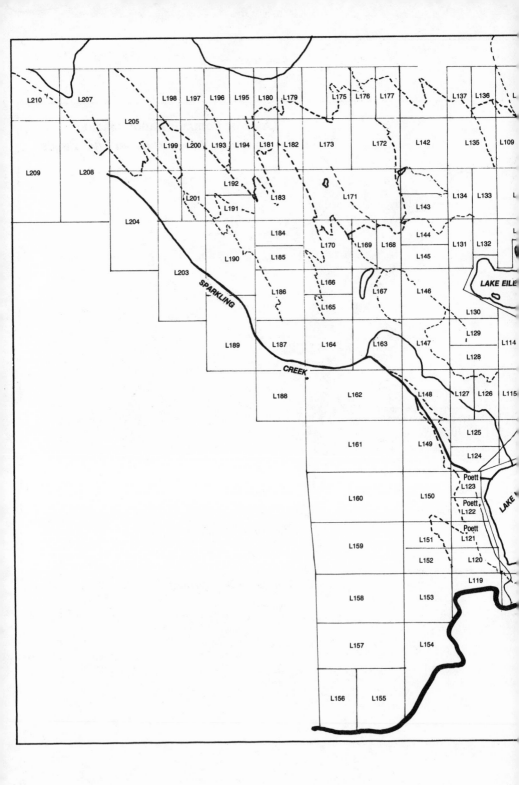

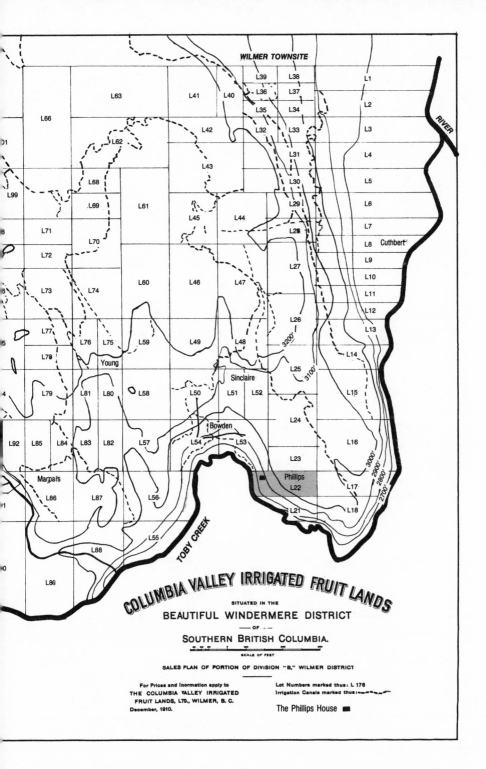

Redrawn from a 1910 *CVIFL Co. map in the Provincial Archives of British Columbia*

LETTERS *from* WINDERMERE

CANADIAN PACIFIC RAILWAY,
ATLANTIC SERVICE,
R.M.S. EMPRESS OF IRELAND
APRIL 6th, 1912

My dearest Mother and All,

Here I am on board the ship and can hardly imagine it really is me. I thought of you all a great deal yesterday but all the same I felt glad that there was nobody to see us off. I got through it alright as it was but I am sure I should not have made such a good start. Jack's eyes simply were sparkling as he thought of being on "the wander" again, and so I managed to choke down my feelings. The boat train went in two parts. Our seats were in the second train, so we did not leave Euston until 12:30. The good Mrs. B. cut us three packets of sandwiches which we enjoyed very much en route, and we got to Liverpool at 5 o'clock. We got our luggage on board and Jack rushed off to get me a postcard to send to you. Before he could get back to me we were off, and that is why you did not hear. I felt very sad about it, but have been extravagant and sent you a wireless this morning to make up. Thank you ever so much for you letter, Mother, and for the wires. I also had letters from Nelly, Auntie Louie, and Mrs. Dainty, which was very sweet of them. There was a lovely box of flowers—lilies and violets—in my cabin at Liverpool. I expect Elsie was the kind friend who sent them. After dinner I found another box in my cabin from you, so the cabin is gay with flowers.

It was smooth last night and I managed to sleep fairly well to the noise of the rush of waves past the porthole. There is a vibration under the berths all the time as if at any moment you may go "up aloft." Jack sleeps on the "top side." He got up this morning at 6:30, as he thought, for his bath, and when he came back announced the fact that the clock was back an hour, so it was only 5:30! However, even at that hour the steward brought in tea and "he" went for a walk on deck for an hour while I read the *Strand* magazine. And then I was pulled out of bed to be ready at the first chance of breakfast. Meals are most wonderful things, and if you like you could eat enough to last you for twelve months, I am sure! Minced veal and poached eggs, sausages and mash, steak and onions for breakfast. How Stewart[1] would enjoy it!

We have been marching round the deck for an hour and now I am sitting in the sun and writing to you. The sea is a glorious blue-green, and on my left is the coast of Ireland, very plain and clear; the waves have white tips and although there is a stiff breeze there is no swell. I only hope it continues, but we are not in the open ocean yet. I think we are on the sea until Thursday. After all "from land to land" is four days, but there were two days in sight of land as well. I keep on thinking how you would enjoy it, and I keep on picturing Freda[2] on her way to see me, but expect that is a long way off yet. I wonder about sending *Punch* out every week. We did not order it as we forgot, but perhaps the family would enjoy it and send it on to us. . . . As I sit here, I can hardly believe it is "me." In fact, I am sure "me" is gone and it is a fresh somebody. . . . The music salon and the writing and reading rooms on board are most luxurious and fitted up like a palace. I don't suppose I shall spend many minutes in them, though, as Jack's craze is fresh air. Please tell the boys how very much we enjoyed the dinner at the Coliseum the other night, but I could not thank them properly at the time. It will be nice to look back upon.

Sunday. How are the mighty fallen! After lunch yesterday the ship began to roll and I began to be very ill. I went and lay down in my berth until 5 o'clock, and then sat on deck feeling very funny until 8:30, but went to bed and was again very ill. This morning could not face breakfast, but Jack insisted on my getting up at 10:30 and coming into the fresh air and I am gradually reviving. I had two inches of cold chicken (on deck) for lunch, and the boat is certainly steadier than it was. The boards of the deck seem to jump up into your face and bang your nose, but I am *not* the only one who is seedy. We do not get to Canada until Friday after all as we are using Canadian coal and only running at 16½ knots an hour instead of 20. Tell Freda I live in my fur coat and continually bless her!

Wednesday. I felt fairly seedy on Monday and again yesterday, and all I wanted to do was just to sit still. I know Mary and various people on board with whom to chat, but there are no other women going to Windermere on this boat. However, Jack has discovered two men going who are not bad, and the wife of one is coming out two months later. Will you tell me where the medical book is when you write as Jack asked if I had got one? Is it in the wooden box? — though I don't suppose we shall be able to touch that for

1. Stewart Oxley, an elder brother.
2. Daisy's sister, the youngest in the family.

some months to come. I expect I shall always be looking for things I cannot find and yet know we have them.

The twelve o'clock bell has just gone. We have a bugler for meals, but I am sorry to say I do not love the sound. My staple lunch is a little cold chicken, a thing I usually rather dislike! The sun is shining today and the water is deep blue and looks fairly smooth, but the boat keeps on slowly and *deeply* swinging through the rollers. I am no sailor bold. But it might be a great deal worse!

Thursday. We had an exciting day yesterday watching icebergs—but it was terribly cold. They were just fine!

This has to be posted early tomorrow. Am feeling better today.

Much love to all, and write.

Daisy

CANADIAN PACIFIC RAILWAY,
ATLANTIC SERVICE,
R.M.S. EMPRESS OF IRELAND
11 APRIL, 1912

Dear Mrs. Oxley,

We will probably reach Halifax tomorrow and though Daisy has written you a long letter you will probably want one from me too, to say how Daisy is. For the first twenty-four hours we had perfect weather, and up to that time all went well. Beyond refusing to read her letters and telegrams that awaited us on the ship I don't think she showed any signs of homesickness, and was always keenly looking forward to each day of the journey. We have had a first-rate voyage, and with the exception of one day no signs of roughness, but always a big swell which has made several people ill and prevented nearly all the ladies from attending meals. Poor Daisy was no exception. Most of her breakfasts were in bed, and her luncheons on deck, but I think she always managed to come down to dinner even though she didn't eat much. The long time on short food has pulled her down a bit, and if she doesn't pull up on the train I shall stay at Montreal, Winnipeg or somewhere and give her a complete day's rest; but they tell me the train waits often a couple of hours at some places, and Daisy, who is very much against stopping anywhere, says this will be enough for her. She says she has stood the journey very much better than she expected to, and better than she has stood any other—which I believe is not saying much—but she is not the worst sailor in the 1st Saloon by three or four at least. She has always managed to be at least six hours on deck—usually ten—and has done a good deal of walking up and down, and writing.

All other news will be give. you by Daisy herself.
Best love to all.

Yours,

Jack

My dearest Freda,

I had intended writing a few lines every day, but with the jolting of the train I have found it rather impossible. The last day on board ship was Friday, and being fairly smooth I managed to enjoy it for at last I had got to know quite a number of people on board. We stayed at Halifax to put off the mails, but only saw the place from deck at 7:30 in the morning. We got to St. John early Saturday, and had breakfast soon after 7 o'clock. Our train did not go very early as we are 2nd class, and so Jack and I went off and explored the town. My first impression of a Canadian town was certainly disappointing, such a mixture of the finished and unfinished. Certainly a great impression of dust and dirt, and the painted wooden houses in a fair-sized town look strange. The roads are all dust and not paved, but the atmosphere is very clear. We landed in brilliant sunshine, though it was very cold and I wanted my fur coat.

Most of our friends on board ship, or all I should say, were 1st class and all went on at once, but we did not start until 12:00 o'clock in the morning. Jack discovered a Mrs. Young and her two little boys and a baby girl on board ship going out 2nd class to join her husband, Captain Young, out in Windermere, so we went down and offered to give her a hand, for which she was very grateful.[1] Her hands are more than full, as you may imagine, as her boys are a perfect "packet." Mrs. Young is a very delicate woman so I think we were a bit of help. It is nice to know somebody *nice* on the train as most of the folk are of the farmer order, and the carriages, etc. are not at all luxurious; but I am keeping fit and have been able to eat on the train. We get out at various stations and have a walk up and down, and we are able to buy bread, etc. We have just had lunch (currant bread and potted meat, apples and chocolate, ending up with a cup of tea), and the "infuser"[2] is of the greatest value, tell Mother. Tea is evidently "the drink" of Canada, and as

1. The Youngs will play a part later in these letters. Mrs. Young, daughter of a canon at St. Paul's Cathedral and able to trace ancestors on both sides back to the Domsday Book (A.D. 1088), was married to a retired army captain. Descendents still live in the Windermere Valley.
2. A gadget like a double spoon with holes punched in it, that could be filled with tea and immersed in a cup of hot water.

beer is 1/- per bottle on the train Jack feels he cannot afford luxuries. We have breakfast and an evening meal in the dining car, but we feel we must be economical. The whole thing is really great fun, and we shall laugh at it all later on. There are cooking stoves at the end of each car and the folk camp out and fry sausages, and bacon and eggs, etc., and a good many of the women put on overalls and tackle things. Our lunch basket is a great comfort. The sleeping arrangements are really most amusing as the seats are made into beds and curtains are let down, but you see a leg going into a trouser suddenly come out under the curtain or a lady doing her hair is suddenly exposed to view. Jack chuckles at it and thinks it very primitive. I feel with him I am well protected, but when Freda comes out she must come 1st class, where it is quite nice.

There are four girls on board ship, all going out alone to see friends in different parts. The Captain looks after you, and you soon make friends on board ship. I picked up a good many hints from people who live out West, though not in our part. The only thing is to write home for everything, I am told, even in the way of lengths of ribbon and lace, etc. for trimming. Little things that are flat come out easily by parcel post. There is the Express Delivery Company for urgent things, and try the C.P.R. It will take 14 days for you to get a letter or for me to receive one, so I must get used to thinking in advance.

It is very wonderful to see these immense tracts of land and so few houses and people. We started in hilly country with fir trees, and quantities of water and lakes everywhere. Of course, just now they are all frozen, but the rivers are just beginning to melt, and such rivers and lakes you never saw. We are just passing the Ottawa River, frozen like a huge ice-field, and a winter road across marked by fir trees. I left writing yesterday as the train was jolting so very much, and here we are again today, still moving on. We are nearing Lake Superior and the country is hilly, as it nearly all has been so far. It is more of the nature of the Chobham Common[3] than anything else I can think of. There are fir trees everywhere, and what look like silver birch. No leaves yet, of course, and mostly brown undergrowth; though where there is grass it is "dirty" colours, and the snow is lying everywhere in patches. We continually pass rivers, very wide as a rule and all frozen, and many lakes; all of them are very broken in shape and have many little islands about. There are huge stone boulders of white and reddish stone in all the country we are now passing through. We go miles and miles, with no sign of a hut or house and no people, but the sun is shining and the vastness of everything is wonderful after the size of England. I am travelling in the train quite well for me, and only get a little headache at times. All the same, I shall be glad to get to Golden and see what our part of the country is like.

3. An area of heathland south of London.

We have to pass through miles and miles of prairie before then, however, and we only hope we shall pass through the Rockies during the daytime. There are black men on the train who make up the beds. Jack complained he was not called early this morning, and the man said, "I call you early, Massa, but you was in dreamland!" It is much warmer today, and we have just had 15 minutes to walk up and down a wayside station—which was lovely, I can tell you. Mrs. Young's little boys are fine pickles, but they stand a little bit in awe of "Captain Phillips," I think which is a good job for their mother. We hear the Columbia River is not open yet. If so, we shall have to motor from Golden, but of course now the ice is melting fairly quickly. We are stopping in a few minutes at a small station, so I will post this and continue later.

Very much love to you all.

Your affectionate sister,

Daisy

I had this note-paper given me by a friendly official on board the train and it may amuse you!! Quite American swank!

GOVERNOR-GENERAL'S CAR,
APRIL, 1912—WEDNESDAY.

My dearest Mother,

The train seems fairly still this morning so will try and send you a few lines more. After I last wrote we got to the borders of Lake Superior. The line follows round the lake for some long way and the scenery is very beautiful. The lake is not one lake, apparently, but many, all connected. They are such beautiful shapes. They are broken with islands in the middle on which grow numerous fir trees, and the effect is very pretty. The shores are more or less hilly, and mostly of rocky formation. I should say the highest is about 600 feet, but the fir and larch trees seem to grow on a handful of soil. Of course, it was all frozen when we passed. Halfway down we had a snowstorm, and when it was over the *whiteness* of the snow everywhere was very beautiful in the sunshine. We keep on stopping at little places, and get about ten minutes to stretch our legs and buy bread. They are mostly lumbering stations, and the men are very weird. Some of them look quite wild. With their tanned faces and rough skin coats and caps they remind me of the men we saw in Holland, as well as the type of man too. I am sure we should rave about the scenery if we had a few miles, but when you get hundreds you somehow get used to it, and it will be even finer when the ice has melted. We got to Winnipeg at 2 o'clock yesterday, and only had time to send you a card as we changed trains there, and have now got a much more comfortable one. The railway station was magnificent, and the station-master came up and had a chat about England. He was going to take us over the station hotel, which is a wonderful place and well worth seeing, but "all aboard" was cried, and up we had to get. There are no whistles on the trains here, but each engine carries a huge bell and you hear a train coming far off by the booming of the bell. The engines of the trains are most magnificent things, about three or four times as big as the Great Western Railway ones, which seem like toys in comparison. These are all black and dirty, like so many things in Canada, but they are magnificent and fill you with admiration.

Every place was full of the terrible disaster yesterday,[1] and we do feel and are thankful we are safe. In all probability it was some of the same icefloe or field. We realized that our ship suddenly changed its course and went right south. We were then only 400 or 500 yards from the huge icefield in which were many huge bergs, and we were many hours passing it. The cold was intense, and I have never felt anything as icy as the wind. Our Captain was very worried and said he had never seen ice so far south before. Luckily for us, we passed it nearly all before night, and we did not get into the fog which they usually get, but of course the crew were prepared and all on the look-out. The Captain told me that sailors "smell" icebergs miles off.

I am getting used to the train and have not felt very seedy at all, but I shall be glad to get there now. We are now travelling through miles and miles of prairie. It has quite a fascination of its own. There are farms just here and there, and it is slightly undulating all over. The sunset and sunrise were very magnificent, deep rosy red. The air is very fresh, but when the sun shines you soon warm up. We get to Calgary tonight at 7 o'clock. We are going to get out and have a few hours' sleep in a bed, and then go on at 3:30 in the morning so as to pass through the Rockies by daylight. We get to Golden at 10 o'clock in the morning and Windermere in the evening. It is difficult to write with talking all round.

I have a small girl I dress in the morning as she has no mother. The Brand's Essence[2] has come in, too, for a girl on the train who is very ill.

Much love to all,

Daisy

---

1. The sinking of the *Titanic*.
2. Brand's Essence of chicken or beef, a jelly that was considered very nourishing and suitable for invalids or for those unable to take solid foods.

HOTEL INVERMERE
INVERMERE, B.C.
APRIL 20TH, 1912

My dearest Mother,

Let me see, where did I get to? I think we had got to Lake Superior or beyond, and then of course we got to Calgary. We arrived about 7 o'clock in the evening, and after booking our luggage we had a walk round the town and went to a café for dinner à la Canada. I never enjoyed a meal so much as I was on "terra firma" once more. They put the train into a siding and told us we should go on at 3 o'clock the next morning. However, when we woke at 7 o'clock we were still in Calgary, so up we got and sallied forth for breakfast in the town, as they told us we had 40 minutes. We were just going into the café when a lady rushed in after me and said, "You are Miss Oxley, aren't you?" It was Miss Edwards, the Reverend Gilbert Edwards' (Canon of St. George's) eldest daughter. She made herself most affable. She was only passing through Calgary with her brother with whom she had been staying in China. Wasn't it funny, but it was awfully nice to see a familiar face from the "Old Country," as it is always called. Calgary is quite a nice place, and growing like wildfire. I met Mrs. Pryce-Jones on the boat, and she says her husband is simply making a fortune.[1]

We left Calgary at 8 o'clock, and then I had one of the days of my life. The scenery through the Rockies is the most beautiful and glorious you can possibly imagine, and when you are passing through it all day at the rate of 40 miles an hour you simply cannot imagine the size and vastness of it all. There is a wonderful spiral tunnel that is a marvel of engineering skill,[2] and the Kicking Horse Pass is too glorious for words. Switzerland is a tiny little place on a postage stamp after it all, and to think this is where we are going to live! Golden is quite a primitive little place like a small Swiss village, but we had a good hot bath in the hotel, had some dinner and then to bed. Captain Young met his wife here so her troubles were over, poor little woman. It was very nice to have made her acquaintance, as doubtless she will be within several miles of us. Her husband has been out here some little time, and has got his land cleared and the barn built for them to live in for a start.

We started from Golden at 8 o'clock on Friday morning (breakfast everywhere here begins at 7:30 so I shall have to reform). The boats have not begun running yet as the snows have not melted and the river is not full enough, so a motor brought us and the Youngs here. We were only allowed a bag each so we had to leave all our boxes behind. But I am gradually altering all my ways, and by the time you next see me I shall be a very different person, I am sure! The process takes place slowly but surely, and you

---

1. Pryce-Jones, a prominent Calgary merchant of Welsh background, ran a flourishing mail order business.
2. The Connaught Tunnel.

gradually find yourself altering. We had 90 miles to come from Golden — as Jack says, the farthest I have ever been from a railway! The scenery was lovely the whole way as the valley runs between the Rockies and the Selkirks. You have snow-peaks on each side, and the country is like Chobham Common or Bagshot[3] with the river running through as well, and the colours like Switzerland. The railway follows the river all the way along for the first 40 miles, but that is as far as they have got at present. However, it will be here in 18 months. If you and Freda come next May or June you will come by the river, which is a most lovely trip. They hope the boat will run next week. It was a glorious motor run — but the road! We were bumped up and down, and rushed round corners. But it was a very power-ful car, and we came along in grand style and took all the hills at full speed.

We arrived here, *Invermere*, at 4:30, and this will be our address. Not Windermere. So please alter the address. It is a most lovely spot, like Lake Windermere in England, with snow-peaked mountains on each side of us, and the air is dry and clear. The hotel constitutes the place chiefly at pre-sent, but there are heaps of people buying land every day so in 12 months I am sure it will be "a place." There is a Captain Robinson[4] and a Mr. Bowden from Reading here. Do the boys know the name? There is Captain Young and family, and a General also in the valley already, and although far from the hotel I know I shall be very happy.

Will continue later. We still depend on "home" for all papers and news, and shall look for the mail day.

Love to all,

Daisy

P.S. I shall have to wash, so will you see if you can find me a handbook, a small one, on the subject, and ask Mrs. Lakewood how to wash handker-chiefs. I have soaked them but they will not come quite clean. Do you soak in cold or hot water, and do you use salt in the water?

G. A. Starke, Manager
HOTEL INVERMERE

INVERMERE, B.C.
20 APRIL, 1912

Dear Mrs. Oxley,

Here we are, more or less at our journey's end. From start to finish of a

3. Part of the heathland near Chobham Common south of Windsor.
4. Captain Robinson was a bachelor and retired army captain who would return to England at the start of the First World War.

very tiring and at times very uncomfortable railway journey Daisy didn't show the slightest signs of fatigue, and though she says now she is very glad it is over she is looking quite fit. We have got as far as we intend going and will probably settle here.

We arrived yesterday afternoon and I intended going round to see land to-day, but the motor which was to take us broke its axle as the last passenger stepped into the car so our ride is postponed till tomorrow. There were only about five occupants of the farm lots of Invermere last year, but I should say at least sixty have been sold this month. I regret not having come out a week earlier as some of the best plots have been taken up. It is impossible to give any opinion of the place. One man you meet says it's a terrible place where fruit trees won't grow and where nothing that was advertised in the pamphlets is ready. Another will say the soil is excellent but it will be a good time before profitable farming will take place. The scenery is certainly splendid and all that is written in those pamphlets will be true in about a year's time; but the place has grown quicker than they expected and they are not quite ready for us. There is a party of three men and two ladies who have taken a big lot, and the senior member of the party, a Mr. Bowden, has farmed a good deal in England. He has advised me to take a plot next to him and is coming out tomorrow to help me select land. He is a first-rate chap and I have a good deal of confidence in him,[1] so shall probably settle on "Lot 22." It is a little more than I expected to give, but with an experienced man as a neighbour I feel inclined to pay the extra amount. There will be plenty of people all round who are all more or less financially situated as we are, but servants, white or yellow, are quite out of the question. There aren't any and we shall have to do all our housework ourselves, but everybody is in the same boat and the only two ladies I have heard of here at present—wives of a General Poett[2] and a Captain Young—both undertake it cheerfully. I take it Daisy will too. There will be many other ladies in the place shortly.

Your affectionate son-in-law,

J. N. Phillips

1. As it turned out, this confidence was misplaced. As the letters will tell, Mrs. Bowden was too frail for pioneering, and neither she nor her husband would live long. The Bowdens were sad, early casualties of the English venture in Windermere.

2. The Poetts, were well off, educated, and refined. Daisy would particularly like and admire Mrs. Poett and the gracious life that she and her family maintained in Windermere. Mrs. Poett's background was German.

"IN CAMP,"
NEAR TOBY CREEK,
WEDNESDAY, THE 24TH APRIL, 1912

My dearest Mother,

If you could only see me here, sitting beside the tent surrounded by pots, pans and an out-of-doors cooking stove, I really think you would hardly know me! I told you we motored from Golden to Invermere as the river was not open, and that Captain and Mrs. Young, the nurse and three kiddies came up with us. We spent Saturday looking about the place as they could not take us out to see the land. The reason was that a motor came to fetch us, Jack and I, and a Mr. Bowden (who I told you came from near Reading and is a farmer) got in, when the landlady exclaimed that something was wrong with the back wheel. We got out, just in time for the shaft to break and for the car to turn over on its side! We were very disappointed, but no wonder that motors come to grief here. It is up and down hill—and such roads, deep with dust. You always know when a cart is coming by a cloud of dust, you see nothing. My feet will never be respectable any more. Brown boots and shoes and stockings will be the thing for years at events, I can see. Nevertheless, the scenery everywhere is glorious. You never get out of sight of snow-capped mountains. On Sunday Mrs. Young's little boy had a temperature, and he telephoned for the doctor at Wilmer, about four miles away. The doctor came and said it was pneumonia, so he was wrapped up and laid flat on a mattress and taken in a cart to Wilmer. Mrs. Young was very upset at parting with him, and as she had to pack up and go off to camp on their new ranch, I went down with Captain Young. The doctor and nurse were both nice and both young. "The Hospital" was about four rooms and is a little wooden cottage! But still, all the same, it is a hospital and there is a doctor within hail.

We saw this plot of land on Sunday afternoon. It is about 3½ miles out of Wilmer (uphill all the way!), on a winding and dirty road or cart-track, you would call it. It is a 28-acre lot. Jack only wanted 20, but he liked this, and Mr. Bowden, who he thinks can help him, has taken the next big lot of about 80 acres and is working it with a friend of his who has just left the service, a Mr. Robinson. All the land is being bought very quickly, though there is hardly anyone living on the lots yet—but they are coming! Captain and Mrs. Young have got a lot, about ¾ of an hour's walk from here, and at present they are our nearest neighbours. We wanted to get nearer them but the land was not so good as this, and ¾ of an hour's walk is nothing out here! We have a tent ⋀ nice mattress, blankets, lamp, etc., lent us by the C.P.R. until our barn is built. That is the next stage, while the land is being cleared, and after that, by the end of the summer I expect, we shall get the house.

The place where we shall build the house overlooks Toby Creek and is on the edge of a sort of ravine. We look right up this to snow-clad peaks, and as I sit here I can count five snowy peaks and ten conifer trees. All the land is fir treed, and as we burn the wood in the stove it smells very nice. It is quite hot in the middle of the day but fresh and cold morning and night; in fact, more like Switzerland than anything else. Everyone is doing general farming about here at present as you cannot plant apple trees on virgin soil. In fact, we cannot grow much this year, as the irrigation system is not finished at present and this is a very dry place. Potatoes and rye, I think, will be all for a start, but the clearing, and posting and fencing, will keep Jack busy for some cosy time. We went round to see the irrigation works on Monday with Mr. Bennett, the civil engineer, and had lunch in a lumber camp. Quite an excitement to have a lady there, of course. Long tables covered with oil baize. Great dishes of meat stewed with potatoes, dishes of tomatoes, plum duff[1] and open jam tarts; and tea. You have it all on the same plate and just pick it out of the various dishes with your knife and fork. But I was so hungry. I never enjoyed a meal more!

I walked over to see Mrs. Young yesterday afternoon while Jack went to Wilmer, and coming back I lost my way and thought I should never find the tent. I took a wrong track and all this forest of firs looks alike; and of course I never met anyone to ask. At last I got back to the Irrigation Camp and asked if one of the men would take me to "Lot 22." I met Jack on the way back, in a fine state. He was on his way to the Camp to turn out some of the men to look for me! I still have not found my bump of locality.

These flowers enclosed are like the red anemones we get at home. They grow all over the place and look so pretty. We live very simply in camp. All food is very expensive, even bread, which is 6d. a loaf to buy. For this reason I must make ours as soon as I get an oven. Everyone does here to save expense. We eat heaps of bread and jam, and cheese and rashers of bacon which are easy to cook, but so far we have had no meat. It is very expensive and very scarce at present, until the boat comes up with supplies. They think it will be up tomorrow. I boiled a large kettle-full of water and had a nice hot bath in a large washing pan we have bought, just after Jack went to Wilmer this afternoon. No chance of being caught in the act! but the men have just come to arrange about the clearing and I expect they will begin in a few days. The sound of explosions is a very common one as they use dynamite for the large trees. I am wearing my old brown skirt and golf jersey, and only wish the skirt was much shorter as the dust is so deep on the roads. This, of course, smothers anything in the hat line, so I am wearing my purple felt. Everyone here is living in the rough at present. The oldest residents up here are a General and Mrs. Poett. They only came last sum-

---

1. A solid pudding often made with dried fruit wrapped in dough and boiled in a bag.

mer, and we met and were introduced to them yesterday. They have grown-up daughters who run the house. Servants cannot be had for love or money, and a Chinaman here gets £120 a year.[2]

I wonder if a fine cooking apron like the pigskin one of Stewart's could be had in a cheaper leather, as that is really what I want for this camp life and Jack has not one? Any time a parcel comes, some water-softener would be a great gift as the water is so hard and I have to wash. I cannot get the stains out of handkerchiefs. What can I put in the water?

Much love, and looking for a letter soon.

Your affectionate child,

Daisy

COLUMBIA VALLEY IRRIGATED FRUIT LANDS LIMITED.

C. H. Davidson, Jr., President.
R. Randolph Bruce, C. E., Vice President.
Basil G. Hamilton, Sec.-Treas.

WILMER, B.C.
24 APL 12

Dear Mrs. Oxley,

I have come in to Wilmer shopping and, having an hour to wait to see someone, will write you a short letter. We have bought Lot 22 as we hoped, and our address will be Wilmer, B.C. and not as previously stated. The view from our house will be perfect. We are about 300 or 400 ft. above Toby Creek and only about 50 yards from it horizontally, so we look down a semi-precipice across a valley, up and down the creek, round the big curve of the creek to high hills two or three miles off. Above these hills, forming the background to the whole, are the Selkirks—snow-clad mountains about perhaps thirty miles away but appearing only five or six miles off. The country all round is thick with patches of thin fir trees. We are three miles from Wilmer, 3 from Invermere, 3½ from Athalmer. There is no post office at Athalmer, so we've chosen Wilmer as our postal address but will soon alter it back to Invermere. We were paying £1 a day for the two at the Invermere Hotel so we decided to go under canvas on our plot, and yesterday Daisy and I moved out. The company lent us a tent, stove, and blankets, and as all our baggage is behind us we are living as best we can. I'm used to it and see no change but Daisy enjoys it thoroughly in spite of yesterday's occasional

---

2. The cost of Canadian labour will be a constant refrain in these letters because of its threat to a way of life supported by servants.

rain. Today has been like all other days, perfect sun and a bit cold at night. Our nearest neighbour is at present a mile and a half off, but as the plots fill up they cannot be more than 600 yards. Mr. Bowden will have a house, marked "x" on Lot 53 — a much better view than us but his is a larger plot and much more money. Lot 22 is much more money and more acreage than we intended having but the view is so good that we decided to take it. The soil is much above the average, and with an exceedingly nice man and good farmer next to us on 53 I thought it best to take the larger plot. I am in here to sign a contract for the building of our house — the plans of which will be sent to you later — which is to be finished in five weeks' time. The stable will be finished in a week and we shall be in that as soon as it is finished. I am negotiating the purchase of a house and shall be very pleased to have it for one seems to have no spare time, and the two or three miles backwards and forwards to town is too much. I have entered the names of the people we know occupying plots. Several more have been bought — 30 or 40 — but only a few of the purchasers are on the land. Very little of the irrigation work has been completed and I doubt — according to information — if we shall get much of a crop in consequence this year. This will be a big financial loss, but there is no labour available and it's no use making a fuss. Once we are on our land living is fairly cheap, and we can tide over for a time till we get a return for our money as we shall be living below our income the whole time. Daisy was very good in looking after Mrs. Young and her three children coming over in the train, and has made a great friend of her.

This is a very hasty letter and I have no time to read it through, but Daisy was saying this morning that she mustn't miss a mail so I'm writing against time to give you one this week. We are both very fit and enjoying ourselves.

Yours sincerely,

J. N. Phillips

WILMER, B.C.
SUNDAY, APRIL 28TH, 1912

Dearest Friddles,

Jack wants you to go to the Stores and ask them to send out to him at the above address 100 soft-nosed 303 cartridges and 20 soft-nosed 400/450. There are varying amounts of cordite in the latter. He is not sure of the amount of grains he wants for this, but Kenny[1] will send you the lid of one of his old boxes which will give it. In return for all this he sends you three 1d. and one ½d. stamp (which, by the way, are of no use to him), which will help to pay your bus fare from Paddington to the Stores!! I believe the

1. Kenneth Phillips, Jack's younger brother, who was living at the time in Stafford, England.

English mail comes in tomorrow, and if so shall hope to get a line. The mail to England leaves here on Wednesday so I shall try and write on Sundays if I can.

We are still encamped in our tent, and make ourselves very comfortable. We have a mattress on the floor with lots of blankets and an eiderdown, and though the nights and mornings are exceedingly fresh I have not felt the cold as I find the best way is to put on extra clothing. We have the hamper which is a great treasure, and have bought various pots and pans. A packing case is the table and Jack's small valise and my dressing bag are our only luggage so far. We could only bring these in the motor with us. They said the rest of the luggage would come from Golden in three days but it is now a week. I have only got my shoes with the "flat bows" which I was wearing on the train journey, and only one pair of stockings but they are all hole and no stocking in the foot, but in spite of this I am quite happy and enjoying life thoroughly. This bracing air makes me feel very fit. My cabin box did not fetch up at Golden but my large box was there so I fished out my old brown skirt and golf jersey, and wore them on top of my grey, as the only way of wearing them! and I am jolly glad I did, as the skirt is fairly well spotted already. Luckily, too, I found a blue overall in the box, so what I have worn out in the shoe and stocking line I have saved on my clothes. We have a little camp stove just outside the tent, like a square box with a tall chimney. Of course, you burn wood, but there is no scarcity of that anywhere. I find I can boil a kettle and use a frying pan, but the oven is no good.

Everything in the eating line out here is a fabulous price. Bread is 6d. a loaf, and that a small English one in shape and size. Butter 2/-per lb., Sunlight soap 5d. a cake. Jam 1/- per lb., bacon 1/3d. per lb., and so on. Meat is very difficult to get until the boat comes up, and all the supplies in the shop are very low. But we live on bread and cheese, and jam and eggs, and have tea at every meal, as we have our water in two barrels nearby and the cart comes up from Wilmer, about 3½ miles every three or four days, to bring a fresh supply. I seem to spend half my day washing up, and washing handkerchiefs and towels and clothes. The water is very hard, so what my hands will be like in a few months time I dare not think. I am wondering if plain glycerine would be a good thing. I think I asked Mother or you to try and get me a small handbook on washing, how to get out stains on handkerchiefs, underlinen and table linen. I don't know. I only know you have to soak things the day before, if possible. When we get our house built I shall have to make bread as well, so shall write to Nellie and ask if her friend at Malvern could let her have a recipe. They use dry yeast out here and I dare say I shall find out in time, but Mrs. Young, my nearest neighbour, is a beginner like myself. I should also like a small 1/- handbook on poultry, if you will look about and enquire for me. . . . Quite the simplest thing about feeding, etc. is what I shall want. You might send me a couple of back-hair nets, and two fringe nets, 2¾ dark brown, in your next letter. Also, another thing I want is rough gloves to slip on. I should think shammy housemaid's gloves in a small size, or an old pair of the boys. With these wood-stoked fires you have to open the door and put on wood every 30 minutes or so, and I find the wood ashes and sticks of wood stain my hands. I have written to Timothy Eaton for a catalogue,[2] and shall hope to get my sewing machine from them. They are the best firm to deal with, I am told, but are in Winnipeg, and of course everything takes ages to get out here. I wish the old one was coming, but that cannot be helped now.

Jack went down to Invermere this morning. He started at 9:30 and did not get back until 1 o'clock. I don't feel a bit lonely when he is away as I have a good bit to do, but it is just like being in camp the other side of the copper-house, with no traffic about and no chance of seeing a soul. We have got a little terrier named Roddy up here with us for the summer. He really belongs to Mr. Stark, the proprietor of the hotel in Invermere, but he has attached himself to Jack and it is very nice having him as a pal. I do wish I had a camera. At times the mountains are so beautiful, but I expect they are rather too distant to come out well, though the clear air makes them look quite close. Of course, there are pines everywhere. Our tent is in the middle of pine trees; and there are larch here and there in the lower parts, which will be very pretty when they get their bright green leaves.

Now about the house. We have settled on the plan and I hope to send you one later. The sitting room runs through the middle, our bedroom and kitchen on one side and two small rooms on the other. One of these will be a spare room, and one I expect will be used for stores. It will be most exciting when the furniture comes, to see how it all fits in. What about Stanley's[3] fly rod? Does he ever use it now or would he part with it at a reduction? If not, enquire the price of one at the Stores, enough to catch trout of a foot long, 3 or 4 lbs. in weight. The birds here are lovely in colour though they do not sing much. One that we see a lot of is bright blue all over and looks most unreal. In fact, it is the colour of "the blue bird" in the play; another is the woodpecker which has a lot of red about his head and breast, as well as brown and white plumage; and the robins are as big as blackbirds.

They have begun cutting down some trees today on the site of the house. It is difficult to get labour here as well as everything else but we shall get it all done in time for you to come next year, I hope. I shall feel much nearer you all when the mail begins to come regularly. I have had no letters yet and we have heard no news of the outside world. I have only been a little

---

2. Founded in 1869, the T. Eaton Co. established an enormous mail-order business with customers in pioneering communities across Canada.
3. Stanley Oxley, Daisy's eldest brother, who lived in Windsor.

homesick once, but I shall be always so busy I don't expect I shall get another attack.

Ever so much love to you all. Always your loving sister,

Daisy

WILMER, BRITISH COLUMBIA,
WEDNESDAY, MAY 1ST, 1912

My dearest Mother,

I cannot tell you how awfully pleased I was to get your two letters, one written on April 4th and one on April 11th, and also Freda's. Monday is the day the mail comes in so now I shall always look forward to Monday and feel I can almost touch you. All our news of the outside world will come from you as we do not even see a Canadian newspaper here, so all you can send will be exceedingly welcome. Wilmer is our best address, we find, as that is the most direct place from here, a little over an hour's walk, and all downhill on a sandy, narrow road. This in itself is not nice, but the pine woods with the lake below and the mountains—"toujours" the mountains—are very lovely. Wilmer, Invermere and Athalmer are all little places round the lake and all this land which is being developed and opened up is on the flats, or slopes I call them, running up from the lake. Our second tent which Jack bought on our way at Golden came up yesterday so we fancy ourselves today, and it is much more comfortable in every way. The tent cost £5, but even then we save very considerably on our hotel bill, and it certainly suits me as I am feeling very fit and Jack says I look very well. Of course, it suits him down to the ground. I wish you could see him crawl out of the tent in the morning in his pyjamas (very dirty, as we did not get our boxes until yesterday), his boots on, and proceed to blow on the embers of the wood fire in the little camp stove. Then the next thing is to boil the kettle to get water to wash in, as it is very fresh here in the early morning. Then he usually chops wood until I am up, and then the next thing is to cook the breakfast. We usually have bacon and also fried potatoes, or eggs. Frying is the quickest and easiest thing when you cook in a wind, I find. Jack usually then goes off to work about ten minutes from here on the other end of "the estate," where he is levelling the site of the house. We have had about twelve pine trees cut down and the roots blown out with dynamite. Today Jack is up there having a huge bonfire of all the green branches. The trees themselves, I expect, he will sell to the lumber company and make a bit. We shall want every penny we can get this year as there will not be much return from the land. The sound of explosions is going on all round on the different lots that are being cleared.

Certainly we are pioneers of this place. Of course, we never see a soul here as there is no road or even a path to our tent at present, but I walk over to see Mrs. Young in her barn about every other day. General and Mrs. Poett have a nice large bungalow and a good bit of land about 3 miles from here. They have five daughters, I believe, and are most charming people. Mrs. Poett is very like Mrs. Rough, only talks faster, and is very charming. They found their way to our tent in their buggy yesterday afternoon and as we were out pinned a piece of paper to the tent asking us to lunch on Sunday, which will be very nice. We met them down in Athalmer where we had walked to get a few stores, and Mrs. Poett told us we should have bread and potatoes. There is no meat to be had in the valley at present, for love or money, but of course you laugh and accept gladly. I expect they will be able to help and advise me in many things about the house, as they came out last July and went through all the stages: tents first, then barn, and then house.

I have just left off as a wind has got up and put out the fire, and Jack comes back at 5:00 and expects a large kettle of boiling water for his bath, which is a large zinc washing pan which will come in later for a rinsing tub when I do my weekly wash. At present I do a daily wash of handkerchiefs, towels, cloths and collars as everything quickly gets dirty in a tent, but it is gradually breaking me in. I have only just sat down for the first time today, except ten minutes for lunch. It takes me some time to tidy up and fold things in the morning, and wash up and wash, and by noon we are ready for lunch. Today I took it out to the scene of the burning. The tea was in the Thermos flask (which please tell Mrs. Rough we love dearly), marmalade sandwiches on chunks in one of the plated boxes out of the hamper, and cheese sandwiches and hard-boiled eggs in the other; and the plates, etc. wrapped in a towel quite à la British workman. The hamper, of course keeps us going with knives and forks, etc. and was most useful on the train. We cannot get fresh milk, so the powdered milk and all the things you gave us have been most acceptable, especially the glasscloth and the knitted dishcloth. Roddy, the small dog, was brought up as a companion for me, but he much prefers master to missus and is not with me many minutes.

. . . Things move very slowly out here and so do people. The first load of timber for the barn came up this morning in a huge wagon drawn by two horses. It will make about half the doors I should say, but enough for the second half may come tomorrow. A man makes an appointment for 8:00 in the morning, and if he turns up at 4:00 in the afternoon you are lucky. Poor J. N. P. finds this very trying as he, of course, is always on the tick. I say we shall get like it soon, but I am reminded that I am not a civilian's wife in this case as in so many others.

We were introduced to an Admiral Storey at the C.P.R. office yesterday. Jack asked him the usual question, "Do you know anything of farming?" "No more than a cow knows about Sunday," was the reply. He was just off to England to bring out a family of five! He has bought a lot of land and ordered his house. His wife is staying in Wilmer to look after things and pick up the ways, which I assure you are totally different. The great thing here is to shake hands with everybody, and if a friend is with you introduce him on the spot.

Later on this evening I am going to open my boxes and get out some boots and stockings, otherwise my old golf jersey and an old brown skirt is what I live in. The skirt is fairly messy already. Overalls are things I shall want a lot, I can see, and I shall also be very hard on stockings. Anyway, I have got all I want at present, but as I think of anything I shall mention it, if you will keep a list of a parcel to be sent "some day." Certainly, tweed clothes will be the thing, and plain hats of good style, tweed in winter and of the good sailor type in summer. If you ever send me anything always think of dust, won't you? Also, notepaper is frightfully bad and dear. Another pad like this when a parcel comes will be the best. Your letters took 17 days coming, but they may be a little quicker when the boats are running regularly....

Friday, 4 o'clock. Jack has got to go off to Wilmer to sign the contract for getting the land cleared, and I have just washed and put on a clean collar (my way of changing at present) so will send a few lines more. I walked to Wilmer with Jack yesterday, about 3½ miles, to the C.P.R. office to settle about details of the house, and to buy and settle on the stove. While there the Civil Engineer asked me to walk out and lunch with him as he was just going out. His wife is a very nice little woman, a Canadian, and it was awfully nice sitting down to a table having a tablecloth and everything proper. She has no help of any sort at present, but she managed to cook the lunch and bring it in without covering up a very nice skirt and blouse, so I expect I shall be able to do it after a little practice. It made me feel I do not want a big house, all the same. They have two sitting rooms and five bedrooms, and a lovely large verandah. All the floors are polished, with rugs, etc. about, and their walls were buff stucco. I think ours will be grey to start with, and we can colour them ourselves afterwards. There is certainly a lack of finish about everything out here, but life drifts along very easily.

We were introduced to the great Mr. Bruce[1] yesterday, and went into his house to see his fireplace, which is of rough cobble stones. Ours will be the same, only much smaller. His bungalow is charming and he has a nice garden, but this is the work of five years. You do not make money or do anything in a hurry, I can see, out here; but if you jog along patiently it is

---

1. Robert Randolph Bruce who established the Columbia Valley Irrigated Fruitlands Company in 1911. The son of a Scottish Presbyterian minister, Bruce came to the Upper Columbia Valley in the 1890's as a surveyor for the C.P.R. and by 1900 became the C.P.R.'s land agent there. A decade later, with financial backing from friends in Toronto, he bought a block of C.P.R. land and advertised it in England as prime fruitland. The Phillips were among those who responded to this advertising. See the Introduction.

alright in the end. We are not having central heating, but a fireplace in the sitting room and a good stove in the kitchen. If the bedrooms are very cold we must use heating lamps. I am looking for the Waring book on country cottages and cannot find it in my boxes, but have found Mrs. Beeton.[2] The boxes and parcels you and Freda did up so carefully took a lot of time and bother, but I appreciate the writing on the lids I can tell you and every little thought a thousandfold.

Much love to you all. I am always thinking of you,

Daisy

MONDAY
MAY 6, 1912

Dearest Freda,

I am going to walk to Wilmer in a few minutes to fetch the mail and to post this letter to Mother and enclose this line to you.

The last few days make me realize that the sun will be exceedingly hot in a few weeks' time, and I wonder about a shady hat. I wonder if one of the soft grey hats the Eton Boys wear would be easily posted and not expensive. Try one on yourself. I should say a large size and with a "chic" piece of ribbon would not be bad. If not, a sunbonnet might be posted out, and look out for a sort of Liberty square or scarf that will take the place of the green ribbon on the mushroom I have got. . . . A small account book like we use for the washing list at home will be useful, and a screw pencil. Also, this bracing air is trying for the insides of one. Eno's fruit salt you see on the shelf of every store. The B & W Vegetable Laxative Pills were very good, and I have to take them about three times a week. I suppose they are things you can take fairly regularly. Ask Mother, and send me more when the big parcel comes. You might send off a book on poultry (Cassels 1/- or something quite simple), and also one on gardening, giving simple vegetable growing as well as flowers. . . . We have had no news of the world since we left and so should very much like the *Observer* every week. My old brown golf shoes with nails would be useful here. Anything old as long as it is tidy, and a box of

2. Waring and Gillow, Ltd., *Country Homes. How to Build, Decorate, Furnish and Equip them at an Inclusive Cost,* London, 1911. Waring and Gillow were furniture makers with showrooms in Oxford Street, London. Their book contained house plans, most of them in cottage revival styles, suggested furnishings, provided detailed price lists, and offered inclusive costs. The numerous house drawings, floor plans, and views of furnished rooms undoubtedly mirrored up-to-date, middle-class, Edwardian taste in England. *Mrs. Beeton's Cookery and Household Management* was the classic book of its kind since first published in 1861.

things can come as "Settlers' Effects" up to six months, as long as we get things here by September when the boat stops.

Very disjointed, but will write you later.

Ever so much love,

Daisy

My dearest Freda,

Your letter and Mother's I got yesterday afternoon, another Red Letter day. I walked down to Wilmer in the afternoon and felt very hot and dusty when I arrived. I called at the Post Office, which is a little store where they sell groceries, and at the end of the shop there is a sort of rabbit-hutch (this is the Post Office). The man gave me three letters. I glanced at them eagerly. All for Captain Phillips, and official-looking documents at that, and my heart felt rather heavy. I walked on bravely to the C.P.R. office, which is a little wooden house, painted white, with a green roof and a flight of steps leading up. I said, "Can I see Mr. Bradie about my kitchen stove?" "Oh, certainly, Mrs. Phillips, and we have some mail for you." I am afraid I forgot all about the dimensions of the kitchen stove and came back without them, but I had got some letters to read, and that is enough for one day, I can tell you. There were three for Jack as well, and at present they are our only literature!

You are a splendid letter writer and no mistake. I envy you, for I wish I could describe all this district round Windermere Lake. It is really glorious. I am sitting here just outside the tent in the shade, for it is very hot this afternoon and brilliant blue sky. But this morning it was quite fresh, and you could see your breath in the tent. I felt a bit shivery cooking the rashers at 7:30, for that is the time we breakfast. I have to wear my thickest knickers then and at night, and change during the day. I am wearing my old wincey blouses in camp, and am thankful I have got them. I love camping out but I have to wash my blouses and clothes and put them out on the grass to dry, and wear them rough dry as I cannot heat an iron on our little cooking stove. If you drop the soap it is covered with pine needles and the dust seems to work through everything, but you just eat dust and all! In fact, you can get used to anything. I had a glass of fresh milk at Captain Young's the other day and thought it was the most lovely thing I had tasted for months. We live on condensed milk, of course. Stanley mentions roast lamb in his letter. I said to Jack, "That makes you feel a very long way off, doesn't it!" But it made my mouth water all the same. I don't suppose we shall see lamb until we come home one day. Our great dish is haricot beans, as I soak them and boil them with tinned tomatoes. Otherwise we have bread and cheese for the meat course, and bread and jam for the sweet course; tea or cocoa; and dried figs for dessert!

We are going to order a big supply of things from Timothy Eaton as soon as we have a house, as things are at "famine" prices in Wilmer. You see, the boat stopped running last October and has only just started coming up with supplies, so we are in the hands of the small store-keeper at present. I expect I shall always be writing home for small things, for instance, all the lace. If one wants any for toilet covers, etc. it is quite impossible sort of stuff. The very commonest and cheapest stuff like you see on the very cheapest underlinen at home is all you can get, and I have got the various catalogues from Pryce-Jones and Eaton. Then I shall want cord for my pillows when I make them up, but I expect these sort of things will come in the envelopes Mother speaks of. I have tried to get turkey twill to make cushion covers for the verandah, but you cannot get it out here. Cushion covers at Libertys[1] — if you ever see a cheap and effective sort going you can invest in it, but always send something for its back and some cord. I wish I had brought out some dhurries,[2] as they would be so handy for throwing over packing cases for an extra seat, or putting on a camp bed. But I must just rub along at present as the house and the land, and the fencing and the clearing of the land, all mount up.

I think we shall only have about four acres cleared this year, and try to get the house fixed up and fairly straight before the winter. We have begun the barn, and also the house quite close to the barn. Of course, the floor is laid first out here, and then the walls rise round it. Looking at the floors, it looks about the size of our dining room at home, but it is very deceptive! The sitting room runs right through the house, a window at each end, size 12′ by 21′. On the left front is our bedroom, 12′ by 14′. Behind that the kitchen, 8′6″ by 11′, and off that a small pantry, 3′6″ by 6′ (no room for Jack in there). At the back door is a platform where you can put pots and pans, and do washing. On the right front is a room 8′ by 10′, which Jack calls his den. And at the back a room, 8′ by 10′10″, which will be a spare bedroom and storeroom combined, as we are having a lot of shelves put up. The sitting room is grey stucco, very rough sort of stuff, but we are told it will keep the house warm. Jack's den is all wood inside, dull stain in a dull brown colour, and not the yellow varnished wood they are so fond of here. We cannot afford a white painted house with a green roof, which looks so pretty here

1. The first of many references to Liberty and Co., a Regent Street store founded in 1875. In its early years the store specialized in oriental goods and fabrics, and later popularized contemporary design in the Art Nouveau style that Daisy, her mother, and sister Freda all appreciated.
2. Woven cotton rugs made in India.

among the pines, so the house will just be brown stain, and the verandah made with peeled logs. And I think I shall have a bright green roof. The architect, who also is a carpenter and builds the house, says red, but I do not think you will like red and brown when you come, and as several other people are having red I want green!

A man who is helping build the house came over the other day to our camp for water. (Huge explosions have just been going on and I see roots of trees being tossed high up in the air, and clouds of dust. This is always going on in various parts where they are clearing. Jack says it is exactly like the bursting of a big shell. They use dynamite for the big trees and then put a long chain round the roots and drag them up out of the earth. It is the work of two horses as a rule.) The man then said, "I know your face very well as Miss Oxley. My 'fiancy' lives at Windsor and is a Miss Cole. She lives in Gloucester Place." He then produced a photo of his fair lady whom I then recognized as a girl who I think serves in one of the tuck shops in Eton, and I expect Stewart can point her out to you.

Jack has gone off to Athalmer this afternoon to buy a saw and to get provisions. I had been washing all the morning so thought I should prefer a couple of hours with you, and it is a three-hour walk there and back. The dog, of course, goes with him! He also takes an old potato sack to bring back supplies! He is wearing out his old khaki uniforms as they are the most sensible things for dirt. I shall have a khaki drill skirt when I am in need of anything new, but it will not be this summer. I do hope the Stores have sent off the Madras muslin for the curtains. It has to come by post, but it is no good worrying out here. I shall get a sewing machine from Timothy Eaton, and expect it will be about £4.10.0. with freight.

I had my first experience of "first aid" last week. I was here alone and heard someone calling out. I went out of the tent and found a man coming across from where they are building the house. "I have got a nail right through my foot, Mrs. Phillips." He had hammered one of those long nails right through his foot. Luckily, I had that little "Scout box" in my trunk and so was able to wash it with boracic and bind it up. The man who comes round with a large cart to fill up our water-barrel appeared shortly after and was able to drive him down to the doctor at Wilmer. This reminds me you might send my triangular first aid bandage when the box of various small wants comes out, and if any of them can be put into a biscuit tin, the tin is worth its weight in gold out here. (Here comes the watercart so I must go and help hand out the buckets.)

Thursday. I have just finished washing and tidying up the camp so will snatch a few minutes before taking Jack up his lunch of bread and cheese. Before I forget, I should very much like one of his side-face photos if you will send me one, and some day a frame that will fit the photo. I shall have to get you to send me a few frames later on, I expect, and mind you have yours done soon and put on a big mount so that it will fit Evelyn Manning's frame, or that will be a white elephant. I believe I have seen talc instead of glass at Mrs. Marley's, but perhaps it would not look nice, and my house has got to be nice!! A 1/- pocket knife is a thing I should find very useful too, and I wonder if some ribbon corsets would come cheaply by post? I have no means of finding out up here, at present anyway.

The last two days have been baking hot, quite like July at home, but today there is a strong and cool wind blowing and I am glad I did not leave off my thick underclothes, as I felt very tempted to do so. We walked over to lunch with General Poett and family on Sunday and had a great time. They have a large house on the lines of a Swiss chalet, on the border of a most lovely little lake and, of course, a vista of snow mountains beyond. There are five girls so they get on fine. One does the washing, one the baking, one the chickens, and one milks the cow and does the dairy work. They are most charming people and make fun of it all. Mrs. Poett had cooked lunch, which was a tough piece of beef steak (the first meat for ten days so received with applause), salmon croquettes, tinned peas and potatoes, and jelly and cream. They say they will help me, but they are a long way off and it takes about 1½ hours to get there. It was quite nice to sit down to a meal with a tablecloth and, of course, out here I should say they are very well off and can go in for luxuries in the way of tinned food, etc. Sausages are nice but expensive at 1/6d. per tin, and so we find everything. We have had no butter for three days. The boat has stuck and nobody can get any until the boat comes unless you have a big supply by you. I fry bread in lard—in fact, there is nothing I cannot fry now! And we get dried peaches and prunes, and later on we shall be able to buy fruit, I expect.

I am so glad you like the brooch. It was Jack's taste. I thought a big "merry thought"[3] would be useful for this, but Jack said his idea of a *nice* brooch was a bar of gold with a single diamond, so he went off to the stores on his own, and returned triumphant with the brooch.

Sunday, May 11, 1912. Since writing the other part of my letter it has got much hotter and, in consequence, a mosquito has arrived and as usual taken a fancy to me. At the present moment I have got a pad of Hazeline over my right eye for the little beggar took a fancy to that part of my anatomy last night. Jack has written to Kenny for his mosquito curtain to be sent out, so later on we shall be alright. We have just moved into our barn and it is certainly more comfortable than a tent—or I should say it is much cleaner and one can stand upright too, which is a great thing! We have a table made of a few planks and two chairs, and above all two long shelves on which are arrayed all our provisions: marmalade, cheese, bread, eggs, etc. The house is quite close and they are getting on finally with it, and when the verandah

---

3. A brooch shaped like a wishbone and considered to be lucky.

runs round on the two sides it will be quite as good as another room.

I am always wanting silly little things. When I looked in my boxes this morning and found all the things I have got I felt ashamed to ask for more, but please keep account and I will settle with you later. A ball of medium string will be very acceptable when the parcel of oddments comes. Canadian string is soft like darning cotton, and no good! Also, what I do want in spite of all my boots and shoes is a pair of shoes I can wear in the house and yet wear outside. I think perhaps brown ones with a strap across, but glacé is no good here, it cuts too soon. If not, a pair of shoes like I had and Mother used to have. (They have flat heels and broad toes and a strap across.) Perhaps they could be had with more pointed toes, and look more elegant but suitable for working about in the house—but remember we are in the wilds of the country. I have more than enough fine clothes; it is the work-a-day tweeds, shirts and overalls I shall live in! An overall of dark blue and white spot would be useful when I have new ones. You should just see the one waiting to be washed after camp life! Of course, it is from continually making up the stove with wood. The ashes are very dirty, and I have to clean my pots and pans with wood-ash—good for them but bad for my nails! Jack is busily employed cleaning my boots. We have begun to make a patch to sow a few vegetable seeds next week.

Ever so much love.

Your affectionate sister,

Daisy

A few flowers enclosed, though I fear they give you no idea of the "real thing." The pink and white bell shape is the plant that grows everywhere. The others are a violet and the plant like the cyclamen, etc.

WILMER, BRITISH COLUMBIA
TUESDAY, MAY 14TH, 1912

My dearest Mother,

I was awfully glad to get a letter from you, a letter from Freda, a card from dear old Stewart, several Rottingdean[1] cards, the *Observer,* and *Punch.* Yesterday evening we felt awfully rich I can tell you, and Monday is a day, quite the most important in the week! I feel you write so much to me and I will write as much as ever I can, but really one's time is fairly well filled up now, so what it will be later I know not. It is alright about the Medical Book; I am sure we shall not want it here. If anything serious we can always

---

1. Rottingdean, a seaside town in Sussex.

get at a doctor, and although some little way off he is *there*. I feel ever so fit and am quite sunburnt, ditto my hands, but they are nearly always dirty now — except at mealtimes and on Sunday!

Brilliant sunshine day after day is very nice, and the blue sky makes such a lovely background for pines! Always pines, remember, no other trees. There is a rough sort of grass everywhere, but a little low shrub like the wortleberry of Wales grows everywhere under the trees, and the grass springs here and there. The mauve flower I sent, like an anemone, is over now, and there is a low cherry bush about that has lots of wild white blossom; and a little yellow flower I do not know the name of; also a little magenta flower like a baby cyclamen. It is so interesting as all the new flowers and plants open up and show themselves.

We have now got one stage further on and are living in the barn. It is nice to have a board floor under our feet again instead of "dirt," as they call soil out here. It is a large roomy place made of peeled pine which looks like matchboarding at home. It has two windows which are only holes at present, and a wide door that is never shut day or night. I am being brought up in the fresh air entirely now! We have a wooden table made of lathes by the carpenter — while you wait, or about half an hour! Being the afternoon and all the work done it has the red and white check duster spread in the centre, and a white cheese jar filled with wild cherry blossom! And the potted meat jars we brought out are also filled with cherry blossom, in each hole that will be a window some day! Two kitchen chairs and Jack's Roorkee chair[2] which I am now sitting in, the boxes arranged all round which act as washstands, etc. with a towel spread on them, and a bed with heaps of double blankets. The Canadian blankets are excellent, very warm and heavy and double length so they turn up at the bottom and keep your toes warm; the air-pillow and Miss Buckland's pillow, for which I have blessed her many times, and an eiderdown complete the furniture. The *Windsor & Eton Express* and *Punch* just now make me feel we are just in touch with the world and no more.

Jack is kept busy from morning to night with lots of pick and shovel work. It is hard work in the sun, but he is thoroughly enjoying life all the same. He has written to Mr. Phillips,[3] — Did I tell you? (but do not mention this when you write) — and you doubtless saw his resignation in the *Gazette*.[4] We are now working very hard in the garden, or rather a patch where we can grow some vegetables as soon as possible, as this I think will be the only way of getting them. Jack has dug it up and the earth is loose and loamy and light brown, not dark like the garden at home. It is full of large lumps which all have to be broken and crumbled in your fingers before

2. A folding safari chair made of wood and leather.
3. Jack's father from whom he was estranged and to whom he had probably written about his marriage. See the Introduction.
4. The published announcement of Jack's resignation from the regular army.

planting. Jack got some little onion plants in Wilmer yesterday when he went for the mail and provisions, and we were putting them in last night. We could not get finished so this morning your little daughter was up and had cooked breakfast and eaten it and was planting onions again at 7:30 so as to get them in before the heat of the morning sun. I always have a rest after lunch and we usually go to bed quite by nine o'clock.

We still have a little camp cooking stove but it is no good for baking. I tried some scones this morning, but they are more like thick biscuits than scones. The Maggi soups are nearly all gone. They were most useful and so good, but we now go in for pork and beans, and also have had some tinned salmon which is quite good, and Canadian! We went to tea on Sunday with the Cuthberts.[5] They live about 45 minutes from here, down by the lake. Tell Freda "Mrs. C." is the one we saw the photo of at the C.P.R. putting the tiles or shingles on her house. He was an engineer and a very clever carpenter and wood-carver so their bungalow is very nice and so are they. They have been here a year and so this year are making a show on land they had ploughed and cleared last year. Mrs. Cuthbert is quite young and very pretty, also very capable, and you just need to be that here. She will help me, I am sure, later on if I get into difficulty with my breadmaking and washing. I saw the first process of soaking the yeast-cake when I was there and hope to go again to see the next process, but everything is so far away you cannot get there and back between meals if you stay any length of time. Everyone is most kind in trying to help, I must say, and that is very cheering. The Cuthberts gave me 15 strawberry plants and they are planted now, but I fear this baking sun is very trying for them. I have just been up and rigged a tile propped up by a stick over each plant to try and shade them a little, as we have no manure. We only have two barrels of water so we save all our washing water and dish water for the garden. It really looks very like soup!

Jack has marched off to Athalmer today to see about a horse. He has heard of several but "Mr. Right" has not come along yet.

The house is getting on and they are now putting the shingles on the roof, but of course the other part is not nearly finished. We have had the sitting room window built out in a little bow where we shall fix up a seat, and we have long narrow windows instead of deep ones to try and be original and different. You see, ours is the first bungalow to be started this spring as we passed the plan and did not haggle too much about the price, but everyone who goes to the office is shown everyone else's house. Mr. Malandane motored up yesterday and brought a Captain White[6] who had just come out

5. The Cuthberts were of Irish background. For many years Mr. Cuthbert was secretary of the Columbia Valley Irrigation Company. After the First World War they moved to Nelson, B.C.

6. Like Jack Phillips, Captain White was a refined army officer who had served in the colonies. He was a bachelor and would return to England early in the First World War.

to see our house. "Oh, that window is pretty. I shall have one like that. A stone fireplace, that's nice. I shall certainly have one!" This is the sort of thing. Mr. Malandane took some snapshots, and if they come out and we get one I will send it some day. I had just come off the garden patch where I had been kneeling in my overall! Luckily I had washed it in the morning, but it does not last long as the camp stove is such a dirty little brute.

Our house is right at the far end of our property, quite ten minutes or more from the road upon which nobody seems to walk, but it is used occasionally by lumber wagons! There is a fine view of Mount Nelson, a snow peak, from the end of the verandah, and far below is a torrent at the bottom of the creek. We have the Selkirks on the one side and the Rockies on the other. Of course, they are foothills, but peeping over here and there you get the snow-capped brethren. This is a grand country and no mistake, but I do not think I should care to live on the Prairies.

I have ordered my sewing machine from Eaton at Winnipeg, and hope to get it in six weeks. No news of our goods yet awhile. I saw one of the boats come up to Wilmer last week, a white flat-bottomed two-decker, exactly like the pictures one sees of those on the Nile. A big turbine at the back painted red makes a most quaint and fairy-story sort of vessel! It is a very pretty journey up from Golden which you will enjoy when you come next year! Please thank Freda for the postcards.

Wednesday. They (the postcards) now adorn the walls of the barn, put up with drawing-pins, one of the many little things that have come in most useful. I also discovered another old glass-cloth today. It will be a great treasure, as the first one has had much hard work and is rather "holey." I have just been resting for an hour, but the mosquitoes have *made* me get up. They love my arms and neck, and make such a noise buzzing. It was 82° in the shade yesterday, so you may guess it is fairly warm for May! But the nights are cool which is a great thing, especially when you have no cool sheets but only blankets. Did I mention a pair of ribbon corsets among the many little things? If they will come in an envelope I think they would be so cool for working about in the house. . . .

Flora sent me a very nice letter, and of course was surprised to hear I was married.[7] I feel quite an old married woman now, and quite settled down. It is impossible to think I was in England two months ago! Jack has settled this morning to have five acres of land cleared next week, all he can afford this year, but shall hope to do more next and put in some apple trees as well as potatoes. We shall be able to do more when we get a water supply. At present we have to drink tea always, and mostly cold tea. It is just something to flavour the water, or rather to take away the flavour, as we put one tea-

---

7. Flora Nicholson was a school friend living in Perth, Australia. Her husband was a fruit farmer.

spoon of tea to a large teapot of water! We see some Indians about when we go to Athalmer but they seldom have much warpaint on, and mix up Canadian clothes with bits of their own. A snake darted across our path the other day when we were walking, but Jack soon hammered it on the head. This is the third I have seen.

Whit Sunday. Your letter posted on April 30th Jack brought up yesterday as he went down for supplies. The boat is coming more regularly now, and we can hear the hoot down on the lake, although we cannot see it from our plot.

Will write Freda next week. Much love to you all.

Your affectionate child,

Daisy

WILMER, BRITISH COLUMBIA,
WEDNESDAY, MAY 22ND, 1912

My dearest Freda,

Your turn, isn't it, this week, so here goes. It is a pouring wet day, the first we have had since we have been here, and the clouds are right down over the mountains. All would be well but "the barn" is leaking! I was wakened this morning by splashes on my nose, and now there is only one dry spot in the centre by the door. That is where I am sitting to write, and not feeling in the best of tempers. I have covered up a few things on the bed, but the trunks and boxes round are sopping and there is a sound of dripping in all the available pails and basins. However, as Jack says, it is good for the crops—but alas!, we have none put in at present.

The great excitement this last few days has been the clearing of six acres of the land. I love to see the men working on a tree with their double saws, then a call, a crash, and down comes the tree. They are such lovely straight things, some of them, and two of ours were 90 feet high so the fall is a great sight. Then, when the felling is done, along comes an old boy, whom I call Guy Fawkes, who makes a hole with a crowbar and in goes some dynamite. You then hear the cry of "Fire" and you clear out of the way as quickly as you can and take shelter behind the largest tree you can find. The explosions are fairly heavy and up come these huge roots, and pieces and branches go up a tremendous height and very often fall at a great distance away. The next thing, they saw the trees into long lengths and drag them along with chains and pile them. Then all the branches that are lopped off are piled in bunches, and you have nice little bonfires all over the place. Then the huge roots are dragged off with chains and a team of horses, and put on one side to be burnt in "the fall." It is not safe now as it is so dry.

Yesterday the men began ploughing, and of course it was very rough at first but one acre of potatoes is going in on Monday or Tuesday and this will prepare the ground for apple trees next year. Another couple of acres will have rye or grain of some sort, to be cut green ready for feeding the horse when we get one during the winter. We have only just enough water for ourselves at present, so have decided not to get a horse just yet, though it means many long walks to Wilmer to bring up food as we can only bring four loaves at a time. Picture me with a potato sack on my shoulder with cheese, butter and bread therein, and a tin pail in the one hand and a walking stick — the tin pail containing eggs that *will* rattle! I usually go down on mail day, which ought to be Tuesday. However, there was nothing yesterday, but I had a letter from Mother on Saturday, and I expect there will be something if I can get down on Friday. The house is at a standstill at present as they are waiting for the window frames, but hope they will make another start soon. This is a country of waiting and possessing one's soul in patience, but it is very enjoyable all the same — at present life is simply a picnic.

We have got a little bit of vegetable garden started, or rather, the seeds are planted, and now the rain has come I hope things will make a start as I miss my vegetables very much and just long for a dish of greens sometimes, and stewed rhubarb I should just adore! But we shall doubtless have some later on, and I believe I shall learn to do without anything in time. Two days ago Captain Young came over with his wagon and brought us two pillows, pillow cases and sheets. It was just lovely to feel a clean sheet under my chin, and not a scrubby grey blanket, but I don't believe Jack appreciated it one little bit! It was very kind of Mrs. Young. Their things are arriving by degrees, and they had sheets and pillows lent by General Poett, so did not have to do without. I went over to their barn and took my washing in a bundle under my arm and did my ironing there. Mrs. Young has *three* irons, and underclothes certainly feel much nicer ironed than not, I find, and certainly blouses *look* nicer. My Harrod's[1] skirt is my chief joy as it is nice and short for walking in the dust, and just the thing for out here. My old brown is a sorry wreck and does for messing about in camp, but afterwards the only thing to do with it will be to *wash* it; of course, it is rather long for out here! I find my old mushroom hat the most useful and comfortable at present as it is so shady, but colours fade very quickly in the sun and my favourite green, I expect, will be the best sun-colour. Everybody is most kind out here. The old man who brings us up the water brought us up a loaf of bread on Saturday his wife had made. He heard me remark the week before how dry some bread was we had got, because we could get no other. Then there was no butter to be had in the store, and the man who sells the hardware took me round to his house and gave me a pound. "Let me pay

---

1. A large department store in London.

for it." "Oh, no, you give here!" It makes us rather afraid to say we are short of things, but we shall be able to give back later on, I expect. Here comes Jack looking like a drowned rat in his Burberry! I must make some hot tea to try to warm things up.

The Madras muslin has arrived at Golden. It was sent on by the Stores, you remember, by parcel post, and we hear there is something to pay. You will by now be home again and settling down to work, I hope. Don't give up, whatever you do, but try and go up to Brangwyn[2] or somewhere like that for a term, and get bucked up. Not feeling well has made you a bit depressed about your work, I know, but struggle on and it will all come right. Don't go in for helping in the house and leaving your work. That is *not* your duty so don't persuade yourself it is, but stick to your drawings. I think you will love these pine trees when you come. And I keep on seeing "subjects." The mountains are much more in the distance than they were in Switzerland, though I think the level of our house is 3020 feet.

Jack heard from Kenny last mail that Mr. Phillips is very ill indeed, with kidney troubles, and Kenny had been to see him. They do not think he can possibly live out this summer, but don't speak about it in your letters at present as Jack wants to hear all the news. I am sorry that Gertrude is going, but you do not realize how luxurious it would be out here to have *one* servant. It always seems meal times or washing-up time. In fact, you might call yourself a "general"[3] only you are your own mistress. Even then, it is horrid to see a dirty kettle and know that if you want it clean there is only one pair of hands that can do it. You will become quite domesticated when you come out to stay with us, so for the present stick to art! Thank Stewart for his card, and tell him I am looking forward to a letter from him! Another of my accomplishments is barber, and I really manage to cut Jack's hair in good style. His one idea is to get it short, and mine not to cut away all the twist in it! However, the looking-glass is very small and he seems quite content. All sorts of different flowers are coming out, but none of them last very long, that is the sad part; and soon I expect we shall have wild strawberries and gooseberries. I shall think of you on June 4th.[4] The river Thames seems very far away, and Lake Windermere is really too far off, and at present I have only seen one canoe! I am sending a book about the district, and the pictures will give a good idea of the kind of scenery here. The little log book is rather a dream of the future, but we hope it will be true some day.

Friday. I had to go to Wilmer yesterday afternoon for bread, and to my joy I found a letter from you and one from Mother, as well as *Punch* and the

2. A reference to a school of painting run by the artist Sir Frank Brangwyn, R. A.
3. An all-purpose servant.
4. June 4 at Eton College was the social event of the school year with processions of boats between Eton and Windsor, boat races, and fireworks. For the people of Windsor, too, it was a popular day.

Express. You talk about the value of my letters home. You cannot picture what yours mean to me out here! It is so nice to feel we are more or less in touch now, and I am only about a fortnight behind everything you are doing. I love to hear all the little details of the spring-cleaning and the gardening, and who has been to tea, and sit and picture it all when I get my quiet hour in the afternoon which I get if I am in the barn and have not to go down for supplies. The doctor at the hospital gave me a few lettuce plants yesterday as he was thinning his out, so we have put them in and hope they will thrive. It is much cooler again after the day of rain, for which I am not really sorry, as for the time the mosquitoes have disappeared and my bites are healing up nicely. A horse walked right across our garden last night, and so I am afraid a good many of the seeds will not come up, which is very sad. The horses stray about in herds of seven or eight and we often get a procession across the land.

This is a great place for studying natural history, and there are quantities of little grey squirrels about with lovely tails, and some other funny little things called "chip-monks" that are rather smaller than squirrels and have stripes on their backs. They are always playing about the lumber that is lying about the house, and there seem to be endless birds with a good bit of colour, and lovely dragonflies, some peacock blue and some with wings like gold-dust.

The Madras muslin from the Stores has arrived. It cost 2/- by parcel post, but we had to pay $2.85 duty, which is about 5/- in the £. But Timothy Eaton or Pryce-Jones are no good for anything like Madras muslin. The Canadians are evidently not people of taste, and all the old rubbish from England is shipped out to the Colonies. . . .

I have come to the conclusion that the winters here must be very cold and rather severe. A sledge is the only thing you can drive, and you are more or less shut off for several months and get rather tired of seeing nothing but snow. But my "fresh air" treatment will have hardened me by then, I expect, and there is always lots to do here to keep you warm. The great thing is not get your supplies frozen, and Jack is busy with pick and shovel digging a root-cellar. This is all I have time for this mail, but will write to Mother next week.

Ever so much love to you all, and to *you.*

Your affectionate sister,

Daisy

WILMER, BRITISH COLUMBIA,
WEDNESDAY, MAY 29TH, 1912

Dearest Mother,

Your very welcome and splendid letter of May 5th was as usual gladly received and enjoyed. There is usually perfect quiet in the barn for about half an hour when we bring up the mail, while we each devour our letters; and our evening meal is always late that night, though usually a very chatty one, talking about and picturing you all. It is so lovely now to feel we are in weekly touch with each other. Wilmer and Windsor feel quite close when the letters come, and we forget the vast stretch of land and water between. I am so interested in hearing all about the spring-cleaning, and you tell me all the little details I love to know. Stanley's room will have quite a strange face, and I am glad Freda is so pleased with her room. Tell her I think it badly needs a little table in the centre to make it perfect. . . . I do hope Freda is really better and will be able to enjoy her summer, and that it will not be too hot for you both like last year. I think it would be a great idea for you to go with Freda . . . either to Port Avon or Auvergne, but personally I don't think Scotland would altogether suit Freda's style! Anyway, don't spend all your pennies this year but try and save for one or other of you to come to B.C. next summer.

You talk of the chasms and the gaps on the railway journey through the Rockies, but the extraordinary thing is that there is nothing of the sort. The whole thing is so gradual, and you *never* look down what feels a great height. You feel as if you are on a plain between the two ranges. This wonderful double or spiral tunnel takes you through the only part that would or used to be steep, and then you go in the tunnel at the top and come out in a valley below, and can look right up to the entrance of the tunnel. The railways line winds round and round the whole time and the train goes slowly so that you can enjoy the scenery the whole time. You often wait twenty minutes at stations such as Banff, and can get out and walk about and see more of the surroundings. The boat trip from Golden must be beautiful. You would come that way any time after the middle of May, and in the same way you could come by boat across Lake Superior, and so make a break in the railway journey and it would take no longer. We are always talking about your coming. Jack is the one who is always planning it, saying "When Mrs. Oxley comes next year, we will do so and so." I am sure you would like it, Mother, in every way — the beautiful surroundings, the simple life, and the quiet of it all which makes it so much easier to work hard and not get tired.

Sunday. No time to write again until now. This has been a most exciting week in many ways. We have had two mails, and each one large. The letter from you and the hair nets arrived, for which many thanks. Also a letter from Daisy Mac. Then came four *Cornhills,* the washing book, and the medicine book; two *Pictorials, Punch,* and the *Overseas Mail.* Jack was delighted with this and says it has much improved, and I think he has read every inch with his pipe after our evening meal. We were most interested in the *Titanic* enquiry.... Will you tell Stewart I will answer his letter shortly. I feel quite close to the home people now, which is very nice. I think we have had all letters from Windermere and Invermere now, and things will begin to come to Wilmer only, but if not, everything comes on in time. I wonder if you have sent off the things yet, for everything in the way of a parcel or small case... will come "Settler's Effects" at £9 per ton. Some of our things are at the wharf, but we have not got them up yet. When there is a full load... they will come up on a wagon with a team of horses.

Last Sunday, Mr. and Mrs. Cuthbert came up to tea in "the barn." They live on *Lot 8.* All the way from us to them is downhill, so you see it is a pretty good climb back each time we go for supplies and the mail. I usually have a rest by the roadside when there is a mail, and have just a peep at the letters. I am getting quite expert at carrying a sack on my back now! Monday we spent "culling" potatoes before sowing them. Mr. Bowden (Lot 54) came over to help and show us how to do them. Then he and Jack spent Tuesday planting them, Jack paying him instead of a man who would have been employed otherwise. We had to hire a ploughman, and then they just follow the plough and put the potatoes in. Nearly an acre, and the other three acres are sown in rye. Now this piece will have to be fenced in. The posts are made of some of the smaller pine trees, peeled, and four strands of wire. The whole place will have to be fenced by and by. These fences are springing up everywhere as various lots are taken up.

The parson called on us on Wednesday evening about 7:30. He had been making a round of visits, and had called at the barn in the afternoon and found me out, as I had gone for the mail. We were sitting surrounded with letters and papers, having finished the pork and beans, so the parson had to be content with bread and cheese. I had been to buy eggs off Mrs. Cuthbert on my way, and she had given me a loaf of brown bread. Sad to say, the parson liked brown bread and made a very big hole in it. He is a young fellow with a black moustache and a round face, a Canadian, and not bad but rather boring. Mrs. Young came over on Thursday, the first time she had been here. Captain Young drove her as far as the entrance to our lot, as well as one small boy. She will not come often, I expect, as she is not a good walker, and that is where I certainly score out here at present. I was doing a little darning and patching Jack's pants. Things will wear out when one is working hard, I find. My washing is certainly improving, and the book is splendid. Thank you ever so much. Also the medicine book is very good, I think. Just enough, but not too much. This climate will keep away sickness, I hope. Tell Freda it will brace her tummy up when she comes! I am feeling very fit, and am quite brown and freckled. I went to Athalmer yesterday as I had worn down the heels of my boots, and a dirty old Swede is a cobbler down there. I have had some slippers (for wearing in the barn) made by the Indians; they had one of my slippers for size. They are just flat foot cases made in thick hide like very thick chamois leather, and have most lovely needlework on the toes in emerald green, scarlet, and bright blue, and, of course, no heels. The Indians wear them in the form of short boots with lace holes, but these are something quite special. The Indians are very fascinating, with their black tails of hair and their white teeth, with a placid smile always on their faces. I have not seen one in full "war paint."

I am cooking some steak today which I got in Athalmer yesterday, but I have only one saucepan for everything and the frying pan is invaluable! Toby Creek is filling up now, and we can hear the roar of water below the house although we can hardly see it. General Poett's lot is 121 and 122 on a lovely little lake, and you see, a long way from us! We did not have to pay on the postcards, tell Freda. Jack is writing a line, so will close for this week.

Much love all round, dear Mother.

Your affectionate child,

Daisy

WILMER, B.C.
2 JUNE 12

Dear Mrs. Oxley,

A short letter only to supplement Daisy's and to explain our frequent change of address.

We are in the Windermere District and about equi-distant from Wilmer, Athalmer and Invermere. The office of the company, hereinafter called the C.V.I. (Columbia Valley Irrigation), is at Wilmer and the few stores in the country are as good at Wilmer as elsewhere, so as we frequently go in to the C.V.I. offices to stir up a lethargic and lymphatic management, we find it best to have our letters sent there. I have drawn a rough map. Later on the C.V.I. offices will move to Invermere which will be a residential place. It will then be more convenient, as Athalmer develops, to shop there. Later on we may have our letters addressed there, but not yet.

At present everything is working perhaps rather differently from what I expected, but quite as satisfactorily. There has been a larger number of people than the company expected out here and, coupled with imperfect management, we have been pestered with small delays, but every assistance the company could give they have given cheerfully, and much more liberally than one has a right to expect. The Customs have been very good in passing all our stuff through duty free: new silver, furniture, and everything.

If you do send out any more kit—and we are always thinking of things—will you clearly mark on them "Settler's Effects." This allows them to go at a cheaper rate and may avoid customs duty. They must, to go as effects, contain a certain amount of old clothing or something of that sort. I do not know, but would suggest the C.P.R. would send out boxes as well as the Express Company, or if there is any doubt the advice of the A. & N. Stores[1] is always worth following.

The outdoor life has done Daisy all the good in the world. We are both very fit.

Yours sincerely,

J. N. Phillips

P.S. We are always wanting something, but would it be possible to cut out the *Gazette* from the *Daily Telegraph* on Wednesday and Saturday and send it with the *Windsor & Eton Express* for Jack's edification? It would be very gratefully received!

Much love,

Daisy

FRIDAY, 7:30 P.M.
JUNE 7TH, 1912

Dearest Mother,

These have just come, so send them to *you* to have first peep.

No. I. Is taken from point due south of house with the photographer (Mr. Malandane) back to slope down to Toby Creek, and contains besides selves one Captain White (who arrived out a fortnight ago and has taken land about a mile away) on Jack's left; Mr. Bennett between them; the company's engineer; and directly above me on the roof one Mr. Clark, contractor.... The window on extreme left our bedroom. Front door has small window on either side which forms one end of sitting room. The window below Captain White's head and the one round the corner are the "smoking room" windows. The window on the extreme right will be the place where, when you come, you curl up among the marmalade, the macaroni, and the milk.... This is the front of house which looks up Toby Creek to Mount Nelson in near distance.

N.B. The roof has today been painted bright green.

---

1. The Army and Navy Stores in Victoria Street, London, published a large catalogue and sent goods around the world, serving as a crucial link between England and English people throughout the empire.

No. II. Taken from the west, gives a good idea of surroundings, shows also second window of our bedroom.

No. III. Same position as No. I, a week earlier. Gives a good idea of windows when finished. On right is Jack, resting from his labours and wrestling with root cellar.

N.B. He has a vest on!

No. IV. Is taken from east side. The open space in east wall is where a bow window has been put, quite our own idea but going to be largely copied by the architect in his future plans. The man on right is standing immediately above the kitchen door.

No. V. Is a large flume (aqueduct) which brings the water from seven miles off to our "patch." It is here passing over a dip in the hills. The figure on the left Mr. Bennett, the one on the right Captain White. This is the biggest flume they have in this irrigation scheme.

We both appreciate the *Daily Mail* very much, and if we have them shall not need the *Observer* as we feel postage is so high. The *World's Work* and *Cornhill* are both very much appreciated, and so also *Punch.* I hope you realize now that every letter you have sent has been received and very much appreciated. Work always ceases the moment a letter arrives, whatever is going on! Dora will be pleased to see the overall in use. Please remember me to her and Harbour, and also to Price. Our financial position at present prevents us having a servant, but we live in hope.

Ever so much love, dear Mother,

Your affectionate child,

Daisy

P.S. The day after we arrived at Invermere we telephoned Windermere to send our letters on to us here.

P.S. What *depth* ought the little valance board to be above a window to put a "cottage frill" on? And what depth frill, do you think? I want it to look like the window in the bedroom at Dulverton. Things move so slowly here I expect there is time for a reply before I make my cretonne curtains. Also, if any boots or shoes are ever sent out get Freda to wear them and do not let Price polish them too highly. Though I long for well cleaned boots they soon spoil on the dirty roads.

WILMER, BRITISH COLUMBIA,
SATURDAY NEXT BEFORE ASCOT
[APPROXIMATELY 8 JUNE 1912]

My dearest Mother,

By this mail we are sending you the plan of the house, with footnotes by

Jack. I am sure you will like it and be interested, and if you and Freda can make any suggestions in any way as to the fitting up of the rooms we shall be only too pleased. I thought the cretonne would look pretty in the sitting room as I have had the windows made as nearly like casement windows as I could get them to understand out here. They had to send away to Golden to have them made, and now they have come they are rather on the small side, but they will be different to other people's, anyway, and I hope to be clever enough to rig up a window seat. The difficulty, of course, will be making the mattress cushion for the seat as you cannot get anything in the way of stuffing here. Perhaps a brown blanket and some hay and papers will be very uncomfortable but look well! Anyhow, I shall have a try. The Madras will come in for the other rooms. If the frilling does not look nice I can cut it off and put plain hems, and the *next* set can be casement cloth.

I shall not have time for a very long letter as I have written to Mrs. Wall and also sent a line to Stewart. Your letters are always so long and interesting. I know what a long time they must take, and very often I expect you write them when you are tired and ought to be reading the *Daily Mail!* But I love to have them, and they make me feel there is still a little place left for me and Jack as well, as your letters to him have given him very much pleasure. He has had so very few people in his life of late years to be really interested in him. When I read to him or he reads your home letters he usually at the end says, "Bravo, Mrs. Oxley!"

Ever so many thanks for the gloves. They will be most useful, and now I have found my new red gauntlets I am well set up. These do for everyday, and pull-on chamois ones for Sunday are all I want until the winter. The poultry books have come and will be most useful, as I expect we shall start with pullets in September or October. I feel quite ashamed of myself for asking for so many little things. It all takes time, I know, doing them up and sending them off as you and Freda do. Please thank Stanley for parting with the mirror. It is splendid, and I had not really seen myself properly out here until it came, as cracked and starred glass is not very interesting! I see now that I am very brown, and I think rounder in the face than I have been for some time. This would be the climate to do you and Freda a world of good, as the cool evenings and mornings prevent you from being fagged with the heat. I am sorry to hear that all the servants are on the move, but do hope Harbour will stay until after your summer holiday and also that the new cook will settle down in spite of her fine clothes! Tell Harbour (if you like) that I often think of her when I am sweeping and washing up. If ever I come back to England I wonder if I shall be able to manage servants!

In spite of my new surroundings I feel quite sure I have not altered and never shall. Jack will see to that for you, I am sure, and as to talking like a Colonial that will be quite impossible. At present I find that my English is not perfect, and when I talk of "going to go" and that bacon *wants* mustard, he tells me the bacon does not want mustard, but of course I may (but this is "entre nous"). I have to boil the drinking water as at present it is brought up to us in barrels twice a week. Jack usually goes in for cold tea but it is very weak: 1 teaspoon to a large teapot of water, in fact, just enough to flavour the water. All these things may sound to you like hardships, and to a certain extent I suppose they are, but you quickly get used to them, and Jack has always been through something much worse. Things will be alright when we get into the house, and in many ways much easier, and we shall have every comfort ready for you and Freda when you come. Jack said last night, looking up from his Mail, "I would rather see Mrs. Oxley out here than anybody I know, and her suggestions about the house would be awfully nice to have." So you will pause and consider how it can be done, won't you? The wild roses are out now, everywhere. They grow on very low, small bushes, and are very sweet to smell, and various shades of pink.

What bad news about Harbour. She does seem to have bad luck. Freda seems to be getting very domesticated, but I hope she is not giving up her work. She can learn to do all sorts of things when she comes to stay with us. The sewing machine has come from Eaton's but is still in its packing case like the rest of our things. If we open them they may get wet, and the barn must not get too untidy, as occasionally we have visitors!

Mr. Phillips is very ill, and I should say cannot live long. Kenny has been to see him twice, and now he (Kenny) has unfortunately burnt his arm rather badly.

This must be all for this week, I think. I do hope Ascot will go well and that you will not be very tired.[1]

Much love from us both to you all. I think of you every day.

Your affectionate child,

Daisy

The following alterations have been made in the plan.

(1) Windows were found to be too high (Daisy was not quite tall enough to see out of them) so they were lowered 1'4".

(2) As the house faces S.S.W. the verandah, instead of running halfway down the right side, was brought halfway round the left side.

(3) The small front room marked Bedroom, 8'0" x 10'0", is to be called the Smoking room, and has a front window added to it. It is to be walled with wood (stained "oak"). The remaining rooms light grey plaster.

(4) The small Bedroom behind will have long shelves on the back wall and will be used as a storeroom for the present.

(5) The Living room will have a fireplace 6" wider than the plan.

---

1. The Oxleys would not attend the Ascot races, but the Oxley firm printed the race cards. This lucrative contract made May week a particularly busy time for all the family.

(6) The kitchen stove will be in the corner near the chimney to allow the stovepipe to run up the chimney. The roof bright green, and the house a medium light reddish brown. Chimney red.

(7) Verandah posts will be rustic logs.

The roof is already painted and looks very well. It is roofed with "shingles," thin cedar boards that look very much like slates — are about the same size and put on in the same way.

The house is the prettiest we have seen here up to date, and shows good workmanship for the country (which is perhaps not saying very much). We shall be very glad to have any suggestions from you.

J. N. Phillips

WILMER, BRITISH COLUMBIA
THURSDAY — "ASCOT" WEEK

(JUNE 14, 1912)

My dearest Freda,

I was awfully pleased to get your last long letter written at your bedroom window so early in the morning. In my case, it is necessary and easy to get up in the morning as in this way I can get my washing and warm work done before the sun is too hot, but if you are not feeling quite strong yet I should not do too much of it. I *am* enjoying life very much although it is so different. I have not been in a room with a door or window shut for so long it will seem quite strange when we do get into the house. The simple fare seems to agree with me as I feel and look very well, I know. The fact is not that I have not got enough but before I had too much in some way, more than is necessary, I suppose, but I enjoyed it very much too and it is nice to look back upon. I am glad you are looking after the garden, and I often try to imagine you working hard when I am up in our little vegetable patch, usually early morning or at 7 o'clock or so in the evening. There is seven hours' difference in our time. You are seven hours in advance, and I often say to Jack, "What time is it now at Windsor?" . . .

Jack is quite looking forward to your visit as well as Mother's, but to make him perfectly happy he would like to hear you were going to be married too. I tell him he is crazy on the two subjects, fresh air and matrimony! The ordinary *Daily Mails* have both come and it was very nice to see them, but we have come to the conclusion that the *Overseas* gives us all we want, except *his* dear *Gazette!* Thank you ever so much for all the parcels and books you have sent and the care with which you pack them, as I know it takes time. The waistband corsets are the joy of my life now it has turned so hot, and I think of you every time I put them on and take them off, and I won't say how many hundreds of other times. The tears so often come into my eyes when I get a parcel or letter I think Jack is sometimes puzzled, but I have to explain they are only tears of joy and not of sorrow! I do hope Mother's cold is much better and that she will get through this busy week alright. I have been going through it all with you both helping to tie down those silly salt and mustard pots for the hamper, but I expect you do it much better than I ever did. How I should like one of those lovely long lettuces to eat this hot day! We have a number coming up in the garden that are now as big as a thimble!

... How I should like to see all my friends for just one minute and you for many minutes but I am always looking forward to your coming, and then I tell Jack he will be quite out of it for a bit. He is awfully good and kind and realizes, I think, how much I miss you and how much you miss me.

I have found a friend in Mrs. Munsen, an Irishwoman, the wife of the man who brings up our water from Wilmer. She makes lovely bread, and as a great favour makes six loaves for us every week. I think I told you she sent a loaf as a present and Jack liked it so much I asked if she would mind, though as a rule she does not make to sell. She is more of the stamp of Lizzie Bailey, but here these people are so grand and this sort of man can earn from $4 a day, so *we* dress with great style. Her little wooden cottage is always very clean and she is going to show me how to bottle cherries as she is shortly going to do some, in "sealers" or airtight bottles, and she has promised to show me how to make bread! She and her husband have taken a great fancy to "the Captain," I think, as he chats when he goes for the bread.

Mr. Munsen has a wagon and a team, so Jack employed him to bring up our things. The packing cases are now outside the barn and I am longing to open them. The wonderful grey box came up last night and the other two packages, so you can tell Rainer they have travelled well and the band round the boxes is a good idea. One of the barrels of china from the Stores is missing and Jack's brown leather trunk, but they will turn up in time, I expect. His tin uniform case with his lovely riding boots was broken at the bottom, but the boots are not even scratched, which pleased him greatly, bless him! I don't think he will be half so worried if the sideboard is scratched, but that will worry me!

They are now working on the house again and the windows are in, the only casement shaped windows in the district at present, as I told you. And now the outside boards are going on, this way——, and the boards overlap. The roof is bright green and the house is to be stained light brown. I want a green front door, if we can get it, and I hope that will be different as well.

Captain White and a Mr. Bennett have two lots near Lake Eileen. I have met them but have not been to their lots. They are both bachelors and are working together. I do not often see the Miss Poetts, it is such a long way to walk, but I see them occasionally when I am in Wilmer as they drive in for shopping. The eldest is very fair with blue eyes, and very pretty. They are all very fine looking girls with a bit of dash, more like the Captain Gooches used to be perhaps. They usually wear simple gingham dresses with very nice muslin Peter Pan collars and cuffs, quite Debenham & Freebody[1] in style, but I have never seen them in their working kit. I have been wearing my plain blue cotton with my brown Jay hat and a brown bow on my white muslin collar, and Jack very much approves. I have got all I want for this summer in the way of cotton frocks. The only bother is the washing, or rather ironing, but Jack says I may take them to the Chinaman. He also has an idea that the English are made of money, and charges accordingly.

I am enclosing a picture of a cooking stove as nearly like mine as possible. Of course, you burn wood which is sawn up in lengths and size according to the size of your fire box. There are about forty trees piled up near the back door at the present time, ready for sawing into cords. This is work one can do in the winter. The stoves have "holes" for the pots or kettles, and you can have four or six. I have four on mine, and one ring is graduated for smaller saucepans, etc. Otherwise I buy pots and pans to fit hole "8." You use the big oven for bread. It pulls down from the top. The long box (I), is called the heating box, to heat plates and dishes or to keep things warm, like the rack on English stoves. I have a small cistern (II) on the right, which takes the place of a boiler and you dip out the water. You get wonderful stove polish you put on with a brush like enamel so there is no hard rubbing, and once a week will keep it going. *You* can do this when you come! The good Mrs. Munsen has boiled us a piece of bacon, and that and boiled eggs make a good breakfast, bread and cheese and jam and cocoa for lunch, and every day now I make a batch of scones with brown flour, and the dirty little stove usually manages to bake them well, as they only take twenty minutes. Last night I made some rissoles of tinned salmon, and tonight "Welsh rarebit" will be the pièce de résistance. I forgot to say there are three men now working on the outside of the house, one of them an Italian Count!, a very good-looking youth of about twenty. He is getting experience of carpentering, and is shortly going to take a ranch on the prairie. I think we shall call our estate Heston. . . .[2]

Jack heard about Kenny this week. He has burnt his left arm and hand very badly, with burning turpentine, and I suppose the shock has been pretty severe. Thank Mother ever so much for sending Jack's side-face photo. I like it very much indeed, perhaps better than the others, but none of them are half good enough or do him real justice. I wish you could see

1. A department store in Oxford Street, London.
2. After Jack's boyhood home. See second page of photo section.

him sometimes with his dirty face, and more than dirty vest when he has been working on the land in the hot sun for three or four hours. I often taken his lunch down to him, like the wife of a true British workman. However, nearly all our meals are picnics at present which is very jolly, and bread and jam is good stuff when you are hungry. Jack says he will never be able to live in an English house again, but nous verrons! You ask about the roof. It is tiled, with "shingles" which are tiles made of thin cedar wood, and when painted look very nice and I think you will say artistic as well. The "saddle boards" or pieces that come so ⋀ on the roof, will be white, and the window frames too, I think.

Jack was awfully pleased with the book on crops you sent me. His eyes sparkled and it gave him great pleasure I could see, especially as you had taken the trouble to write in it. The information too is most interesting and useful as he has no Farmer's Handbook. I have just been down to the "patch" where Jack is working and the potatoes are just coming up—great excitement, when you have cut and planted them yourself! We were busy early this morning sticking the peas and they were coming on beautifully as we had rain a week ago! We get very little, and that is why the irrigation is so necessary. They are building or digging the ditches but they have not reached us yet. We have to "cultivate" and keep in all the moisture there is. The soil is quite different to that at home and is much more porous and more golden brown in colour.

Mr. Bowden's house is now being built and they will only be ten minutes or so from us. They have the best view of any site on Toby Creek and look right down the valley. Their house is fairly big with five bedrooms, but Mr. Robinson is living with them and they have a farmhand, Smith by name, who they brought from England. A girl friend is coming out with Mrs. Bowden in August, who I think I told you before is the head of the domestic training college at Reading, and she will "run the show" for them, I expect, as she is a splendid cook and knows all about washing, etc., Mr. Bowden says. I do hope I shall like Mrs. Bowden, though I expect she will be a good bit older than I am. I see Mrs. Young about once a fortnight, and Mrs. Cuthbert occasionally, and like them both very much, but I am far too busy to be dull. All the same, it is nice to talk household matters with another woman occasionally. Jack is always perfectly sweet and kind to me, and most unselfish in every way and ready to help me. I am a lucky girl and ought to be very happy. He is so proud and interested in the house as he says, and one hardly realizes he has never had a place he could call "home" since he was about twelve years old!

I expect I shall want various little etceteras for the house later on, but as far as possible I think I shall ask you to get them at Liberty's as those things will suit the house best, sideboard runners, and perhaps a tablestrip. . . .

I have not described the fireplace properly, I am afraid. Instead of tiles all round the grate as at Dulverton, we are having rough stones put in cement round the grate, and the shelf above will be of cement and the plinth round... also of cement. Then a large wire fire guard, which the blacksmith in Athalmer will make, I expect, fits right into the fireplace, and as the wire is fine it will prevent sparks popping out. Mr. Bruce and General Poett's houses both have these guards and they look very well, of black wire with little brass handles attached and mounted on brass rods like we use for curtains. Jack had two letters from Kenny yesterday, and I one from Mother and one from dear old Gilbert[3]. Kenny has suffered agonies with his burnt arm, and will not be able to use it for some weeks. Also, he wrote to say that Mr. Phillips has passed away and to tell Jack particulars of the funeral, etc. He was buried at Twickenham. It does seem strange after having to keep all my doings "dark" because of him, but I really think Jack wished it as much as anything because of his aunts, and he hates having his affairs discussed (entre nous)....[4]

WILMER, B.C.
23 JUNE '12

Dear Mrs. Oxley,

Our baggage with the exception of two cases has been landed within twenty yards of our house. These two deficient cases were those that (I expect) could not be shipped by the *Pomeranian* and were sent out by another ship. They may be in Wilmer now. There is a great deal of stuff on the quay but our carman hasn't seen them, and I cannot at present spare the time. We don't feel anxious about them, though. Nobody hurries much, and a fortnight more or less in delivery is nothing. We have opened nothing, but the cases look in first rate condition. The missing cases contain most of the china and glass, and some old clothes of mine. The silver is alright. As our stuff was marked "Settlers Effects" we had to pay no duty—not a penny—and I am writing to Golden to try to have the box you are sending out passed through duty free.

My father had been suffering for some ten days, was given up almost at once by the doctors, and I am sorry to say died on the 30th May last, but this I suppose you have heard already. I am sorry for it all because I feel we had lost touch with each other for so many years that he was almost a stranger. Our position—Daisy's and mine—will be slightly improved by

---

3. Gilbert Oxley, Daisy's youngest brother.
4. Jack's marriage to Daisy was kept secret from his family. He was not in contact with his father and stepmother and with only one of his aunts. See the Introduction.

this, but it will only be slightly for there is not much left of the Phillips estate.

I don't know if you ever do intend coming out here but the opening of the Panama Canal will improve the comforts of the journey immensely; or if it is not opened by next year or whenever you intend coming I should most strongly advise the lake route. You go, I think, to Quebec, tranship to a lake steamer which takes you to a place called Fort William on Lake Superior (this saves a couple of nights on the train), and join the train there. You would find, as everyone else does, that the train journey is very trying for so many days on end, and the freedom of the steamer is a cheerful exchange. It may be more expensive but I'm sure you will agree afterwards. Any time after April 15th each year is warm enough for the journey as a rule. Daisy tells me you might come out and live in a hotel for some time. There are few hotels costing under 16/- a day, by no means inclusive terms. This is a cheap country until you employ labour, and as hotels must employ servants the guests have to pay. Unless, therefore, you are prepared for a liberal expenditure I should recommend coming to stay with us for some time until you are able to get a grip of things yourself instead of from C.P.R. pamphlets which, though perhaps absolutely true, don't say how much money all these luxuries cost. Needless to say, we shall be awfully pleased to see you, and living in the country is so cheap that a six months stay wipes out the expensive journey entirely.

Yours sincerely,

J. N. Phillips

WILMER, BRITISH COLUMBIA,
JUNE 24TH, 1912

My dearest Mother,

Your last long and welcome epistle was written from your bedroom in a temperature of 68°. It is considerably more than that in the shade here to-day, but it is very beautiful all the same and there are lovely lumps of white cloud about, tell Freda, and a gentle zephyr is rustling the notepapers as I write. Jack is sitting resting in the shade as he has just come up from the potato field, reading the *Overseas Mail* which he dearly loves. He is covered in dust with a very dirty face, in an old flannel shirt, khaki breeches and puttees, and nearly black arms and neck he is so sunburnt. All the same, I really believe he is happy as a king, and very proud of his 28 acres. He is also drinking cold tea, which is his chief beverage. He encloses a letter to you, which is really written I think to tell you of his father's death. Kenny has just written the bare particulars, but we shall hear more later. I fear there is little regret or sorrow from them both, and when you know the particulars as I do now it is hardly to be wondered at.[1] You will see Jack is most anxious you should come and see us. I know and see he has a very tender spot in his heart for "Mrs. Oxley." Don't write and say it is impossible, will you? You will never really have the faintest idea of this lovely country until you come, or what our house is like, and if you wait too long I know you will begin to say you are too old. And if you wait for us to come back to England I fear you will have to wait a very long time, as I don't believe Jack would ever tear himself away even if he could afford it. . . .

The remark about your staying in a hotel is a chance one made by me some time ago, as I felt perhaps you would think we could not afford to have a visitor, but I think this simple life with lovely surroundings and beautiful air would quite set you up in health. One piece of our land sloping away from the house is like a piece of a lovely park. It only wants a few deer. A hind came across the other day and looked lovely. I keep thinking how you would enjoy your crochet and your book without having to walk any distance. The men are now busy putting up the fence posts and enclosing the estate. We often get herds of unbroken horses wandering across and grazing, and although they look very charming they are a nuisance now the rye is coming up. We always know when they are about as one of them has a bell. . . .

Yes, we get letters twice a week now, on Saturday or Monday, and again on Thursdays, and the papers come at various intervals. . . . We always ask for letters whenever we go down on the chance, and there is usually a paper if nothing else. You are so good, Mother, to send so many things, but it is lovely to get them out here. A little parcel or a book is quite an excitement, I can tell you. The gardening book is splendid! Just what we want. The peas are growing splendidly and so are the lettuces, but it is difficult to give them all the water they want. But it is coming and the irrigation ditches are being built, and now they have got a gang of Greeks in to work. Labour is very hard to get. A good gentleman called Mr. Zamir is now digging a cellar under the house. This is most necessary, we find, to keep stores cool in summer and warm in winter. One supply of provisions has come from Eaton's and we shall write for more a little later on before the boat stops running. The logs are now all coming down the creek, and as it curves and turns continually they get jammed in great heaps and have to be broken up, so you occasionally hear an explosion below. Later on the "log-driving" takes place, which is most interesting and exciting too, I should say. Kenny's burn has been pretty bad, but his last letter says his health is improving. I am longing to open the crates as they are piled up outside the house. Jack says,

1. See the Introduction.

"What is cretonne? Shall I like the curtains, I wonder?" I only hope he will. In case I upset the frying pan I have got oil in the Scout box which has proved most useful for various cuts Jack has on his fingers. On Saturday we found the oil of lavender and white birch waiting at the post office, so I have used it nightly on my face, and the mosquitoes have no longer bitten my eyelids for which they seemed to have a great weakness before. I was very grateful for the oils as I had used up the little bottle of ammonia I had, and I have now written to Eaton's for some witch hazel. I have only had one bad swelling on my eye, and then Jack went over and borrowed Hazeline from Mr. Bowden and it soon brought down the swelling. I have found the South Kensington cookery book, but I have not come across Waring's country cottage book that I thought would help me in the arrangement of my curtains. The sewing machine has come from Eaton's and will shortly be taken out of the packing case, I expect, and kept busy for a time, but sweeping, washing and cooking will still have to go on and I shall have no Mrs. May to help. But I shall manage it somehow, and work is good for one, as I feel very well. My wedding ring, which used to be loose and come off when I washed clothes, etc. and cause me great anxiety, now fits tight. Did I tell you one day I went down to Invermere with Jack, and when I got into the hotel found I had no ring on? Jack thought it hardly looked quite right, but this is *entre nous*. It may amuse you, all the same.

I do hope you are feeling better and got through Ascot week well with the new cook. I wonder if you were able to see Miss Muldoon? How I would have liked to see her again. I am wondering if you *can* dispense with a new Dora, but perhaps it will be best left until after your holiday, if Harbour stays on. One cent is the charge they told me at the post office for a postcard, and I did not pay on the Rottingdean cards, tell Freda. I have left this letter until rather late this week as each afternoon I have *had* to mend socks and stockings. It is frightfully hard on these here, but it will be better than nothing, won't it?

P.S. for Freda. Will you get one of my photographs and take it to the Stores and buy a *nice* frame for it. Pay or rather draw the money from Jack's account, and give it to Dora as a small wedding gift from "Captain and Mrs. Phillips." This is Jack's wish and I should like it too, as the servants gave us such a nice present and Dora did her work for me so very willingly.

In great haste, with lots of love to you all.

Daisy

N.B. Jack remarks, "Please return sock!" I forgot a stick of sealing wax in my other order.

[Jack's writing]   From Scott Adie
                                115 Regent's St.

2 pr hand-knit homespun yarn Stornoway Hose, extra-thick, grey or Lovat, 6/6d. per pair. Size of foot as sock enclosed. If these can be had in tops only (without feet) so much the better, but it's not essential.

13/-

2 pr extra thick heather mixture socks to go over the stockings, so should be at least one inch longer in the foot and of strongest material. Don't be argued into smaller sizes because tight socks mean frostbite—socks a little too big don't mean frostbite. Army & Navy Colonial Stores.

1 pr grey shooting anklets, canvas with buttons, size about 11″ at top, 12″ at bottom.

About 3/6d.

6 pr fancy Oxford mat pants, waist measurement 36″, price 3/4d. each. Army & Navy Colonial Stores, Large. These are short things that only come down to the knee.

£1.0.0.

Would you find out how much my deposit is in credit at Stores and let Scott Adie know of my address so that if socks are satisfactory I can write for more.

I enclose a sock for size and a sample of Oxford mat.

WILMER,
27-6-12

Dear Freda,

Daisy and I want a writing desk for the smoking room. The ordinary roll-topped desk—which we should like to have—is one inch too large to go through our door so if we have one of any size it must be a knock-down. I wonder if you—the next time you are at the Stores—would ask them to show you some designs or if there are none made at present if they would prepare you one or two; the original cost ought not to be more than five or six pounds but if you find one can only have a perfectly impossible desk for that amount we must go a little further in price. It is too late to have it sent out this year so there is no desperate hurry about it. The desk ought not to be more than 42″ wide, 30″ deep, 52″ high, and should be of dark oak of the roll-top desk pattern, i.e. plenty of drawers and lockers. The roll top, though, is not essential. If the Stores are not satisfactory perhaps Maples[1]

1. A furniture store in London.

could do one. Would you also ask the auxiliary to send me their catalogue especially for knock-down furniture. Many thanks for the fishing catalogue and the farming book.

Yours sincerely,

J. N. Phillips

WILMER, B.C.,

JUNE 28TH, 1912

My dearest Freda,

Here I am again at the end of the week and I have not begun to answer your splendid epistle received last Saturday. Jack and I walked down to Wilmer in the cool of the evening for our bread. A boat had just come in and brought your letter, and also a very welcome packet of oil of lavender and oil of birch from Woods the chemist. I wonder the little parcel got here safely. The bottles certainly were wrapped up in corrugated packing, but no string round and the sealing-wax at both ends had come undone. I expect Mr. Woods is getting blind in his other eye! I like the binding of your epistle very much, and you are certainly getting most efficient with your needle and thread! I was so interested in hearing all the gossip. Fancy Jennie being Winifred's bridesmaid! Perhaps it will be best not to have a new Dora at present, but later on I believe Mother will find it better than having someone in to do the cleaning and mending and to carry gossip backwards and forwards! I don't hear anything about art. Don't give it up, whatever you do. I shall insist on your painting all day when you come here, and you will not be allowed to be indoors one minute! Fresh air is a cure for all ills so stick to it, and you will certainly please brother-in-law. I am most interested in reading the "New English" crit.[1] in the *Observer* and gathered it was not as good as usual, but you evidently were pleased and enjoyed it.

I wish you could have found the exhibition of Canadian pictures... but the reality will be the thing, won't it? Of course, we have heaps of lovely clouds and lovely sunsets too. It is not always blue sky. It has been frightfully hot one or two days this week. We have no thermometer at present, but one is coming from Eaton's. At Athalmer I heard one evening it had been 92°, and 93° indoors. However, it is much more bearable than last summer at home as it is not *moist* heat but *sun* heat, and the mornings and evenings are lovely. We had a thunderstorm Wednesday and Thursday and now it is quite cool with a high wind like the seaside feels, and walking down to see the potatoes this evening I wanted my golf jersey. The potatoes are all just showing their heads, and the rye is able to bow itself daintily in

---

1. Review of the Annual Exhibition of the New English Art Club.

the wind, and now the fence posts are all up—230 of them—round the estate, and the wire has come today, and two gates, so we shall soon look quite swagger. The gates here are made of thick iron-tubing, and the gate filled in with wire in squares. Four strands of wire are all round the estate... so stray herds of horses will no longer come and roll on the rye and deeply grieve and make irate the Lord of the Manor, or rather bungalow! When we hear the bell we know the horses are advancing, as horses and cows wear bells here as in Switzerland. Down comes the hunting crop and away goes Jack, cracking for all he is worth, always returning frightfully pleased with himself at scattering the enemy! There are many other wild flowers now appearing. They are so difficult to press, but the prettiest are like campanulas, and my vase is always full of something. I was outside making scones yesterday and heard a humming near my head and the most lovely little humming bird came darting round the flowers. He was about as big as a dragonfly, with a very long beak, a scarlet throat, and shot green and blue wings. He had his fill from the flowers and in a second was gone like a flash. We have seen one or two eagles hovering over the barn when the thunder was about, and they cause much alarm among the small birds. Then there are prairie chickens wandering about, and blue grouse. Later on I expect we shall have some for "the pot."

Mother asked about foundations to the houses. Well, they have none as they are raised above the ground. Five upright pieces of wood on each side of the square, about a foot above the ground and the flooring is hammered down on these. This is the first floor only on which the sides of the houses are built. They lay another floor on top of this later, which will help to keep the house warm. Jack is banking up earth on a slant all round the house, and then we shall put large stones on top and try and make a sort of rockery with various small plants (perhaps nasturtiums?) next year. No ferns grow here. It is much too dry, I expect.

Saturday. I was *made* to go to bed last night and not finish your letter, so am continuing this in the morning. I have just been "cultivating" our little patch, and the water cart has not yet come so I cannot wash the towels that want it so badly. When you have a husband who comes home in the evening as dirty as a farm labourer you can imagine what bath towels look like—also pocket handkerchiefs, also vests, also flannel shirts! But I am getting quite clever at washing soft things. Also my darning is improving, I find, with much practice. My two recreations at present are writing letters and darning! Tell Mr. Lightfoot when you see him that I am a most interested reader of the *Express,* and most critical. English papers are so sane and truthful. The advertisements in the Calgary paper (which we usually get our bread wrapped up in) are too absurd! The picture of the airship was most interesting, but when I think of airships, Military Tournaments, Earl's Court, and Ascot, I feel I cannot possibly be in the same world as you all.

This has been a most exciting week as first of all I washed my hair! Wood's shampoo reminded me so much of our bedroom but instead of a gas stove to dry my hair I went for a walk round the estate, and in half-an-hour in the sun and the wind it was quite ready to put up and I had not been caught! Stray lumbermen often come across, and you never know if anyone will come riding along (of course, always men, never a woman!). I went down to buy some eggs from Mrs. Cuthbert on Wednesday and had tea with her on the verandah. Her bungalow is a very sweet little place, white, with a green roof, and very pretty inside. It is so nice to drink out of china and have a nice teacloth, etc. She is very sweet, and I like her very much. I had not seen her for a month and took her two *Pictorials* with which she was very pleased. Our tongues wagged terrifically, I am afraid. You do not talk servants here, but provisions and gardens! They have just got the water on, and are very excited. Mr. Cuthbert has been busy all spring building his "flumes," and now the water is coming down and running in and out of all the rows of peas and beans and strawberries. They will begin to grow like anything, I expect. They have put in apple trees and bush fruit this year (they have been out twelve months), and are going in for gardening more than farming. Their land is on the lower "benches" and ours on the upper, so their irrigation ditch was dug first. We should not have time to cultivate much land this year even if we had water, but it will be lovely not to have to use washing water for the garden. The peas are getting much taller, but the sweet peas are only 4–5″ high. Everything is much later here, as you get night frost right up to April.

The enclosed is from Jack. He has made up his mind on a rolltop desk. We saw one in Eaton's catalogue but it will not go in at the door. So will you see if there is any sort of desk made, about the size . . . and of course not too expensive? I feel we are always asking you to do things, you don't mind, do you? Our hands seem so tied out here. I think perhaps Maples might have something, oak for preference. If you go to Maples you might ask if they send out their catalogue to the Colonies. I expect they have it printed on thin paper like the Stores. The Waring "Country Cottage" has not turned up. Some day will you ask them to send one out. It would be more than useful in explaining how I want kitchen shelves, etc., arranged. I hoped to find it in the grey box, so now am sure it somehow got left behind, and no wonder.

We had a very sad day yesterday. We started opening the "Rainer" small crate which I thought contained pictures, *in case* any glass had got broken so that we could write and order any that wanted replacing. We discovered in it Jack's pictures (by you), and he was very pleased with the alterations you had made. The corners of the frames had broken out, or rather opened. Will you ask Mrs. Marley if there is a proper way to try and mend them. Is it best to take out the glass and then try to hammer them together? You understand, the mitred corners have sprung open. Then the table top—alas, the two candle sconces were loose and had been rubbing up and down the polish so the poor carving looks as if it had been gnawed by a rat. The edges of the table too are chipped. The few books were quite alright. Then the big case. I am sure Mother and you could never have seen Rainer pack it, or your common sense would have told you it was wrong. There was *no* packing, and of course *everything* is smashed. I am not blaming you as I know things had to be done in a very difficult way, but I thought Mr. Marley was to pack the pictures. There were no shavings, and no hay or straw, and pictures and china all among furniture with only one wrapping of newspaper. I do think it was badly done. The photo frame of Daisy Mac, the group of the Mac boys, and the four ointment pots were the only things *not* broken. I do feel so awfully sad and sick about it, as having a larger house we wanted them *all*. I think Stanley had better see Rainer and tell him, but I am writing a letter at Jack's dictation. All the picture glasses are broken. The little Japanese print frames have suffered least. They are only scratched and I may be able to black them with stove polish, I hope. The two brown Greuze frames[2] are badly knocked. The one we brought from Paris that Mother so kindly sent out is smashed, as also the two water colours of my own that used to hang over our bed. Then the Nicholls photo of horses has the frame split. The "Angelus" is badly damaged, and the other frames all have chips or pieces out of them. So my poor sitting room will not look half so nice as I had hoped. My china all broken too, so I am glad of the few bits of brass. I wish I had bought a few oriental vases or ornaments at the Stores, but I must wait and hope some day to get a few things out by post. Things seem to travel so well that way, for instance the shaving-glass. So in years to come when Mother has paid all those many bills for me and you want to send me a little Christmas gift, risk an ornament or a photo frame. I shall get you to go to Goods on Audley Street some day and send me a few of those little fruit plates for the sideboard shelves. The chair rails were smashed and the seat scratched, the lower shelf of the little carved table is in half, and the chest is quite antique as all the edges are chipped and the top badly marked and scratched. Another commission, will you go to Halliday and ask him how I can make all these white marks and scratches dark again? Should I use stain or oil, and if so, should it be hot? There is no such thing as a furniture man in the neighbourhood. All these things would have looked so nice in the sitting room, just the thing, in fact, and now it will be a bit bare. The trays are quite alright, and the new mirror frame too, as it was on top. But that is no use without a mirror, is it?

I wonder if the Hallidays are coming to Toronto? Oh dear, I feel very sad over all my silly little treasures. Mrs. Young's big engravings with glass have

2. An ornate frame associated with the 18th-century French painter, Jean-Baptiste Greuze.

come without even a crack, and all her small bits of furniture. I cannot make out how it is, but there was no packing to take off the jar. I do hope the silver will be alright. Perhaps later on Mr. Marley could make one or two frames if I send measurements, and send them without the glass, and we could frame them ourselves. Jack is splendid at everything but, entre nous, he is no carpenter. He cannot be everything, and he is so good to me I must not mind about this. I have heaps of nice linen and house things like that, perhaps better than other people's, and I had been looking forward to the Windsor cases more than the Stores. I think I must forget about it. Evelyn Buckland lost everything, didn't she, which was far worse. But I feel it was a waste of money for Mother to pay for this, and she was so more than good. I am going to Wilmer presently with Jack. I hope there will be a letter from you.

Goodbye for the present, old girl. Take care of yourself.

Love to all,

Daisy

WILMER, BRITISH COLUMBIA,
JULY 5TH, 1912

My dearest Mother,

I have been trying every day this week to sit down and have five minutes at my "home" letters but without success, and here it is Friday before I begin to answer yours of June 9th though I have since written to Freda. I was glad to hear so much news and little details about Windsor folk, but best of all to know that you were really better, and I do hope you will keep so now. Try ever so hard to keep so, for my sake, so the next time I see you you will not have altered a little bit! I have no business to dictate to you . . . but this life out here has made me realize how silly I was to worry over silly little things that here I have to do without and do not really miss. I am sure when you come you will look and feel ten years younger, and when you think of me think of a slightly rounder face, very brown and freckled for me even. My hands have got harder and do not get half so rough or dirty as they used to, and I suppose the same with my face, as my lips and skin used to peel. It is the dry air, and the alkali in the air, whatever that may be.

I hope . . . the new cook proved herself a treasure in Ascot week. I am sure Harbour would rise to the occasion and do all she could to help you and Freda. I hope, too, you will be able to meet Miss Muldoon later on. The side-face photo of Jack I like very much, and shall keep it for my own special. He has sent a good many to his various regimental pals and they seem to meet with approval, but I do not think they are really *quite* good enough. Did you go to Freda Dainty's "At Home"? I expect Park House looks awfully nice now it is all new, doesn't it? I am afraid the wedding presents have been a bit of a worry as to which was the best way to send them. But Jack quite approves of what you have done, and all we can hope is that we do not have to pay much duty. We want and shall value all the things out here more even than in England. Even if the silver takes all day to clean I shall have it out and appreciate it so much, after all these weeks of enamel and white metal and doing without, but in the meantime I am learning how to do lots of things (even to helping move big packing cases with a crow bar), besides possessing my soul in patience.

However, the house this week has been painted, or rather, we have had the house stained. Rather a light brown (umber) is the colour, so Freda will know, and the window sashes or wide outside pieces dark Irish green like the roof, also the doors green, and the window frames in bars to match the saddle-boards or slants on the roof which are white too. I thought it would make it look a little brighter and cleaner, though the painter assured me they were quite correct in *Calgary* all green, and thinks my taste very bad. The inside of the house is in the same state as we are waiting for the plasterer and lather. The lathes are packed up outside the house, but the good man is doing a house in Athalmer and will not be hurried. There is only *one* of everything and they are frightfully independent. To think of all the unemployed in England! The painter has come on here from General Poett's. They had their house built last year and have only just got it painted! But it is a very large house and lots of rooms (it is two storeys and not a bungalow). They have their rooms done with beaver board, and each room is painted a different colour, like distemper. Beaver board is like *very* thick smooth cardboard, and as it is narrow it is panelled into the rooms with lathes of wood which are stained, and the effect is very nice. However, I think plaster must be warmer and show fingermarks less, and it is certainly not so expensive!

I am afraid my last letter was rather a sad one, but please forget all about it. I did not mean or want to blame you in any way, you understood that, didn't you? But only to let you know so that you could tell Rainer, and, of course, being the first things I opened with great excitement I was a bit disappointed. However, some days when the apples grow we shall be able to send home and get a few new frames sent out. We have now got some glue, but find the corners are all done with nails. These have sprung open and have got a bit strained so the glue will not hold them as they will not fit truly, and in most cases the corners have split. I have got Freda's lithograph of you in the barn—the glass was not broken! And from the painter I have got some lamp-black and some linseed oil and have been touching up the frame. I have also been rubbing linseed oil into the carved things to try to tone down the scratches, but of course it will not take out the ruts! We next opened Jack's pictures which were packed in his travelling chest of drawers. Not one was damaged, only the glass on his chocolate box,[1] which he has got in a frame, was broken. They were just stuffed in with letters and photos and ties, etc. so perhaps Rainer's crate was not heavy enough. However, if ever you move I thoroughly recommend the Stores. The way their things are packed is simply splendid. The cases have all strong wooden battens round and take a long time to open, but not a thing scratched so far. The cases are first lined with waterproof paper, then a thick layer of straw, each thing wrapped in paper and tied up with string and bars of wood nailed across inside to keep the different layers of things steady. We have begun, or rather Jack has begun, to put the chairs together. I can only hold the pieces! They really do look awfully nice and do not show any join, and the leather seats are nice and large and nicely padded. The sideboard looks rather like a jigsaw puzzle but I expect that will come alright when we find the top and bottom! At present the barn is full of brown paper parcels, legs of chairs, etc. The table looks awfully nice, and I think the cretonne is pretty. Jack does not know if he likes it or not! But that is his fault entirely, I tell him, as he left it to me. With regard to the writing table, that is his piece of extravagance, but I think the only thing we shall get about that size is a bureau, like you have in your bedroom. I could not think of the name the other day, and I believe I have seen them at Maples in black oak. Jack, of course, wanted a roll-top desk. They have them at Eaton's, but they would not go in at the door. Most of Eaton's furniture is atrocious, but Jack says roll-top desks are American and the same all the world over. He has so many papers and things a place to keep them is most necessary. He has five bags in the barn, and when he wants a thing he never knows which bag it is in, and he can never wait a second for anything, of course, so you know the result!

It has been very hot, but we have had several thunder storms and now it is quite cool and I am wearing my golf jersey this morning. But, of course, I am virtually out of doors. It is like living in the summer house at home as the barn is not finished and has no window frames. We had terrific rain in the night. I have never heard such rain before, but Jack calls it tropical and takes no notice. However, it is lovely to hear it as the poor peas in our little garden were quite yellow and without water. Things grow so slowly. Seven strawberry plants are doing well, but the rest are dead. You can see the thin green rows of potatoes in the field now, and I hope this rain will increase the crop. But you cannot expect a big one the first year without water. This soil is very porous and a small shower has no effect whatever except you see "spots" all over the soil, and of course directly the rain ceases everything

---

1. Probably one of the souvenir boxes of chocolates that Queen Victoria sent as Christmas presents to soldiers in the South African War.

dries in an hour or so, even wet and muddy Burberrys and breeches, *and* boots! We have got our first supply of things from Eaton's, and even with the freight they come much cheaper and are very good. We had great fun opening the cases, and now they are stored in the loft or roof of the barn. When we wanted to get them up there we found we had no ladder so we set to and made one in an afternoon, and the new saw was a great success! We shall not touch many of the things but keep them for the winter, and next week order a second supply so as to have plenty. A man is now digging a cellar under the house and this will keep the things from freezing in winter and melting in summer. Eggs are now 45 cents a dozen, so I have sent to Pryce-Jones for some Waterglass[2] and shall put down and keep them for the winter.... We do not get meat, but gradually I get not to miss it, and we live like fighting cocks now. Plenty of eggs and bacon for breakfast, cheese and potted meat and jam for lunch. When we eat jam we *eat* jam and lots of butter! Last night we had macaroni in onion sauce, and sardines and hard-boiled eggs on fried bread, pork and beans, and various dishes of this sort. We always have stewed prunes or stewed apricots going and once or twice we have had rhubarb. Jack is able to work *hard* on this, and I feel very well and am certainly not thinner.

We went over to tea with the Youngs on Sunday, and I expect this week we may walk over and call on the Poetts for tea. When Mrs. Bowden comes we shall have neighbours twelve minutes away! I tell Jack the place is getting horribly crowded and he will want to move! I think he would like to be a hermit, but I am not going to let him. If he wanted to be a hermit he should have remained a bachelor.

I have no time for more just now. We do so enjoy *Punch,* *"The Pic,"* and the *Mail.*

Your affectionate child,

Daisy

WILMER, BRITISH COLUMBIA,
FRIDAY, JULY 12, 1912

My dearest Freda,

I believe I have two letters of yours unanswered, but all the same I try to write you and Mother alternate weeks and don't know how I manage it. You seem to have had a great time with Elsie in Town and I expect your tongues wagged pretty freely! Thanks ever so much for all the trouble you have taken, as well as Mother, about the box. We shall look forward to its

---

1. A solution of silicate of soda used for pickling eggs.

arrival, and whether we have to pay much or little will be forgotten when we see the contents. The scarf arrived with your letter written on June 9th, and I think it is lovely. Just what I should have chosen myself, and thanks ever so much. You must not mind if I ask you to do ever so many things for me, but just take your time and do them when you can without it being any bother. All the same, I love to think you are doing things for me and I believe you really like it too, and it is so comparatively easy from *my* point of view, of course.

As you say, fancy delicate Elsie gadding about as you describe. All the same, she seems to think from her letters that a colonial life is very hard and that I am wasted out here! I have written to tell her she is quite mistaken, but all the same I am sure a colonial life would not suit her. It is hard to a certain extent because it is all so different. But there are so many things that compensate, and in my case I am so well looked after I shall not come to any harm or grow lean and scraggy! Women are what Canada wants. There are such heaps of men, but all the same I hope bands of Suffragettes will not start coming out. *They* are not the sort that are wanted. . . .

Yes, I have worn my Jay hat a lot and it has been much admired. Jack very much approves and I think will safely trust you to choose another for me some day! I find it goes with everything. The other Sunday was wet and rather cold, and I wore it with my new "grey Cobden," and my grey crêpe de chine blouse (my silver blouse, as J. N. P. calls it), and it looked quite nice with that too. I told Jack you had got one like it, and he remarked, "I liked Freda in that hat with the red feather. And the blue coat and skirt with the red touch on the collar was quite what I liked too!" This pleased me as I like him to approve of you too. . . . Now for the Panama hat. It arrived on June 30th and is a real beauty, just the *very* thing for everyday wear out here. It is not a bit too big in the head. I have draped the scarf in a most fetching fashion and it looks very "chic" and the blue goes perfectly with my cotton dresses. The duty is from 20–30 per cent on cost of goods, and we had to pay 22 per cent on this. It was marked "Hat from South America" and was packed in a Liberty cardboard box, an oblong box, but of course it was firm. It was well papered with strong paper and string, but otherwise no protection and came without a dent. By the same post came a small box from the Stores, with a white felt hat that Jack had ordered for working in the field; also some gun oil. So we were both strutting about in our new hats and trying them at various angles!

I am awfully sorry to say I never received Lisa's letter or the small piece of green ribbon, but as you sent them before you went to Rottingdean I fear they went down in the *Titanic* too. Everything else has come, I am sure. The *Cornhills* and the *World's Work* are most welcome guests. I read the picture crits in the *Observer* to try and keep myself up to date! And I imagine you walking about in costumes, mostly grey or blue. Is that correct? This finishes (mosquito blood!!) answering your letter written on June 9th, I think.

You will be sorry to hear that poor old Jack has been in bed more or less all this week. Don't be alarmed, he is much better now and out in the sun for a little today! We had some very wet days, three or four, most unusual here for this time of year. Jack, of course, put on his Burberry and big boots and worked out of doors all the same. But when it rains one cannot dry things at the stove as it is out of doors, and so I suppose he got a chill and undoubtedly has had a severe attack of flu, aching in all his limbs, and burning head and eyes, and a cough and catarrh exactly like Mother gets. He has been rolled in blankets and had lots of hot tea, and for two days was very sorry for himself, but yesterday morning he got up at ten o'clock. While I went down to Wilmer for bread, butter and eggs, I left him the job of washing up, which he did very nicely! After I got back he retired to bed again feeling very weak, but spent the evening reading *Ingoldsby Legends*[1] aloud while I darned! Eggs and milk he is very fond of and has had plenty of, and when I ran out of eggs I gave him milk with a teaspoon of brandy. We get evaporated milk which is much nicer than condensed and is liquid like cream. Last night I tried to make a batch of haricot soup from the South Kensington book, and was quite successful as I have got a little cullender. Jack is much better today and has been cultivating the garden for a little. He is now sitting at the door with me in the sun and reading your book on crops. I went to fetch the bread from the good Mrs. Munsen yesterday. They have a few gooseberry bushes in their garden laden with green gooseberries. They very kindly gave me a large bagfull and a bundle of radishes. We have had stewed gosseberries for lunch (très bon), and now I will soon be cooking scrambled eggs for dinner. Jack is a splendid invalid and the first night when he was ill and hot and burning, tell Mother I very easily got him to take aconite![2] It soon did the trick. Everyone is so kind to you out here. I asked for eggs at the store in Wilmer yesterday. They were very scarce and they had none to sell, but directly I said Jack was ill the good Mr. Taylor went to his house and got me some. Mr. Bowden has been very kind and has walked over each evening. The cabbage seedlings in the garden were ready to be transplanted and he very kindly did them for me. We have now got fifty planted out in the field, and tomorrow I hope to pick a couple of our own lettuce. Though small they will be nice.

I am feeling awfully fit and well, and I am sure my face is getting fatter every week. The lather has been up this week and put up the lathes ready for the plasterer to begin. He promised to come Wednesday, but a week late

1. A favourite Victorian book of humorous poems by R. H. Barham, first published in 1840.
2. The Oxleys were interested in homeopathic medicine, and Daisy undoubtedly brought aconite, an extract from a flowering plant of the same name, with her to Canada.

here is simply nothing! You cannot depend on anybody's word. Jack has been putting the dining room chairs together and they look exceedingly nice. We have also been rubbing linseed oil into my carved things and some of the frames, and it certainly improves things. It was *awfully* good of you and Mother to write to me in Ascot week. I only expected about three lines from one of you and I had a long letter from both, which was lovely. Having two posts a week simply makes the time fly. I only wish I had more time for writing home. I never say half I could say, and sometimes forget what I have told you and what I have not.... I expect I shall have more time for letter writing in the winter. The mail goes out and comes in once a week by the stage and we get parcel post too, so we are not quite cut off! I am glad you found and liked the pictures of the Canadian Rockies. They sound like gems. This spot here is very beautiful, and I hope some day when the railway comes we shall see more.

Mr. Bowden has just been to Victoria for a week, and says the journey from Golden to the coast is simply magnificent and the vegetation is quite tropical. The flowering shrubs, syringa, etc. must be beautiful. They grow so luxuriously but they get heaps of rain. He said that although it is well worth while going to see it all he was glad to get back to this lovely air. He says that in the streets of Victoria you might be in Fleet Street, and that Victoria is very English in every way. I hope we shall be able to go some day, when the apples begin to grow, but they will not be planted until next year....

I have heard nothing of *twelve* ladies coming. I saw *three* ladies who came here with a view to dairy farming, but they moved on elsewhere! The last comers I heard of were a lady and her daughter, but they were going to settle at Invermere, I think, and have one or two acres for poultry. One new store is being built at Invermere, but at present there are no residents in the place, only the C.V.I. offices, garage, etc., the hotel, and the experimental farm which is now being made. I expect there will be lots of small houses and plots at Invermere on the lake shore in a year or so. It is all being planned out. I believe they get tourists at the Invermere Hotel, but they come down by the boat for the trip and have a look round and return, I expect, and they do not worry us on "the heights."

It seems so funny to think of Arthur and Nellie at Windsor and of you all in Ascot week.

I can just imagine old Dandy[3] wandering first into the sun and then into the shade as he used to do, but the new flower bed is there and I expect the lawn looks a little different in consequence. I shall try and grow mignonettes and some English flowers next year. I like your description of the polo and everything like that so much. Have you been to the river much? Remember

3. The family dog.

me to Frank when you see him, and also Mrs. Grix and Mr. Barnes, the fishmonger. When I think of all these people I can't believe I am married and out in B.C.!

I am sorry you did not get a letter in Ascot week. We always post our letters in good time for the mail, usually a day or two before, but of course the boat may stick or the motor break down when it takes them to Golden. There are two of us, and if anything went wrong you may be sure one or other of us would send a card or a few lines. So if you do not hear, *don't* worry. No time for more by this mail.

Much love to you all at home, and a special share for yourself.

Your affectionate sister,

Daisy

WILMER, B.C.,
JULY 17TH, 1912

My dearest Mother,

Your turn again this week, isn't it, though I expect the letters are fairly general property. The first piece of news, I think, is that Jack is better, I am glad to say, and able to work in the usual way. The only thing I notice is that he gets very hungry, and is always ready for a glass of milk between meals! After six o'clock he likes to sit in a chair and smoke and read *Punch* instead of being energetic. But he is very cheerful. Another event this week is that we have had four lettuces from our own "cabbage patch" and, of course, the flavour was most excellent (although perhaps you would object to paying 2d. each for them at Varneys!), and we have lots more coming on. We have been getting an unusual amount of rain. Although it is not very cheerful when the clouds come down and hide the mountains, we have comforted ourselves that it is good for the potatoes and rye. We have not got the water yet, but the irrigation ditch is now dug up to the corner of the vegetable garden so we know that water will soon be on its way. Then, of course, will come the making of the boxflumes to carry the water over to the cultivated corner of our land. More work for Jack, but I don't expect he will get much done until next year as it will be too late this year to do the crops any good. The Company has now got a water cart which brings us as much water as we want, but we find that two barrels every third day is as much as we really want for household use, and the garden has not needed water lately. The peas are growing tall and strong, and the beans which are dwarf are just coming into flower. The cabbages, as I told you, are now nearly all put out in a corner of the potato patch.

Saturday was a pouring wet day, and in the afternoon we could not go outside it was so bad. So Jack wrapped himself up in a blanket and curled himself up on the bed to read aloud while I did some mending. Presently, footsteps were heard outside. "Hello, Cuthbert, is that you?," and in came Mr. Cuthbert dripping wet, followed by his faithful hound, a retriever in like case. Says Mr. Cuthbert, "My wife has been thinking of Mrs. Phillips the last three wet days, in the barn and no cheerful fire, and has sent me up to bring her down to our house to get a good warm up." He had walked up here in the pouring rain, a good ¾ hour's walk, and we thought it most kind. I had not felt it cold as I have got so used to being always outdoors. If damp I always wear my drab golf jersey, and it has been my greatest comfort. Mr. Cuthbert also stated that they wanted us to go and dine with them on Sunday, as they had killed the "fatted calf," or rather one of their fowls, and he hoped it would go round. I thought too that perhaps boiled fowl would do Jack good, but he has been taking a lot of extra milk before breakfast and in the middle of the morning. We got to the Cuthbert's about one o'clock and thoroughly enjoyed our meal of boiled fowl, green peas and potatoes, and a very nice lemon cold sweet and stewed apples to follow. After, while the men smoked, I helped Mrs. Cuthbert to wash up. She is very clever, I think, as she managed to do it all without putting on an apron. But I expect I shall be equally clever in time, and with washing clothes it does not so much matter, especially when you do your own and have no laundry bills!

July 18th. The Cuthberts are going in largely for market gardening and have a good show of vegetables, though everything is much later here. I occasionally buy eggs from her when she has them to spare, as she goes in for chickens. She is very pretty and a little thing, smaller than me. He is Irish, with a pretty twist to his tongue. He was an engineer near Manchester, and is a wiry, spare man with iron grey hair, but very clever, of course, when it comes to building flumes, etc. Their house is very pretty, white with a green roof and doors, and a back-water of the Columbia River runs right at the bottom of their patch. The river winds about and the banks are covered with green withy beds. Now, of course, the current is fairly rapid and the water is full of logs floating down to Golden.

To get to Athalmer we go down hill all the way from here and cross the river at Toby Creek Bridge, and then it is level walking the rest of the way. We get a lovely view of the lake on our way up and down Toby Creek Road and it also bends about. With the foothills of the Rockies rising from it, Jack often says, "That is exactly like the Congo," or "How the lake reminds me of the Nile." But I am always hoping you and Freda will see it some day. The fencing round "the estate" is now complete, and it feels quite grand to go in and out of a gate! We have a small gate fairly near the house, where we can go out when we want a stroll along the top of the creek in Mr. Bowden's direction, and a large gate for carts, etc. down by the cultivated patch.

We now await the plasterer's advent with anxiety. We know he has come in from Cranbrook and was to have come up on Tuesday, but we hear on arrival he indulged in three bottles of whisky and, of course, he is not fit for work at present! This is the silly sort of thing so many of the men do out here. I suppose they get high wages which burn a hole in their pockets and there is no other way they can spend it.

Jack has now finished the six dining room chairs and they look very nice indeed. He has stuck the carved spinning chair together, as we have now been able to get some glue. Today being the 18th we had early lunch and went down to Wilmer hoping to get the letters. But when we got there the mail had not come in and they did not expect it until 6 or 7 o'clock, so I shall get two letters from Freda and you on Saturday, I expect. But I know you have thought of me. After this, I think birthdays will have to be forgotten as I can never get anything here to send you and already I feel you have given me too much.

Your hint about washing the handkerchiefs I have tried, and the salt is certainly beneficial. I kept wondering on Sunday, when I have people to lunch, shall I be able to truss a fowl, but I expect I shall find that out in time like so many other things I feel I ought to know. You certainly want to be a Jack-of-all-trades in the Colonies. On our way down this afternoon we met the eldest Miss Poett driving home from Athalmer, laden with supplies.She is a very pretty girl with fair hair, blue eyes, and pink cheeks. She had on a *huge* mushroom hat with a very pretty salmon pink ribbon, and a light blue cotton dress, with turn-down collar open at the neck, with a floppy black bow; and very pretty earrings, quite as if she was ready for an afternoon on the river. So you see we are not all "ugly frights," though I expect she does not feed the chickens and do housework in quite this attire. On our way back the Company car overtook us on the hill and gave us a lift. On board was a Mr. Malpas who has just bought Lot 86. It is near the Poetts. A retired Indian Civil man has bought another lot in the same direction and he has a grown-up son and daughter. Distance is great, and you are so busy you do not come across each other often, but when you do people are all so nice. Mr. Malpas is going back to England to fetch his wife and family, but as he is a young man I don't imagine his family is large.

July 20th. As I finished writing this on Thursday night, Smith, Mr. Bowden's ploughman, appeared at the barn door and said he had been for letters and found several for us and brought them up. One from you and one from Freda too, so I did have my birthday letters on *the* day after all, and shall get the small parcels tonight when we go down for bread. We may alter our address to Athalmer during the winter and when *I* begin to make our bread, but I will let you know for certain.

What a lot seems to have been going on in Windsor lately, or is it a matter of comparison, I wonder? You are so good at telling me all, and I do appreciate it. Having two letters a week I feel so near and close to you all, and quite forget the ocean between! I knew you would enjoy those photos, Mother, but I wish I could send you snapshots of the surroundings. Freda must borrow one of Stewart's cameras when she comes and bring that as well as the dog! The verandah goes as far as the smokeroom window and leaves off so the spare room has no verandah. The broken line is nicer, we thought, and the spare room has only one window so it does not make it dark. There is no verandah on our bedroom side. We face nearly south, and I expect shall live on the verandah all the summer, and sleep there too in all probability!

The chimney goes up when the plasterer comes, as it is plaster, as also the mantle piece and the plinth. . . . We do not have a big hearth as we have a wire fire guard that fits right across the fire to keep sparks from the wood. In the *very* cold weather we may have to get a heater as well, but the pipe can be fixed to go up the chimney. The stovepipe from the kitchen range will also run through into the chimney. As usual I am writing and resting, so writing very badly! *Your* room when you come has only one window, but the kitchen window and tiny pantry window are both the same side of the house as the "hall" bow window, and then round the other side of the house is only *one* window, the second of our room where I expect the dressing table will be as it gets the direct light. This window looks towards our "cabbage patch" and our little gate beyond. The windows are rather high up but I can see out alright. They are a little small, but are the first of their kind about here. We intended them to be bigger but they really look quite nice. They will keep out the cold in winter, and in summer I think the house will not trouble us much except on wet days. The spare room at present we can use as a bathroom. The ceilings will be plaster the same as the walls, not wood, as I think that would make the rooms too dark.

It is the greatest luck *I* was in the photo at all, as I was grubbing in the garden and only came along just in time. The hat is a grey one with the little wings—I wore it all the time we were in the tent. Now the Liberty hat is perfect, so shady and so light on the head, and withal a little bit of "go" as it is turned up on one side. The thing you think is an iron "girder" round the top of the verandah is a plank used as a part of the scaffold and will shortly be removed. We shall have no blinds but only curtains as there is nobody to look in except the bats! I think I shall use all the cretonne for the hall and so the other rooms will be Madras muslin, but nous verrons! The windows will open à la casement, with a primitive hook arrangement to hold them, I should imagine. We have not got that far yet. They are now just held in place by nails.

I have sent directions in my last letter for "winter comforts," but have now received the Jaeger[1] list. I think one of the knitted hoods would be very

---

1. Jaeger's is another London clothing store with its main branch in Regent Street.

useful and warm. Jack says, have an "attractive" one, so I think the hood and scarf in one piece look nice, 5/9d., and I should think plain white is best. The other sort Jack likes is the bonnet, 2/11d. Perhaps Freda could try one on and select the most fetching. I expect they keep all sorts at Debenhams for winter sports, don't they? Perhaps a warm petticoat that would not be too gaudy would be useful. If Freda has not already ordered the gloves at Sleeps, will she order them to be made like baby mitts, as they are much warmer than the gloves with fingers, and a pair of woollen ones of the same sort—white, I should say. I should think the best way would be to send these things by parcel post even if they come in two parcels. I have golf jerseys, and Shetlands I can put on for extra clothing, Jack's putties for my legs, and he has ordered me snowboots from Toronto. I am sending a cheque for £3 which Jack has made out to Freda.

The sewing machine has come and I am learning how it goes. It was £2.18.0. and is guaranteed for seven years. I know two people here who say they are good. Mrs. Dainty has kindly written me about the valence boards; she *is* kind (so is everyone), and it is such a help to me out here. I will try and write to her by this mail, but I find so little time after home letters, and after our work I suppose naturally Jack and I like a little playtime together. I often look at him and feel he is so magnificent he is wasted out here. But I think he is very happy and contented, and proud of his estate. We are both now writing outside the barn door! There is a lovely soft breeze and the buzz of the mosquitoes and lots of jumping grasshoppers that make a popping noise peculiar to themselves! The enclosed flower is very beautiful and is found in this colour and in pink. It is between a lily and an orchid. Mrs. Cuthbert had them in silver vases on Sunday, and they look lovely.

I must close now, dear Mother. Ever so much love to you all.

Your affectionate child,

Daisy

ATHALMER, BRITISH COLUMBIA
JULY 25TH, 1912

My dear girl,

I don't know how to thank you for your birthday gifts, for they gave me so much pleasure. It was awfully good of you to send me two things. The Japanese print I like immensely. It will go with the set and so help to make a feature of them in our room, and with light grey plaster for a background I am sure they will look awfully nice. The green leather frame is a duck. Jack's side-face is now in it and it suits the photo perfectly. The glasses of the frames were broken but that was no fault of the packing, the parcel might have had a knock. However, we have found a man in Athalmer who has a glass-cutter and so we soon got some more to cut to size. Please thank Mother very much indeed for the pudding. It is more than a treat, and Oh, those chocolates! They were the very best I have ever tasted in my life, and all *hard* sorts too. Also the Maggi soups. What lots of thoughts and time you all give me, but it is a greatest help for during these first months we have had a tremendous lot of odds against us and lots of discomforts besides, of course, much happiness and many pleasures. Things are straightening out a bit now and we are beginning to feel our feet, and I really think I must be a most adaptable person for I have not suffered a bit and feel so well and fit. If you get a bit tired at night, in the morning you feel as fresh as paint and ready to begin again. So don't enlarge on these things when you write, as Jack is perfectly content and happy. I told you I got my birthday letter on July 18th as Mr. Bowden's boy Smith brought them up just as we were going to bed. The two parcels arrived on that day too, so they take about the same time as letters.

On Saturday we walked to Wilmer in the afternoon and went to the experimental garden. Mr. Hanley, the man in charge, is a charming Irishman and took us round and showed us the different sorts of vegetables and small fruits and we had a good feed of raspberries which was lovely. We also saw the water ditches and cultivators at work and, best of all, he pulled and gave us three lovely lettuces, onions and radishes. He also lent Jack a hand cultivator for a few days to do our "spuds." They are trying various flowering shrubs and small ornamental trees such as lilac and maple, and if they stand the cold we shall be able to buy them for our garden next year.

When we got to the Post Office I found the two "home" parcels, and a parcel and letter from Western Australia. As we had six loaves of bread, the vegetables and cultivator, the excitement of it all was almost too much. We were frightfully hungry and it was late when we got to the barn, so I got *cheese and onions* ready while Jack opened the parcels and, of course, we immediately began on chocolates. Flora's present is really awfully nice and unique: a bread fork, at the end of which is the map of Australia for the handle, greatly takes Jack's fancy; two knife rests which are two bars, at one end is a kangaroo and at the other a laughing jackass (these *I* like and I think shall use as ornaments); and a gilt and enamel spoon with the arms of Western Australia. Flora has written me two awfully nice letters and wonders why we did not go to Western Australia for fruit farming.

Mr. Newman, a new man whom the Company have brought in to help folk buy apple trees and lay out orchards, is an Englishman who has lived a great many years in Australia, fruit farming, and has two brothers out there now near Perth. He has come here from the Okanagan Valley where he has a prosperous orchard and a partner. He came up this week and we have decided to plant two acres of apple trees next year to make a start. Our kinds will be "Jonathans" and a "Mackintosh" for permanent, and "Wealthy" for fillers. These grow quicker and bear sooner, but are pulled up when the other trees grow and spread. We are also going to plant about 100 rasp-berries, gooseberries, and red and black currants. The ground is ploughed in the fall. I believe they dig the holes then and plant in the spring, but "nous verrons." The ground all round the house will have to be ploughed too and the garden mapped out ready for the irrigation. Such lots to do for Jack. I think we shall have to afford a little help next year, but 12/- a day is a little thick, isn't it, and we want to go very carefully at present. Jack's idea is to get the house nice with shelves and fittings and comforts. As he keeps on saying, "I have never really had a home since I was 15"!

On Sunday we thought we would explore a little so we set out in the morning with cheese and jam sandwiches, and Jack with his water-bottle and walked to the old "saw-mill" lake, quite close to Captain White's lot, had lunch there and then went on to see the viaduct which I sent in the photograph. The big flume leaked and part of it collapsed last week. As this flume will bring us water "some day" we were rather interested! The men are repairing it, but water when it gets loose is not a very nice thing and the beautiful glen where it is situated was very muddy. A good many Swedes are working on it and the foreman is a Swede. I expect the reason is that they understand working in wood. The best carpenter on our house was a Swede, the cobbler in Athalmer is a Swede, the blacksmith is a German, the men who made our fence are Germans. Where are the English with wages at $3-4 a day, and all the unemployed!

Well, from there we walked on to call on "the General." Their house is now painted and quite finished, and is perfectly charming and artistic. They have the roof, doors, and windows a sort of dull moss green. The rest of the house is a dull terracotta stain. It sounds horrid, perhaps, but the effect is charming as it goes with the surroundings. You sit on the verandah, and in front of you is a most beautiful lake and beyond in the far distance you get the mountains. The inside of the house and of the rooms is done with "beaver board," which is very thick board with a smooth surface, and is painted in plain colours and looks like distemper. The drawing room is white, dining room red, staircase mignonette green, and all the paint is dull brown stain (the stairs, etc.), and though they have not much furniture they have lovely Indian rugs, and draperies and tablecovers, and lots of nice silver ornaments. Each girl has her own room and they have made dressing tables with pretty chinz frills round and little bedspreads and curtains to match, though I believe the beds are folding ones of a variety bought at Harrods! Mrs. Poett looked charming in a navy blue muslin gown, with three tucks in the skirt and a tucked blouse bodice, the only trimming being most beautiful turnover collar and cuffs. She and her daughters have all their clothes made like this, only "Mother" wears a stand-up neck band inside and always wears most beautiful diamond earrings. We began tea as the daughters were out. Two men on horseback soon arrived, Captain Lawrence and Captain Fraser, I think, both men in the 7th Hussars. Jack says that means at least £1,000 a year income. They were on leave and travelling in Canada, and as far as I could gather knew General Poett in India where he was living before they came out here. They had come down from Golden the night before, and returned the next day. One of them said he had large money interests in Canada. His pal had come out with him and he was just looking for a little "pied à terre" so that he could just run over occasionally! The great puzzle to them both was that refined Englishwomen should be willing to do all the work. The Poetts have now got a Chinaman who brought out tea, and the evening before Mrs. Poett had got all the bachelors of the neighbourhood there and they had danced on the verandah. Six couples! The eldest girl is about 21, and the youngest is a good-looking flapper[1] of 16. Then comes a big gap and there are "the babies," twins of four. The Campbell kids, I call them, as they sit on the sofa and hold each other's hands. Jack would call this gossip, I expect, but I tell you everything. You need not comment on it all, but it shows what contrasts you meet out here. Of course, the Poetts are well off, and are now putting in a gasoline engine to pump water from the lake, but we met Mrs. and Miss yesterday in the pouring rain in old, old Burberrys and skirts, and you would not know them for the same. They very kindly left a large bundle of rhubarb for us at Mr. Bowden's, and having stewed the rhubarb I am going to try the leaves boiled as spinach, and put eggs on top for supper.

Jack is going to Wilmer but I will write to you and darn. We still wait for the plasterer. Nothing has been done to our house for a fortnight. It is sickening. I hear there was an artist, a "French Impressionist," here last year who had exhibited in the Paris Salon, by name one Frank Armington, and some of his sketches in oils were reproduced in the pamphlet, "Windermere, B.C.," with the small boy sitting among the apples on the cover![2] We shall see what we can do when you come. The Company will doubtless bring out a new pamphlet! I am now looking forward to Pandora's box. It will be most exciting. I think I told you the wedding presents have fetched up but are not opened yet. It is no good opening much as things soon get knocked about in the barn. Jack's latest treasure is a wheelbarrow, which he takes out with him when he goes collecting firewood! Will you please send your next letters to Athalmer as we think it will be better to have them there during the winter. The Company offices have moved from Wilmer to Invermere

1. A school girl who wore her hair in a pigtail.
2. Frank Armington was an English artist who lived in Paris between 1910 and 1914. A member of the Royal Society of Painters, Engravers, and Etchers, and best known for his etching, he did most of the paintings for Bruce's pamphlet on Windermere. The arrangements are unknown.

and we often have to go there. It is only about twenty minutes from one place to the other.

Poor Mrs. Young's "lady help," Miss Hughes, whom she brought with her has gone, and for some weeks she has been alone, but she is very plucky. They have got two cows as they must have fresh milk for the children, but of course they get more than they want and she makes butter. You can imagine what it is washing for three small children. Their barn is much larger than ours and their loft is big enough for a large bedroom, and they have a bedroom downstairs as well. I went over last week and gave her a long afternoon of ironing, and now I hear that a girl friend of hers from Vancouver is coming to help her for a time....

I have had a long morning's washing, and so am sitting outside to write today (Saturday) while Jack has gone off to get the bread. He is busy hoeing the potatoes at present and weeding. Oh, the mosquitoes do bite, but not so badly as at first as then the bites came up into little blood blisters. They seem so fond of my eyes, but I have a large bottle of Witch Hazel now from Timothy Eaton and it soon takes down the swelling. Tomorrow we hope to take our lunch and go down to the lake and sit there for a few hours. Sundays as a day of rest is most essential out here. We always enjoy being able to laze, and to read and sit quietly. There is a small church at Wilmer, and we are going on Sunday when it is not too hot and we can start early enough. As it means we do not get back for lunch until so very late and feel hot and tired and cross, I think until the autumn it is best to rest and meditate. There is a church at Windermere, but that is about seven miles away on the other side of the lake, and the congregation I should say would be three! When we have a horse we shall be able to drive over there, as I believe it is a lovely spot, but there are no settlers there yet. They evidently thought they would develop this side first....

I feel so ashamed when I get your letters as they are such volumes, but I hope I shall get more time some day. The darning takes me some time as I go through stockings in two or three days. I am wearing my Evans cotton dresses[3] now for Sundays and like them very much indeed. I am so thankful I have got some old underclothes, as camping is not good for them either. A piece of French tape and a *small* bottle of Mrs. Woodman's astringent hair-wash will be useful things to come some day. Plenty of shavings and corrugated paper round the bottle ought to bring it safely. When you want money, let me know. I am not a millionaire and do not want to spend more than I can help, but I don't want you to be out of pocket one penny piece! I like the sound of the black tulle ruche. I see it is correct by the *Lady's Pic.* ... Nelly told me in her letters how you were working in the garden and how nice it all looked this summer. My sweet peas are not in flower yet!

---

3. Probably from the D. H. Evans store in Oxford Street.

The chocs are lovely and so fresh in an airtight tin, and cold Christmas pudding is just lovely. I am a little pig, I believe....

My dearest Mother,

I wonder if you will still be at Whitby when this reaches you or whether you will be home again. Jack had Freda's postcard last Thursday, and I her letter written from there, last Saturday.... Your letters are splendid and I devour them, but I often think they must be written as a self-sacrifice when you are tired, as I know how long it takes me to send these few lines every week. Anyway, Thursday and Saturday are the "best" days of the week and those which we both look forward to most, and now I find Jack is always ready to give up work to go for the letters. Kenny writes nearly every week, and most weeks Jack gets some from Gibraltar,[1] this week from Colonel Lloyd. And, of course, just now there is business going on winding up his father's affairs which are very disappointing. Of course we shall not starve, but the extra money we should have spent on luxuries and a holiday home some day — but this is entre nous.

Meanwhile I am very happy, and I am sure Jack is. He came in to lunch today from hoeing potatoes, exceedingly hot and dirty — we had cheese and potato salad, scones, and strawberry jam, stewed prunes, milk, and lemonade — and said, "I *do* enjoy this life and no mistake," and I think he does. It is a sign he feels quite right again after the 'flu, as for a time he used to get tired very easily. I was so glad to hear old Gilbert had been up to see you.... When I saw the surveyors come along with their measuring tapes the other day I thought of him. Of course, perhaps you have not realized how differently men dress out here. It is difficult to describe exactly, but the boots are very high, in most cases halfway up to the knee, and have very large lace holes with metal rings that show (not blackened like the eyelets in an English boot), a khaki or butcher-blue shirt open at the throat, and a bandana handkerchief round the neck, (or nothing as the case may be), and a soft felt hat. The workmen, carpenters, etc., all wear blue overalls, like very high trousers that brace over the shoulders and no coats to them, and these they slip off when work is finished and they are quite your equals once more, and hardly ever say Sir!

Thank you ever so much for my birthday presents, the Christmas pudding was just lovely. I boiled it an hour and a quarter and found it just right.

1. Where his former regiment was posted.

We ate it cold and made it last, and we had the last slice last night. There are still two chocolates left, and we shall have these as a *bon-bouche* after dinner tonight, I expect, which is to be macaroni and onions.... The mould will be most precious as at present I have not seen china cooking utensils at all, but only enamel and tin. I remember with joy that two pudding basins were included with the dinner service! I am afraid I shall not be able to get the materials for Christmas puddings, so we too shall look to you for one of sorts. I will send Jack's family recipe in case you are able to make them yourself.... I am glad I did not know last year it was my last Christmas at home "as an Oxley," though I still hope to spend another at home with you all some day.

I am very glad that Lizzie Bailey has got the canary, the very best thing you could have done with him, I think. There are lots of questions I have not answered yet, I believe. The ceiling of the rooms—well, they will be plaster too like the walls, and we are going to have a band of stained wood along the wall of the sitting room to take the place of a picture rail, and also a chair rail, as I think these will take away the bare cold look if there is one. But I really think it will look rather artistic, as the fireplace is made of large pebbles and stones that are pressed into the plaster and a lot have turned up to the light in digging the root-cellar! Then as to the water. I expect in time we shall have a large cistern dug, and lined with cement and store water, and fill it with the supply that comes along the ditch and have a tap in the kitchen. We had the house built where there was a big enough drop to allow for this, but it will not be until next  year as for one thing it is a very big expense and for another the water is not along our ditch yet. I expect in the winter they will haul us ice and I shall have a barrel in the kitchen and melt it, and also melt snow! This sounds very dreadful to you, I expect, but remember I have never turned a tap since I have been here and am quite used to hauling water out of a barrel whenever I fill my kettle or saucepan. I believe the average in winter is 10° below zero and is not at all bad, and midday is fairly sunny and warm, but as far as I can make out they have "cold snaps" when it goes down to -20°, but usually this only lasts for a few days. Here we do not get the high and biting winds they do on the Prairies. It is usually fairly still. Jack says he is quite sure it will be very similar to Switzerland, and that is lovely. It does not do to say anything against his beloved B.C., I tell him.

We have got large supplies of jam, pickles, milk and corn-starch (cornflour) from Eaton's and lots of useful little kitchen utensils, cake tins, strainers, etc. They are all expensive for what they are, but there is no demand for *good* things here and they will serve their purpose quite well. I have got a bread-mixer, and you can see one like it in the Stores catalogue. I am getting a washing machine very similar to the one you marked in the *Observer*. Everyone says they are such a help when you come to sheets and table linen, and I shall have a "wringer" attached. Of course, it is a bit heavy going with large things but Jack will step in there once a week and push and turn! I must just go and get the fire going and put on the kettle as he likes a hot bath when he comes in at 5:30. At present it is so hot we live altogether outside the barn. I got up this morning very sleepily when I was told, and when I was dressed found it was 6:35. We have not been having breakfast lately until 8 o'clock, but these hot days it is far easier to work in the cool and now I am writing to you all the afternoon without any rush! No, we shall not have blinds, there is nobody to look in. There is not guttering round the edge of the roof. I expect it was a piece of scaffoldboard you saw in the photo. The windows open outwards and *not* up and down. A good many windows here only open at the top. You push the top *down,* but the bottom will not push *up.* We are not at all advanced but, as Jack says, this country is only about *twenty years old* and we shall improve soon when the railway comes! Many thanks for reminding me about the beans. If I get a chance I shall salt some down. Some day, will you send me the recipe for the "Spanish Onion pickle," as we get dried onions now from Western Australia! They are not as large as Spanish but are mild.

Thursday. Sunday was a lovely day so we took our lunch (hard boiled egg sandwiches and Christmas pudding!) and a large supply of lemonade and walked down to Invermere and sat by the lake. It is very beautiful and really very like Lake Windermere in England, only of course there is nobody about revelling in its beauties like there would be in England. We got to one little place where there was quite a sandy beach and little tiny waves kept on lapping on the shore almost like the sea does in the Isle of Wight! We had got so tired of waiting and watching our house and nothing doing we went to discover a plasterer, Mr. Tainton by name, and found his little wooden shack buried away by the lake shore. However, he has got so much work to do in Athalmer before winter there was no chance of him coming to us. His wife in a blue and white check sunbonnet and apron to match was a picture of country freshness, and she was out busy feeding her chickens. There were several apple trees in the garden laden with fruit, and the potatoes looked as big as currant bushes. Of course, this was a very sheltered spot and very warm and heaps of water, but I think things will really grow here presently in a very prolific way. By the way, the green sunbonnet from Woolacombe is now worn for *use* and not for ornament and is so nice. I went down to help rake between the rows of potatoes to keep the earth cultivated yesterday afternoon and although very hot in the sun I found it better than a hat.

Jack has just told me I must write and tell you why I am writing now, 12 o'clock in the morning. I was getting lunch ready outside and had come into the barn for knives when a gust of wind came and slammed the barn door and fixed it so that I could not get out until "he" arrived and opened the door with a hammer, chuckling all the time, as it seemed to strike him as being very funny. The Express Delivery box with the silver is now in the barn and has arrived in *splendid* condition. We have opened it and all the things are very well packed indeed. All the things look so nice out here, and Dorrie Durant's butter dish will be a gem after having butter for so long on an enamel plate. Thank you for seeing to and sending these. You must not feel about Rainer's box that the "home people" have failed. I have not thought that for a moment. If you had packed them, Mother, I know they would have been perfectly alright. I am so vexed that you should have to pay, and you certainly ought to get some of the money back. The "Way" box is a good thick packing case and Jack says it is a splendid job. But the Rainer cases, I think, were old ones and not very thick, so Jack says men handling them would perhaps think they contained "old rags" or something of that kind, certainly not pictures and china. We spend all our odd moments patching up things, and we have been able to get glass cut which we did not expect. I have quite forgotten it all now, so please don't you worry. I know things had to be done in a very difficult and peculiar manner, but your son-in-law will never realize this, I am sure, though I do occasionally remind him of the fact! He always does things in this way, makes up his mind and goes at it at once, and sometimes if we are going out his hair nearly turns white while I lace up my boots. All the same, if I have a hair out of place I am reminded that a fringe-net is a useful thing! . . .

I often think if you could leave No. 4 and get right away it would really be a good thing. I know you will say £.s.d., but you and Freda could live in a small house with one servant. I am always planning things in my mind, and now I think a small furnished flat in London, somewhere near Chelsea, where you could be in touch with the boys and Freda could work, would suit you both, and the change of scene and everything would improve the health of both! Thank you so much for the "rosemary" sachet. It was sweet of you to think, and it is a lovely scent. Jack quite approves. I will write to Auntie Louie if ever I have time. I have just said, "What a lot of notepaper we use," and the reply was "You do," but it nearly all returns from whence it came! I do hope we shall see you here some day, though at present I do not think we have room for you both, and perhaps could not afford two visitors! Freda must come first and report, and I know she will make you long to come. We have ordered two mats from Eaton's for the doors but don't expect they will come up to English quality.

Much love from us both, dear Mother,

Your affectionate child,

Daisy

My dearest Freda,

I ought to have been writing to you an hour ago, but I was *made* to rest on the bed and find I have lost a whole hour of precious time from 2:30 to 3:30. I always grudge the rest just then. I could so often write or sew as I have so little time for both these things. But still, when I get up at 6 o'clock and keep running about on my feet until 12, and then running about more or less until bedtime at night it is not time wasted. Jack says it is wrinkles saved! So here I am just commencing, and in a minute a voice will be calling out, "Is tea ready?" and the kettle does not boil even. I shall have to get a little one for the house as the present turquoise-blue enamel (nearly black) holds a gallon, but that is not too much when "large" people take a bath!

This morning we were up with the lark and had breakfast and made the bed and swept the barn and had the breakfast things washed and the boots cleaned and started for Invermere at 8:30. It was a lovely morning with blue sky and a soft light breeze, and everything was looking its best. First of all, we went to the "Experimental Farm" and interviewed one Mr. Anderson by name, who is in charge, as to why our potatoes were not doing their best. Some of them are fine large plants and some quite tiny things that are coming into flower much too soon and will not grow. He says what all the "old-timers" say, it is the new soil. It requires such a lot of working and disking and harrowing, and will be better when it is ploughed again and left to the frost. We shall have enough potatoes for ourselves but we shall not make a fortune this year by selling them. Of course, not having a horse at present Jack could not keep the soil "going" as well as other people who have a team. In Mr. Bowden's case he has the practical knowledge and there are three of them at work as there is Mr. Robinson and the ploughman they brought from the "Old Country," but we are not down-hearted yet and look for better things next year when we shall have a horse and perhaps a cow. Your dairy knowledge will come in useful! From the farm we went to the C.V.I. Offices to see about a water tank (I know this will please Mother). I think they will make one where the ditch comes at the top of the land (view from our side bedroom window), lined with planks and then again with galvanized iron. Of course, this is sunk under the ground and is covered with soil to keep out frost. We should need enough water to last four months, I expect, and it will be nice if there is sufficient "drop" to bring a pipe to the house and have a tap, just think of it, into the kitchen!

Since I wrote we have got "the cellar" under the house boarded up and lined with shelves. It is 12′ x 10′ x 4′ and has a trap-door and about six steps down. The cellar is a great feature out here as butter, meat, and stores keep cool in summer, and it prevents bread, eggs, milk, etc. from freezing in the winter. When we first came and started building the house they said,

"Would we have a cellar?" (a lot extra, of course), so we said "No! We would economize there at any rate." But as time went on we found from other people that the cellar is *the* most important part of the house as there you keep all your stores, milk, etc. so we had to pay a lot to get a man to come with pick and shovel and dig it out when the house was up. It is small as compared to many others but we could not afford more, and now the water tank will cost about $200 or more, and so we go on! But by and by we shall be making money, I hope.

From Invermere we walked to Athalmer and did some shopping. This little place has grown and improved a lot since we came, but it is a common little place where the plumbers and painters and storekeepers with lots of money congregate and are building large houses, with lots of rooms and heaps of paint. It has improved because the two little broken-down stores have built new and palatial premises, and the boat unloads here, and the railway when it comes! It is on a low, rather marshy, part of land by the Columbia River. I am sure you are imagining it all wrong. I wish I could make word pictures. Don't imagine a *large* place, for goodness sake. It is only a handful of houses, but there is a pavement made of boards, which is very advanced. Well, we interviewed the blacksmith (a red-haired giant) about some "dogs" for our fireplace. You enter the shed, he goes on working. "Good morning." "Good morning." (Not looking up.) "Can you make some fire-dogs?" "Yes." (Still not looking up.) "What size? Round iron or flat iron?" (Still working away.) After a few remarks more on our side he finds we treat him as an equal, I suppose, and comes down off his perch, and before we finish he is fairly friendly, but "take it or leave it" style is quite the fashion, as he has all the work he wants to keep him going! We then went to the butcher and were able to buy some steak. His shop is a little wooden box without windows, so the door is always open, and it is furnished with a block and a pair of scales! We got 1¼ pounds of steak, which I stewed today with some onions and I enjoyed it very much. J.N.P. thought it might be more tender, but he does not care for meat unless it is *very* good. This is only the second piece we have had as the late butcher broke his arm and this is a new man who kills local steers and turns up his nose at Calgary meat. I expect there will be sheep here again some day. They tell you there was mutton to be had three years ago, but it was all eaten or killed by "kyoties" — it sounds like this, I do not know the spelling. I heard today there was rhubarb "going" in Wilmer so I trotted off to procure some and buy some "sealers" at Bull's Store, as they tell me you can cut it up and bottle it in water without cooking. I am going to try. The "sealers" are glass bottles with screw tops and everyone in Canada seems to bottle fruit (when you can get it). I believe Nelly had some, but I don't know the proper process. In Mrs. Beeton they tell you to put the bottles in cold water and bring to the boil, but I believe there is a different way as I saw these bottles, I think at Herbert's Stores. You see I am in good condition as I went eight miles yesterday and six today, besides all my other trotting about, but of course no washing on these two days!

Friday. While I think of it, the enclosed piece of "rye" is from our crop, which seems fairly good, judging by others round. We are growing it for feed for the horse we hope to have next year!

I am so glad you like Whitby. It sounds very fascinating, and Elsie sent me a p.c. which reminded me of St. Ives! Your drawing of the old church, too, was very interesting. I do hope you have been able to do some work that you really like. It sounds to me rather like a "pen and wash" place. I want you to stick to heads during the winter as I believe when you come here you could make some money in that line—Jack's idea, and he is sure you could earn your passage money! You see, there is no photographer, and I am sure Mr. Stark at the Invermere Hotel would want one of his wife and Mr. Peake at the hardware store one of his wife. They would not be beautiful people, perhaps, but they have all got money, and if you could get one good likeness—voilà, your fortune would be made! Entre nous, I think brother-in-law would sit for you as many times as you like....

"Your" fur coat has been hanging in the sun today and my furs have been out too, but I hope we shall escape moths. We have heaps of butterflies and I suppose they are relations.... Thanks so much for sending your old overcoat. "Old rags" are most useful out here, though you only wear them on occasion.... Jack will not object to the old coat. He objects to nothing *old* as long as it is well cut! You will have to choose me a winter hat by and by. Jack always scans the pictures in the *Lady Pic.* and I expect we shall come across something as a guide in the autumn. He knows exactly what he likes, funnily enough, *black,* so my old coat and skirt are commended. Earrings are quite approved of and large hats, all things worn by wives of men in his regiment, I gather! I wonder if I shall ever write a letter and *not* want anything. My grey "snow-storm" Cobden tweed is wearing at the bottom so will you send me some grey braid, any grey will do, 4 yards, I think will be enough, and later on I expect I can shorten it, when you come perhaps. I shall be so glad to get in the house as I cannot settle to do anything in the barn. It is so full that even if I make the curtains I have nowhere to keep them fresh! There are mauve Michaelmas daisies growing everywhere now, quite as good as those in the garden at home and they are sweetly pretty. I expect they will be nearly the last of the flowers....

Please thank Stanley very much for the postcards of Hunston....[1] I expect he is soon off to Newquay. Daisy writes to say they are going to West Bay this year again, and also that Glen is engaged, but I expect you have

---

1. Hunstanton, the seaside town on the Norfolk coast where the family sometimes went for a holiday.

heard this very likely. I am glad that Mother stayed on at Whitby, though of course I know she would have loved to be at home for "the Centenary,"[2] but the Whitby air will be more lasting. Old Stewart is in Switzerland, I suppose, so we are all scattered. How my thoughts wander about.

At lunchtime Jack said he was off to Wilmer this afternoon, so my letter *must* be finished soon. I nearly always post on Saturday, and the mail is not supposed to go until Wednesday at noon. I am not allowed to use slang or even to mimic Canadians though I can do it most beautifully. You will find a most proper married sister when you come, and not a bit deteriorated! Yesterday afternoon I went to see a Mrs. Green who is camped in a tent about twenty minutes from us. Her husband is an old soldier and has been out here a few months and got work on Mr. Sinclair's[3] land. She has been here a week and has two little girls, the baby a year old. She is horribly unhappy and does not like it a bit and begs her husband to go back. They came from Belfast and *he* was in the Inniskillens and is a very nice man. Jack met him and then sent me to see "Mrs." and "buck her up" (slang) as she was a soldier's wife, and therefore no need of introduction but do what you can to help! She is a very nice woman, and evidently thought she was coming to Paradise! She thought there would be a lot of fruit and eggs and milk. Finding only tinned varieties has been too much for her and she is frightfully homesick. She is coming over here this afternoon and I am going to help her with a grocery list for Eaton's as I have the catalogue. Jack calls out, "Be sure you give her tea" as he has just come up for the crowbar. He is cultivating the potatoes and has just come across a buried tree trunk. I spoke of Sinclair's land. He is a solicitor from Edinburgh, and evidently very wealthy, came out last year and bought land which the Company has planted for him with rye, and has just been for a fortnight. He put Green in charge and mapped the place out and fixed up the house which is to be a very large one, and has gone back to Scotland to return next spring with his wife and daughter. I think he has over 100 acres, 43 of which are to be planted as orchard in the spring. A hummingbird has just darted across my paper and made me jump. We do not often see them.

No time for more. Goodbye, dear old girl. Much love to all.

Your affectionate sister,

Daisy

2. The centenary of the Oxley newspaper, *The Windsor and Eton Express.*
3. Mr. Sinclair was a Scottish lawyer. He would stay in the Windermere Valley until the First World War then return to Britain. After the war he came back to the Windermere Valley and eventually moved to New Zealand.

ATHALMER, BRITISH COLUMBIA,
AUGUST 15TH, 1912

Dearest Mother,

Here I am again, Thursday, and my home letters not touched, but the days slip away and when you have done tea you must wash up, and then Jack calls, "Come and give me a hand!" And so we go on. Your daughter's latest accomplishment is sawing down trees! We have got a crosscut saw and are clearing the trees in front of the verandah on the slope so as to get a better view up to Mount Hammond. Jack cuts a wedge-shaped piece out of the tree with the axe and then we begin to saw, one at each end of the saw with a swinging movement, till we get within two inches of the cut. Whoever gets there first calls out "Two inches," and if the other side is not so near *you* only saw easily. Then a crack, then a call, "Timber!" and down she comes. Don't think I shall get killed! There is heaps of time to get out of the way and I am getting quite expert at knowing which way it will fall. We fell one tree each day directly after breakfast. Very fine exercise, and it makes me ache all round my ribs! This morning I set to and bottled more rhubarb in cold water, as old Patterson down in Athalmer (who is an "old timer" and has a tiny shack and a small garden *full* of rhubarb) gave us two sacks full, so we have two dozen "quart sealers" ready for the winter. One cannot possibly get fresh fruit or vegetables until next May as the summer season is late because of the night frost, although the days may be warm. I find that people here seem to bottle about 60 quarts of fruit and think nothing of it. Of course, we shall when we get fruit of our own, but this year we have to buy it and we have so many expenses. I have only my camp stove. All the same, I am going to try and bottle a dozen bottles of plums next week. You make a thick syrup and slightly cook the fruit in it and bottle without more cooking, as far as I can make out. I must try and get to see Mrs. Cuthbert tomorrow and she may be able to help me, but at present I have no weights or scales to help me as that Stores box is not unpacked yet and the barn is brimming over!

A thunderstorm is now raging and rain pelting down. It is very sad as our rye is just cut and the last few days have been so sunny and warm. Another stroke of bad luck, Jacks calls it, but that is because the plasterer has not yet come to the house. When we go to the Company, they always say, "The lime will be up by the next boat." In fact, everybody always tells you, if you are out of anything you want, it will be in by the next boat! When we first came we believed them, now we do *not*. I have quite given up worrying about things. It is no good as here you are perfectly helpless to help yourself and just take what comes or what the Stores have got and are very thankful! On Sunday we walked across to see a Dr. and Mrs. Turnor.[1] I don't know

---

1. The Turnors came to British Columbia in 1911 from a comfortable background in

the number of the lot, but quite close to Wilmer, about 300 feet above. We cut across country so it was only about two miles and a half. I had met Dr. Turnor and he had lent Jack some papers on chickens and we went to return them. Being good walkers Jack and I find it is the best way to go and see people. They are always pleased to see you, and are not all as energetic perhaps as we are. Mrs. Turnor was very nice, and there are two girls of about 12 and 13, and a little boy about 5. One little girl is rather lame. They have got ten acres on top and the rest of the land is much too steep to cultivate and runs down to the Wilmer Road. Another doctor was staying with them for a month. He had been ill and came from England for the trip, but it does not suit him very well because it is too high. I met Mr. Marples on the road yesterday and he has asked us to go up to see him on Sunday. He is going home in a week's time to fetch his wife and two children, and his house is being built meanwhile. He said he would take us on an awfully nice walk to a big ranch that is over the other side of Toby Creek. It belongs to Jim Johnson. We have heard a lot about his ranch but thought it too far to go until we got a horse. Mr. Marples has found a short-cut, across country, I expect, and that means jumping and climbing over many tree-trunks. The only tracks one finds occasionally are pony trails and then it is easier going.

Did I tell you I had got some Waterglass and am trying to preserve eggs when I can spare a few to put down? I am always afraid how things will turn out, as I am afraid I have diluted the Waterglass too much. Many thanks for the recipe for treacle pudding. I hope to get suet sometimes in the winter, and could get it now had I a kitchen to cook in. Many thanks, too, for the *Daily Mails* you have sent. I cut out the recipes for scones in the last one. All recipes without many eggs are useful, and things in the cake line will be a great deal wanted, also at any time if you see recipes for "doing up" stale tough beef and suchlike. Tonight we have curried haricot beans and stewed rhubarb, and last night we had scrambled eggs and *peas,* the first we had picked, and they were a real treat although boiled without mint! The Waring books have come and are most useful. It is such fun opening these things when they arrive, and we both grab the *Lady Pic.* and *Punch.* I have forgotten to tell you that Mr. and Mrs. Hamilton drove up to see me yesterday afternoon. Mr. Hamilton is a financial secretary and manages the Company's affairs, and I should say Mrs. Hamilton manages *him!* She is a bossy bouncing female and might be a Suffragette if in England, and is followed about by a fox-terrier and a wolfhound, who wandered about the barn. I took him over the house but they would not stay to tea as they were going on to Mrs. Young, but brought me some recent numbers of the *Illustrated London News.* Jack does not like *her.* She has too strong views on

Staffordshire. See Winnifred A. Weir, ed., *Tales of the Windermere,* Invermere, B.C., 1980, part six.

"women's rights," so when we are in the house and she comes my husband will be very busy indeed. This happens when people do not interest him, and I find, entre nous, there are a good many of these!

Friday. This morning we have received most terribly sad news by cable. Kenny caught by machinery and killed. My poor old Jack is awfully cut up about it, and it does seem hard lines but we must wait for more particulars. He and Jack were evidently great pals, and Jack has always so looked forward to Kenny's weekly letters. He had left Chesterfield and was working with his brother-in-law at Stafford, and he and Ada were living at an hotel.[2] His last letter was full of a pretty house with a nice garden that he was going to take and things financially were looking more promising. . . . Poor Ada, it is terrible for her. You may have heard before you get this. But as usual when you wrote to Jack about his father you said just the right thing, not too much, but in that case I am afraid he had no regrets.

I have been making some enquiries about Parcel Post, and I believe things will come alright during winter without extra cost. If you can declare a parcel as value under a dollar we have nothing to pay either. The silver things from Ways were splendidly packed and arrived in *perfect* condition, the case too, but it was a good strong one. . . .

I have ordered my onions and carrots for the winter and they will be put in the root cellar out of reach of Jack Frost. Our meat is hung up to freeze outside—I expect, suspended from a tree! More or less of a carcass, I suppose, and Jack the butcher, but I don't suppose we shall recognize the joint! The great thing here is to have a Wellbanks cooker, and we shall get one out from the Stores next year, I expect, but it is too late now. It is the same sort of thing as a Warrens cooking pot. You steam the meat and then just finish it off in the oven. You will see these in the Stores list, also the cross-cut saw, also a thing you hang on the wall of the kitchen for drying towels, with many arms and when done with folds up flat. . . .

We have got nearly all our picture frames fixed up now and new glasses, so don't worry any more about them as I have rubbed the furniture with linseed oil and I think we can mend all easily, except the little table. Jack is not a great carpenter at present. He much prefers making a wide path in front of the verandah and working with pick and shovel! But in the winter I think he will prefer the house more, if we ever *do* really get into it. You talk about my brown skirt being dyed! I only wish you could see it. Camp life has done for it completely and it has a *darn* of brown wool right across the front where I caught it on a tree trunk! But I use it for cooking and washing and am so very thankful I had it with me. It is hard wear on my underclothes

---

2. Ada was Kenneth's wife and Jack's sister-in-law. Kenneth was the second of Jack's brother to die accidentally. His elder brother, Francis, had been killed in 1905 in a railway accident in South Africa. After Kenneth's death Jack's closest relatives were his many and mostly "disapproving" aunts.

and nightdresses too, and I have only *two* of everything going and have had to darn a "nighty" in one or two places. This was lighting the fire when Jack was ill, so don't say anything about it. You see, we stroll out of the barn quite happily in these nether garments. . . .

No more news as I want to write a line to poor Ada. Jack is not able to sleep and is frightfully down. He says if this had happened a year ago he would have felt absolutely alone in the world. When letters come they will be rather upsetting, and I am afraid he will get one from Kenny tonight. Much love to all. It will soon be a case of one post a week, I expect, and then perhaps you and Freda could take it in turns, and it would not be quite such a tax if you had not much time. You always, both, write such a lot, but I love the letters and I often see no other woman for a week at a time!

Your affectionate child,

Daisy

ATHALMER, B.C.,
AUGUST 30TH, 1912

My dearest Mother,

I really think the most important thing to tell you this week is that Jack has got a kitten and in consequence I am quite "out of it" and feel my nose is truly out of joint! He went down to Athalmer on Tuesday morning and on his return emptied the things out of the sack as usual, and then remarked quite casually, "I have got a kitten in here somewhere!", and since then he has been its devoted slave. It is a little tabby with blue eyes and like all kittens, I suppose, very pretty, but we have really got it to kill mice as we have a great number in the barn, and when we have grain about there will be many more, I expect, so it will not do to pet the kitten too much. At present you see a lump near Jack's waist and go and feel, and find he has put the kitten inside his shirt because he thought it was cold! Or else you see a small head peeping over the top of his sweater as he walks about. At present the kitten is walking about on this paper and that accounts for the blot, so I have smacked it and put it on the floor, but I am afraid it does not understand why. The kitten is supposed to sleep in some straw in a box at the side of the bed, but twice I have wakened feeling something on my toes and Jack has been filled with pity in the middle of the night and put the kitten under the blankets! How would you like that, I wonder? But, ne remarquez-pas, he does not think it at all unusual.

We have put the little tent up again and are sleeping there. The fact is we began to fear damp and so have undone all the cases and have got the things in the barn, so we have had to turn out. There was a little mildew just beginning on one or two pieces of wood, but we have oiled them well and now it has disappeared. There is a little on one of the sides of the small leather chair, and I have oiled that too but there will always be a stain. However, we shall soon get other stains, I expect, when it gets into use. All the things were so beautifully packed and there is not a scratch or crack on anything. All the things were wrapped in papers and packed in straw, and well wadded at the corners where they rested on each other. You might tell Rainer this. It was a great pleasure to open the things from Ways. They were each tied up and written on, nothing had moved, and the case looks like new. So I wrote a line to Mr. Hunnman. Jack was awfully pleased as he thinks no place can do things as well as the Army & Navy Stores, and I am beginning to think the same when I see all his things that have come from there. The chairs are all done and this week Jack has put the dressing-chest together, so we have taken it down to Mr. Cuthbert. He thinks he can straighten it for us as he is a very clever amateur carpenter. Jack has put his chest-of-drawers together and I have washed out the drawers and papered them with the *Express* in proper "home" fashion, and Jack has put a lot of his things in ready for when we get into the house.

Mr. Clark, the Company's contractor, is very tiresome and will not get things finished. They built our fireplace, did I tell you, and then it would not draw. It was pretty to look at, but the top of the grate was partly covered so of course the smoke curled out into the room. As we have been waiting so long and winter is coming so fast, on Monday morning we went down to Wilmer to see Mr. Bruce. He does not take an active part but undoubtedly he is a very large shareholder and I should think is doing all the booming and advertising of the place in England. He received us and our complaints and said he would speak to Mr. Malandane and see what could be done. Of course, he knew all about it. The Company are too greedy and trying to build and do much more than they can possibly finish. When we came *they* were the only people, but now various contractors and small painters and carpenters are coming to Athalmer and the whole thing is a big race. Mr. Bruce took us over his garden which is full of immense vegetables and many flowers. He gave us some lovely apples, "Golden Transparent," off a tree in the garden and four peaches from his cellar as he had just returned from the coast, also a large rose and some dahlias. The next morning the man came up and pulled out the fireplace and rebuilt it. A fire was lighted last night and I think it will draw alright. Talk about patience and courage, Mother, you want heaps of both in the stage we are in now, but it will be quite easy to laugh at when we are in the house and have a little comfort and a fire.

The last two days have been bitterly cold and the snow is on all the mountains round. There is a wind, a thing we get very seldom, but it comes across the snow area, I expect, and when the sun comes out again the sun will melt the snow and we shall be warm again. The hot water bottle was most acceptable in bed last night. I suddenly thought of it. Mrs. Cuthbert and a friend who is staying with her, Miss Miller, who is a governess in Calgary, came up to tea one afternoon this week to show the friend our view. She had a Brownie camera and took two snapshots, but as it was a very dull day I fear they will not come out. I quite envy her the joy of having a visitor, but hope I shall be in that state next year. I have also been down to Mrs. Munson's and bottled twelve quart bottles of plums. I got what they call "a case" here. You cannot buy things of this sort in small quantities, and it will be a good help for the winter. She is a good, kind soul and showed me how to do it in Canadian fashion, which is very simple. You make a syrup of white sugar and water, 7 pints of sugar and 11 of water, I used. Prick the plums in one or two places, boil the syrup, put the fruit in for a few minutes, then put the fruit in the bottles and pour on the boiling syrup and seal as quickly as possible. The folk out here do pears and peaches in the same way, only this sort of fruit you do not cook but just pour on the syrup. However, pears and peaches are luxuries and the great idea of doing the fruit is, of course, to use your own as then the cost is so little. The sealers cost a good bit, but then of course you can use them over and over again with a new elastic band. One does miss the stone jam jars and pans of old England. I cannot say I am used to metal yet, or that I love it, though I expect it is more economical in the long run. I think if I am lucky I shall be able to get suet from the butcher's when we get our half animal and freeze it. You cannot get packet suet here, by here I mean Canada.

The Duke of Sutherland is coming to Mr. Bruce's for the weekend and is to be trotted round to see all the beauties. The Duchess stays in Calgary. I think he has bought a lot of land in Alberta so perhaps they hope he may invest here too. His son was here for some big shooting last fall. I hope it is drier at home now, it was very sad to have it so wet for Whitby, and very depressing. We have had our share or more, the wettest season for years and years, and of course not too cheerful at times under canvas. But we are always hoping for the time the house is really finished. The men came and mixed the plaster yesterday and *say* they are coming on Monday to work, but you can never trust anybody's word out here. If they come, it will take a week to plaster. Then it must dry, I suppose, and then the carpenters will come and put down the proper floor, fix windows, doors, etc., so we may be just in in about a month from now with great luck. We have no more particulars of the accident yet. Poor old Jack often says, "I wish Ken would throw up that horrid colour job and come out here," quite forgetting. Thanks ever so much for continuing the *Overseas Mail*. We look forward to its advent in a way you can hardly understand, and that and *Punch* are Jack's literature for the week! Next year I shall get you to send me out some flower seeds if you will, as the English are much the best. Godetia do well here, and I shall try and raise some antirrhinums. Do the phlox "Drummondi" you speak of grow from seed? Yes, Mother, we have oil and vinegar, the first thing almost we ordered from Eaton's, and the salad is still *very* good. When we get it though the lettuce may be a bit tough. We always pick long before they are ready!

I think the *Centenary Express*[1] was splendid, and Stanley's speech at the dinner quite worthy of the occasion, also the Vicar's speech which I hope sounded as well as it reads. I wish some of the Canadian papers could take a leaf out of the *Express* book, but then I suppose they would not pay as the Canadian loves *exaggeration* in every form. I have found the tube of sec-cotine[2] and it is most useful, as well as so many little things you thought of, Mother, and they all give so much pleasure because of the loving thoughts that you and Freda put into all my boxes. I often feel glad I did not pack them myself after all. Now, as usual, wants and questions. Will you ask Mrs. Littlewood the best way to get out bloodstains from handkerchiefs? I soak in *cold* water before washing and they get faint, but will not come out entirely when washed. Would soda help or only set the stain more? Then, if crinkled paper does not weigh very heavily, would you send me out a roll to make a shade for the second lamp, or do you think a cheap paper shade like we had on approval from Herbert's Stores once would weigh about the same? Either yellow or red, or fancy if there is such a thing. Then, could you get a collapsible shade *support,* not a wire frame. I think I can make one near enough. . . .

In haste for mail.

Your affectionate child,

Daisy

We had *no* duty to pay on the wedding presents, was it not lucky? But the agent at Golden is awfully good and gets through all he can!

ATHALMER, B.C.
THURSDAY, SEPTEMBER 5TH, 1912

My dearest Freda,

I intended writing early this week, but I have had a sty on the bottom of my left eyelid, "one of the very best" I think you might call it, and it has been very painful. It would not come to a head so I referred to my little book and found Hepar. Sulph. advised, with the result that this morning it has broken and now it is quite easy. I have had several since I have been out here but they have quickly disappeared and I hope this will be the last. All the same, I

---

1. The centennial edition of the *Windsor and Eton Express.*
2. The trade name of an adhesive cement.

feel very fit and only longing to get into the house. We have had so much rain, it is rather depressing at times when we have to sit amongst packing cases, and furniture covered up with blankets. It has been bitterly cold and the mountains are all covered with snow. The rain here has been snow up there, and yesterday morning there was a thick frost when I walked across from the tent to the barn for my morning wash. There is no room in the tent to wash, only room for the bed, one chair, the kitten, alarm clock, and the storm lantern. When there is sunshine we forget all the discomfort. Jack cooked the breakfast this morning under an umbrella. For pottering about in and out the barn . . . I never wear a hat, and my hair gets wet and I do not seem to catch cold. I have now got on Jack's gum boots, which are like cavalry boots and come right up to my knees! I have my own brown-lace boots on inside and still there is heaps of room, but they keep my legs nice and warm. I live in my golf jersey and very often my drab tweed overcoat as well, as when it rains it is cold. But when the sun came out mid-day yesterday I sat out in the sun and was too hot in my blue cotton dress. I was busy turning Jack's military overcoat into a civil one by putting on leather buttons and taking off the shoulder straps, etc. It is lined through the body part with thick camel Jaeger cloth and so will be cosy, but I think chilly about the legs. However, he is a wonderful person and not at all a fuss, but he says it is because he is always fit, and soldiers' wives and daughters are always fit and he is going to make me into one! I think the cure has begun already for if you had told me of all the things I was going to put up with and endure and yet be well and happy I should not have believed you! Don't think you will have to "endure" when you come. I will do all I can to make you comfortable and I hope very happy. By then, of course, we shall be in the house and be living a more or less normal existence. I am always trying to look at the scenery with your eyes, and I think you will be able to do some studies with "pen and wash." I think the pine trees will lend themselves to many and numerous studies. I begin to love them as there are such hundreds and yet they are all different, some happy families all living together, and here and there bachelors and "old maids" all on their own.

On the 1st September shooting begins. *We* have had no luck yet but Mr. Robinson our neighbour went out and got several brace of "prairie chickens," a sort of grouse that we have often seen wandering about. On Monday Mrs. Poett sent us some more vegetables. Jack took some of them over to our neighbours and Mr. Robinson gave him a prairie chicken. Jack began to pluck it at once. He took out all the easy feathers and said, "You can finish that tomorrow!" I began to finish it on Tuesday morning and it took me an hour to get all the small feathers off the wings that are no good as pipe cleaners and therefore not interesting! The next was to behead it so I got out Mrs. Beeton and did that fairly successfully. Then, when it came to trussing, I bent it up à la picture in Mrs. B. and tied it round with string in two places. I covered him well with flour and put a lump of lard on his breast, and then put him in the oven and stoked the fire carefully for an hour. By that time he was lovely and brown, and with a cauliflower as vegetable we had the nicest dinner we have had so far in camp. Oh, we had stewed rhubarb last night and we had the bird warmed up in white sauce and mashed turnips. When I tell you I have only one saucepan and a frying pan in use I think I am a *very* clever cook! You will think I am a dreadful little glutton always telling you about food, but I really think Jack does not care a bit what he has to eat. He would be content with bread and cheese and bread and jam at every meal, but I suppose Mother spoilt us at home by her excellent catering. Of course, at first I missed my nice food most awfully and the thought of Mrs. Tull's shop and all the nice cakes actually could make me dribble like Dandy, but I am getting used to things now and perhaps getting cleverer at catering. I have got some curry powder and we get large butter beans. I do them with curry sauce, and with fried bread they are most excellent! I don't suppose I shall ever taste fresh fish for years but we have ordered some tins of fresh herrings from Eaton's and they are very good with vinegar. Ask Mother how to make the white sauce to put over cold fish, like we have on Sunday nights at home. Is it just melted butter with a little vinegar or has it the yolk of egg in it as well? I have had a splendid and most helpful letter from Nelly this week on washing, and several cooking recipes as well. I am glad she is feeling so fit.

Jack has gone to Invermere this afternoon and thought I had better not write home in case I did not send a cheerful letter, so do not comment if this is not up to standard. If the sun shines tomorrow I shall be as happy as ever. In fact, writing to you has done me tons of good. The plasterer has now come up to the house and is working, and the carpenter is finishing the verandah. After waiting *five* weeks and nothing being done and the winter coming so fast, I cannot tell you what a relief it is. I feel I want to cry, but whenever I have felt my pluck oozing away a little bit, I always think how patient and plucky you were about your leg, and pull myself together. How I should love you to see it all and hear what you think. I so often wish I could just ask you or Mother some question about shelves or arrangements, but as it is Jack always comes to me, and that too is how so much time gets taken up, "Come here and help me with this or that." Of course, he has always had his man, and he can never find his tobacco pouch! "Where is my____. Oh, here it is!" is constantly going on. But he is awfully good, and frightfully worried at all there has been to put up with and helps me along by making light of it all.

We heard from Mr. Wall this week that Kenny was crushed in a grinding machine and killed instantaneously. It is terrible for Ada and little Jack. There was to be an inquest, so we shall hear more later, though of course there will be more bother about the estate. Jack wishes he could be at home managing his own affairs, I know. He does like to keep his own things to himself so much . . . .

I do hope my commissions were fairly easy to do. A little later on a hat of the "Jay" order of cloth or tweed, with a feather mount. Jack has not found the exact thing in the *Pic* yet. He is always so interested in the weddings and engagements, and nearly every week he seems to find someone he knows. *Punch* is usually read aloud before bedtime. The *Gazette* too is the breath of his nostrils and although I know it is a trouble it is *deeply* appreciated. Next year when we find exactly how our expenses work out, I hope he can afford to have the *Telegraph* once a week. What a splendid testimonial to the *Express* in the *Standard* Mother sent. Tell Stanley I think his speech was excellent in the Centenary number. *I* should have had the pictures of Charles Knight, Grandpa and Father,[1] but I suppose it was a matter of expense. . . . The Barnardo boy,[2] I think, sounds a good idea. Perhaps later on you should go and enquire, but at present all our capital is taken up. You see, there are so many things for "the farm," and a horse must come before a boy. I may be writing short letters in a week or two and you will know it is because I am *very* busy. In fact, Jack says if you get a postcard only it is the best news you can get as it will mean we are getting things straight for the house.

Saturday. I have quite got over my fit of the blues. I think it was because my eye was so painful, but when Jack returned with the mail there was a lovely long letter from Mother and the book of Liberty patterns, and the very sight of these lovely colours cheered me up, to say nothing of Mother's letter. I do feel so ashamed of myself when you and Mother are always doing things and thinking of me so much. Thank you with all my heart. . . . A postcard from "Mr. Stewart" too, and a photo from Freda Dainty, so the cure was quite complete when I opened my parcel with the lavender bags and the little collars. You cannot possibly imagine the pleasure that a letter gives or the excitement of opening a parcel! Jack is quite as big a baby over it as I am. It is much warmer and I am scribbling this in the morning after breakfast and must rush off and cook now.

Much love to you all, and many, many thanks for all the letters and papers. I feel how much time you give to all these things but it makes me feel so grateful. I wish I could do something for you all, but my fingers will never have much time nowadays. My loving thoughts, many and always.

Your affectionate sister,

Daisy

1. Owners of *The Windsor and Eton Express.* Charles Knight, its founder, sold the paper to Richard Oxley, Daisy's grandfather.
2. Dr. Barnardo's Homes (The National Incorporated Association for the Reclamation of Destitute Waif Children) placed lads of seventeen in employment in England, sent them to sea, or sent them to the colonies. Most of those who emigrated came to Canada where they passed through distribution centres in Toronto or Winnipeg. The reference here is to such a boy who might be assumed to be a source of labour at English wages.

My dearest Mother,

It is not your turn this week, is it? But this is a line to send you every good birthday wish. I hope it will arrive about the right time, but it may be before, it may be after. I can find nothing here to send you as a little gift, and I have had no chance or opportunity to make you anything. I saw a photograph of Wilmer the other day taken by a man at the livery stable. I went and saw his old mother, Mrs. Palmer, and asked if he could print and mount me one and I would buy it. "Oh, yes." Jack and I went down on Saturday to fetch it and were informed that he had run out of developer and could not do it for some weeks. I hope to send it later, therefore, but am so sorry it will not be with you for the day. It is a panorama of the place and gives you a very good idea, but it is not really a good photo.

I am writing this in the morning as I have got a boil on my left wrist and I have got my "orders" to take a day off. Do not worry about it. By the time you get this it will be quite well, I expect, and Jack is a splendid doctor and knows how to bandage much better than I do, and calmly says, "Oh, I did heaps of it when I was in hospital."[1] He is the most unconceited and unvain person I ever came across in more ways than one, and I had not realized until lately what the five bars on his medal really mean and what an honour it is to have them.[2] But do not comment. It has turned out lovely and hot again the last week, and the autumn tints are at their best. I am looking across at the foothills opposite and they are bright yellow, the colour of butter, intermixed with the *dark* green pines, the snowcapped mountains and the blue sky. I wish I could transpose you to B.C. Little low poplar trees grow in most of the low parts of the ground and these all look like gold, and the wild strawberries are crimson. There has been no high wind yet to shake off the leaves.

Rainer is a liar and I should think drinks! I wrote a long letter to him dictated by Jack at his very best so it was not *mild*. The boxes were *not* opened at the Customs, and on opening the Stores cases and seeing how the things were packed I wondered that even the boot trees that were rolling about among the china arrived whole! However, I have seccotined a little of the china together and we have patched up the carving things with the aid of glue, also most of the picture frames but some are quite hopeless. It has been splendid experience. I feel so happy and Jack is so splendid I really do not mind now—only at first—so please don't you. I only hope you have not paid

---

1. Jack had been wounded in South Africa.
2. The five bars were: Johannesburg, Relief of Ladysmith, Orange Free State, Tugela Heights, and Cape Colony.

Rainer. There were a few shavings scattered here and there, but shavings
are no good if the things are not wrapped and covered. . . .

My dearest Freda,

I have driven off my letters until very late this week, so now I shall have a
frightful rush and it will be more scribble than usual. Thanks ever so much
for the postcards with the view of Whitby. It is a much bigger place than I
thought but I really think it looks most quaint and fascinating though if you
like *that* I am sure you will not like *this,* as where there are houses they are
more or less hidden away. Now I want to thank you and Mother from the
bottom of my heart for having those photos taken. I think they were just
speaking, and I can picture you exactly as you are. I think they are specially
nice of Mother, and tell her that her son-in-law very much approves of
them! I like them of you too, in a way, and I can see by your attitude you are
taking great care of Mother. I like *the* hat on you too, only I wear my blue
flowers on the other side. On Sunday I put my hat on "à la Freda," but Jack
likes it the other way best. Who made the cotton frock? Was it Nina, or
Madame Hutchinson as I see she is called in this week's *Windsor and Eton
Express?* My blue and brown dresses are invaluable and I simply live in
them. I know I am tidy even though I have not got a glass that shows my
waistband! Directly I saw the photo I wondered if the bow was mine, and
Jack remarked, "Freda wears a longer bow than you do," and he also
spotted the cuffs on your dress and liked them, so when you come I shall get
you to bring some more "mat" collars from Miss Hutchinson, and cuffs too.
I have got some belonging to my muslin sets, but I try not to turn over my
boxes too much, and Jack always says, "Wait until you get into the house."
    On Sunday we started off about 11 o'clock to go out to Jim Johnson's
ranch. From our verandah we look right across Toby Creek and canyon,
and on the other side, away among the pine trees, quite near the foothills,
we can just see the ranch. Things look much nearer than they are out here,
as a rule but not always, as we get lovely blue distance very often and sometimes it is quite purple. We walked about a mile and a half up the road and
found Mr. Marples encamped near his house, ate our sandwiches and saw
his house. He has a lovely view right over the lake, and a fairly big house.
He has three children, two jolly boys and a dear little girl (I saw some snapshots) and a lady friend who lives with them. He is going home on Sunday
to bring them out and only hopes his house will be finished in time. The
Company are not building it but a man who is a friend of Adamson,

Mason's clerk. He is a great man in his *own* eyes! Well, we walked along the top of the creek and presently Mr. Marples said, "I suppose you have got a steady head?" "Oh yes, of course," I said, and Jack could not say anything as *he* did not know. We went down a very steep winding path, almost like a goat track, but it was awfully pretty. Mr. Marples went first, I in the middle and Jack at the back, and they each held the end of a long supple willow stick which was like a rope and so I got on splendidly. We then got to the bank where the torrent was roaring along and only a plank to cross to the other side! But I got on splendidly and did not feel a quake. I believe *all* my nerves have gone. The water is the colour of the Aare at Bern and comes along the gorge in the same way, only it turns and twists every few hundred yards. Mr. Marples took a photo so I may get one when he comes back again but I expect we shall look *very* small. We then had to clamber up the other side. We saw various new plants, little maple bushes the colour of fire, as already things are beginning to turn colour here and there. Then there was a good walk on flat land, thin bush I expect you would call it, with hills here and there. At last we arrived at the ranch, and Jim Johnson was sitting outside his log-cabin door all in his Sunday best reading the paper. Such a charming man, clean shaven and smart, the type of the good old yeoman stock of the "Old Country." He has been out here fifteen years and when he left England the doctor gave him six months to live, he told me! And now he has lived on his ranch five years. He has fifteen acres under cultivation, and a huge barn and lots of farm buildings besides the log house he lives in. This has two rooms, back and front, bedroom and sitting room. In front was a nice patch of grass and each side flower beds, one mass of colour and every flower you can think of—sweet peas, marigolds, mignionette, godetia, larkspur, and two rose trees put in this summer as an experiment.

After a rest we went round the garden and I feasted on raspberries, and when we got to the blackcurrants Jack could eat but I was afraid. The blackcurrants were as large as cherries! The strawberries were over but the plants looked like small bushes. Then to see the clover, the timothy grass and the alfalfa, and to try and see how he worked his irrigation though he has a natural spring and brook on his ground. He has a large horse ranch as well, and manages all by himself. The men out here are wonderful when there is no woman to help, they certainly know how to make themselves comfortable! About five we rose to take our departure, but he remarked that if we would stay it was just his feeding time. I sat on the steps and talked to him while he got ready, and Jack and Mr. Marples walked round and brought back some loganberries, very delicious, like large raspberries to taste but the shape of mulberries. By this time the meal was ready—fried potatoes, boiled cabbage, beetroot salad, cold ham and brown bread (Oh, such lovely bread and of course his own making). When this course was finished he produced bottled strawberries (by himself) and honey, and "cookies from the Old Country" in my special honour (Huntley & Palmer's biscuits). As biscuits are very expensive here they are considered a special treat. I had a lovely nosegay of flowers to bring back. We got home about nine o'clock and had walked about fourteen miles! ... Monday morning Jack was going to Athalmer on business and as I wanted to try and get some fruit to bottle I went down too. This was another six miles so if anyone tells you I am delicate you need not believe them for when I come home nowadays there is no sitting down in easy chairs but a meal to get ready, a fire to light, and washing up after the meal! The only job I really do not like is washing and cleaning saucepans and frying pans.

Jack has just come along and said, "If you are writing to Freda tell her to bring out a fly trap from the Stores when she comes." I expect you will have to bring lots of silly little things so begin to keep a list in a notebook if you like. Our rye was cut this week, and is not a large crop. We have a small stack at the back of the barn. By the way, your bedroom window looks towards the barn. On Wednesday afternoon I went down to see Mrs. Cuthbert and buy some lettuces from her as we had eaten all our medium size ones (we never give them a chance to grow big) and to pay for some eggs. She had a friend from Calgary staying with her and we had a merry chat and gossip. Mrs. Cuthbert had just washed her hair so she had tea without putting it up, gingerbread and rock cakes (these things are such treats when you only get bread), and on leaving she gave me a quart of redcurrant jelly. Brother John and I have eaten this in two days and I expect Mrs. Cuthbert thought it would last us a month or more! Mrs. Poett also sent us a box of vegetables this week so we are living like fighting cocks, with salad at every meal. The cabbage and potatoes I make into bubble and squeak,[1] Jack's favourite form of veg without meat. Tonight we had macaroni and baby carrots.

Now to the question of clothes. I do not regret bringing anything I have got with me as far as I can see. I have not worn my evening dresses yet but Jack feels sure I shall want them. Anyway, he always ends up saying, "When I take you to the coast. . . . " and as they are both "no fashion" they will always do. If you are getting a new coat and skirt I should say *not* purple or "pepper and salt"—too dark—for preference a tweed of some sort of a rather rough kind, more like the one I had at Fletchers. As you will have your blue-serge and your old tweed, I should say a *short* Harrods golf skirt and jersey. Also a khaki drill skirt (you must bring me one of these too). Tussore silk is very good for wear out here, I see, but for you two plain cotton dresses and one pretty cotton. I think red and white shepherd plaid with black waistband would be nice. White petticoats, *plain* ones I always wear except when tramping. A Liberty hat like Mother sent me and a nice Jay hat

1. Potatoes and cabbage fried together.

for best and a hat for bad weather. Gauntlet gloves for weekdays and chamois for best, and *lots* of stockings. Do not be afraid of bringing old clothes. I get horribly excited when I think of you coming, but I must not say too much or Jack gets jealous! One pair of very good strong boots, black if you like, as doubtless you will have to *oil* them. Instead of blacking, glacé shoes,[2] or brogue shoes, but there is not much use for light boots or goloshes. I will send you a bigger and better list later on but I cannot lay my hand on the letter in which you mentioned clothes.

We have had to put all our packing cases back into the barn we have had so much wet, so I am again living in a tent or rather sleeping. I do not know when our house will be finished. The lime has not come from Golden and everything seems at a standstill. I am very happy and Jack is awfully kind and thoughtful, but sometimes I have to be terribly plucky and it is then the home letters are so good. I do not think Jack really understands yet my keenness for letters, but he is frightfully pleased when he gets one himself. I tease him and say, "Freda writing to you again? I shall have a bone to pick with her!" But I like you to write, it pleases him so, and he fully agrees with what you said in your last letter! Now poor old Ken has been taken Jack will get fewer letters from England. I feel his great bond to the Old Country has gone, but he feels he has a duty towards his small nephew. I do not know if affairs can be settled up now without Jack. He had just given Kenny Power of Attorney. I sometimes wonder if Jack will have to go back to England but he has not said so to me so don't mention it. We have heard no details yet.

It is awfully good of you to start on some work for me. I should like chair backs or a sideboard strip. If chair backs, mixed dull colours, I think, and different patterns in each. Remember, Debenham & Freebody for the wools, or Tranter & Adams at Bournemouth. My chair is 22″ broad and Jack's 25″. If a sideboard strip I should suggest appliqué. Do you remember the background canvas I brought out with me from Liberty's? I got it in the dress department, and I think the colours you should use should be dull blue and green. Just a design at each end of the strip. Just tack the hem round and put French knots or flat stitches along the edge. . . .

Mother would mitre the corners for you. How would a blue strip be, with design in green and terra cotta? I do miss someone to discuss things with! The sideboard is 4′6″ long and the strip should hang a little over the edge. Jack is so fond of the look of wood he hopes we can do without a tablecloth, and if so I should like one of those "runners" or strips to take flower vases. If so, make a note of this for my Christmas present. All the Stores' things are splendidly packed, *nothing* broken. Some of the wood of the furniture has warped a little and there is a little mildew on the side of one of the leather chairs but we are oiling it and hope it will improve. I do hope I shall find my

2. Thin, highly polished leather shoes.

pen soon, it is a wonder I can find anything. Jack loses something every ten minutes but it is always under his nose!

Much love, dear old girl. Give my love to Nelly. Ask Halliday if he sent the bottles of stain and French polish.

Your affectionate sister,

Daisy

ATHALMER, B.C.,
SEPTEMBER 12TH, 1912

My dearest Mother,

I must try and write you a few lines until I am wanted, which is fairly frequently as Jack is putting together the wardrobe! First of all, let me thank you for the money orders, which I shall put into my Savings Bank book with the other money you gave me for the house as I cannot carry a purse about with me here and when one "shops" it is mostly by sending away "paper money." Of course, most of our money here is in paper form, from a dollar and upwards. Jack's bank is The Imperial Bank of Canada, Wilmer Branch, and my Savings Account is at the bank, not the Post Office as at home.

I feel very excited and more than cheerful. Firstly, the weather has altered, and although the mornings and evenings are cold the rest of the day it is sunny and warm and blue sky. Then, also, the house is really being finished at last. The plasterer has gone and although the plaster is not really dry the carpenters are hard at work. Jack's den is finished, matchboarding from top to toe and looks very nice, and until the whole can be stained a light brown I expect Jack will oil the wood. He is mad on oiling all leather and wood, and his tin of Neatsfoot oil affords him great pleasure and amusement. We have a small corner cupboard in the spare room and Jack has his washstand coming. In the winter we shall make a dressing table of the packing cases and stain them ourselves, and I expect I shall get Freda to buy me some cheap and pretty cretonne to make a dressing table frill and bedspread, at the January sales. Mrs. Poett has got some very pretty ones from D. H. Evans. By the way, we are going over there to tea on Sunday as we met her in Athalmer the other day and she gave us a blowing up for not going oftener. I have got a frightfully stay-at-home husband! I *made* him go to tea at the Cuthberts on Sunday as it was too showery for a walk and I was so tired of the barn, and he always thoroughly enjoys himself when he does go out. I like Mrs. Cuthbert so much. She is so sweet and pretty, and oh, so capable and a most excellent cook. They lived near Manchester before they came out here. We came back laden with flowers and sweet Indian-corn they had grown. It is most delicious boiled and rolled in butter with lots of pepper and salt, and then you just take it up in your fingers and bite along. Not a dish to eat at a dinner party! You will see.

I have had *such* a nice letter from Auntie Kate which I will try and answer soon, also another from Flora. She is most excited at my getting married I can see, and begs us to come to Western Australia if we do not like this. It is "booming" too just now, I see, as a fruit-farming place and they have a huge irrigation scheme on. . . .

I told you we are having a window seat in the "Hall," in the recess at the end opposite the door. The window there is three of the little windows, and above, seven panes of plain glass. I have no time to draw but Freda can bring my water colour box if she likes. Jack is always saying, "Freda can bring that when she comes", so I know when Freda arrives at Golden she will be surrounded with boxes so that Jack can hardly see her and in her hand a small valise containing *her* clothes! The other day Jack said, "I should like a ferret out here. We'll get Freda to bring one"! All the same, some day I hope we shall be saying, "We'll get Mother to bring that." I shan't be quite happy until you have been to see this glorious country and our little corner of it as well! I think your shopping day was a great success and the book on canvas patterns from Liberty's has come — most exciting, but we shall not order until the spring. The portiere curtains over the bedroom and kitchen doors are not so much to prevent draught but to save the look of so much *door*, as there are two on each side of the hall, and with curtains we could have the door open and the inside of the bedroom not quite open to the public gaze if we had callers at the door at the end. The front door and brown blanket will look well enough for a portiere in the winter and it would not be worth the freight to send it to Calgary to get it dyed.

I am glad the Roughs are at Datchet as it must be so nice for Freda. I am so interested in knowing who comes to tea and dinner, so always tell me. Auntie K. thinks the garden is looking very nice, I am glad to hear. . . . I often picture you enjoying the piano and . . . wonder when I shall touch or hear a piano again? My golf clubs are still at Datchet, I expect, but Gibson would perhaps fetch them one day and they could be greased and put away until I want them again. Don't give them away. I, like you, think the buses will not add to the high-class element in the Royal Borough, but they may help things by selling a few more Oxley Guides! . . .[1]

We shall be having meat in the winter but it hangs outside and has to be cut with an axe! It is not very tender as a rule so I expect it will be mostly made into rissoles. Most people have one of those wonderful steamers I told you about and we hope to get one from the Stores in the spring. We are spending more on the house than we intended but Jack is keen on having

---

1. Guide books printed by the Oxleys.

things as nice as possible here and we must economize in other ways! Many, many thanks for the various winter comforts you are sending. The long-sleeved bodice will be most useful, I know, and the Shetland veil sounds just the thing. One of the boats has stopped coming already, but now it is warmer the river may rise and then it will be running again. We have got in all our winter provisions, and I think the rifles and Pandora's box will be in time. Mr. Bowden's furniture has just come, *five* tons, and we had one and a half! I wonder where he will put it all, but their house is much larger than ours. All the other houses are larger but I like this in every way *much* the best. I should like to write to Gilbert, Auntie Louie, Miss Crookshank[2] and many others, but I have a struggle with Jack very often over letter-writing as he insists on that *hour* every day to lie down. I say I can rest and write, and he says *no,* and often I have to admit to being tired at 2 o'clock as you see we usually have breakfast at 7:30 and I don't get many minutes to sit down. Aunt Charlotte (Mrs. Bird) who lives in Park Place, St. James, sent me the Christmas pudding recipe as used at Wilton Place. She was the aunt Jack stands a little bit in awe of and who was so exceedingly nice to me.[3] Freda met Edith Bird who is most awfully nice.

It does not do to think of poor Ada. It is simply terrible for her. I hoped you would see it in the daily paper or that Mrs. Ruston[4] would write, but I think she was horribly annoyed with Jack and me over our wedding! It will delay the settling of the estate but money matters will be as before. Ada and the boy will have one half share and Jack and I the other. No mail yet this week as "the stage" has broken down, but I know the letters from home are there and that is good enough.

Much love to all,

Your affectionate child,

Daisy

ATHALMER, B.C.

SEPTEMBER 17TH, 1912

My dearest Freda,

I have addressed my letter to Mother this week as it is her birthday but your letter must not go short. Well, I have had a very happy time the last few days as I have been unpacking and washing the china. It came in two

2. Auntie Louie, an Oxley aunt. Miss Crookshank was the headmistress of St. Leonard's school, a boarding school in North London attended by both Daisy and Freda.
3. Aunt Charlotte was the one aunt with whom Jack was on cordial terms, and when his own daughter, Elizabeth, was born, he asked Edith Bird, Aunt Charlotte's daughter, to be her godmother.
4. Jack's Aunt Alice, a sister of his father.

barrels and out of all the china and glass only the bottom of one vegetable dish was cracked! But as we have four in the service it does not matter a little bit. I call it most wonderful as the glass was very thin. The Stores' packing is really splendid. They wrap everything round with straw and wedge the things in tight so that they cannot possibly move. It is lovely to see nice china and glass again after having used enamel for so long. The plates we have been using are small and therefore the dinner plates look immense, and you feel if you had a full plate like I have often seen old Stewart attack you would absolutely last for a week! Jack's remark about the largest meat dish was that we could use it as a skating rink in the winter, otherwise he could see no use for it. How your ideas do alter, and you are not aware of it until you see something like this, that you used to see every day and think nothing of.

This week we have had a lovely present, an entrée dish from Captain Spring, Jack's greatest friend who is now at the Depot at Lincoln. It is a real beauty, Sheffield design, square shape, and he has had the Lincoln crest engraved on it which greatly pleased J. N. P. My name in the Regiment is "Mrs. Piet," as Jack is always called Piet, and I get many messages from his various friends. Captain and Mrs. Richardson are sending us a Roorkee chair (see Stores catalogue) and it comes by parcel post, in two parcels, which is a thing to remember. And some other Lincoln folk are sending us oil-and-vinegar cruet or silver candlesticks, I know not which but I *hope* the latter. The Richardsons are coming out here when he is out of his present job and want to be near so have written to ask Jack if he would buy some land while it is fairly cheap. But nothing is settled at present. Mrs. Bowden will be here in a few weeks, and Miss Colebrook, the girl from Reading who is coming to keep house for them, is coming out first to try and get things a bit straight. To save her going down to the Invermere Hotel every night she will come over here and have the camp bed and sleep in the tent or on the verandah, and we shall sleep in the barn. Mr. Bowden has been so awfully kind to us but did not think it quite proper for Miss Colebrook to sleep in their camp and so we offered to put her up here. I hope she will be nice. As she is so capable and knows all about washing and cooking, she may be able to help me. Mr. Bowden remarked the other day on the brass handle on the front door as all the rest are copper, so I said it was because a brass knocker was coming, but *he* has one that has been in their family over a hundred years. He is a Devonshire man and knows Dartmoor and Exmoor well, and I should say has not been living long near Reading. I suppose he has the knowledge of farming and Mr. Robinson most of the money, but I know not.

They are digging the pit for the water tank, and the ditch down to the house. The pipe has to be at least 4' underground out of reach of the frost and will come into the cellar, I think, and from there up into the kitchen, and I expect I shall have a barrel standing in the corner. Jack wanted to have a small sink put in the pantry, but everything has cost so much I have persuaded him to leave it for the present. I can manage quite well without, living in a house of any sort will seem such a luxury. I think you will love my little kitchen, I only hope I shall be able to keep it nice. The stove stands cornerwise, then you come to a little dresser that the carpenters have made. Three rows of shelves and underneath two bins that pull out, to hold flour, sugar, chicken food, etc., and a row of small drawers. I think you see these bins in seed shops at home, but everyone has them here, as you see we have 300 lbs. of flour for the winter and we make our own bread. Then comes the pantry door. Enter pantry, shelves all round, and a deep shelf under window to wash up, and underneath a cupboard to keep silver, etc. Then you come to outside door, and then under window a rather long and narrow table, splendid for ironing, and then door into the hall. Very small and compact, but I did not want a great deal to scrub! The painter is now hard at work and has done two rooms. The dark oak looks very nice with the grey plaster and the hall floor. I shall have it stained and varnished, and a rubover with beeswax will keep it going, I hope. The kitchen floor I shall scrub (once a week), and the spare room we shall stain before you come, but during the winter. Jack will take his bath there and, entre nous, the mess when he washes is past all description! I suppose it is because there is such a lot to wash!

Thursday. The boil is certainly better today and does not hurt so much. Jack opened it and put in carbolic and it has just begun to dry up. I have got a pad of lint soaked in weak carbolic too, so hope it will soon be alright again. It is such a nuisance as I can do no washing. Thank Stewart for his long and most interesting letter. I hope to answer some day but for the next month I expect I shall be fairly busy. I got out my sewing machine to begin some hemming, and the rubber ring that winds the spool has broken, and so must wait until I get more from Eaton's. These things teach you to be calm and patient. Thank you so much for getting the stencils at Selfridges.[1] I am sure Jack will quite enjoy doing his own Christmas cards, and think he is quite an artist! I am sure I shall approve of all your purchases for me, so don't worry on that score, but Jack is a great admirer of *hats* and knows what is just right too. I am glad you did not send me any black, there is no need to wear it here, and it would only constantly remind him. He is so excited about the house, it helps him to forget a bit, but he misses the letters which were always so cheery and of course he has a lot of correspondence with the lawyer. I am glad Stewart is looking after you and taking you out and about, and the two long walks you mention make me feel you are really feeling more like yourself. How I shall enjoy walking with you here. Bring a

---

1. A store in Oxford Street, London.

walking stick, as Canadians never carry canes. Jack felt he was quite conspicuous in Calgary with one, but if he walks from the barn to the patch he must have his stick. . . .

I think you will have to bring oils as well as watercolour, and crayon and chalk for portraits. I will find out if I can if you can get oil paints at the Coast. They do not have them at Eaton's, but perhaps at Calgary. Do not trouble about getting new underclothes. As long as they are tidy we can wash them ourselves, plenty of stockings and two pairs of strong boots and some shoes for trotting around the estate, and goloshes. If you do *have* to get new underclothes, long-cloth is much more difficult to wash I find than the thinner sort I have mostly, and the eyelet embroidery is very easy to iron and inexpensive to buy. You will, I expect, have to get cotton dresses and some hats, but besides these all your old clothes will do quite well. Mrs. Poett told me the other day they wrote home to friends and asked for *old* clothes. I don't know if this is true but you understand the meaning, old things are useful. . . . My great grief is I shall have no flowers all the winter. Do you think some *small* Cape-gooseberries would travel in a cardboard box? They would look rather nice against grey walls, I think, but wonder if they are too fragile. I saw *dyed seaweed.* We had it on our table at the hotel when we came!

This wonderful dry air will do you all the good in the world, I am quite sure. You know I was always using hankies. Now I use *one* or *two* a week only and never hawk in the morning like I used to. I am sure you will find someone coming to Calgary, and almost sure as far as Golden. The boat you will enjoy and I think the train will not be too bad. It will all be so fresh and there is so much to see and to amuse you outside and inside. The luggage question is *no bother at all,* and besides you have got *us* at this end, and the others at the other end when you return. The Athalmer Fair as it is called is on Saturday and I am sending my two tablecloths as there is a needlework class. It is mostly farm produce and horses, etc., and will be most amusing, I expect.

Much love to you all from us both.

Your affectionate sister,

Daisy

ATHALMER, B.C.,
SEPTEMBER 25TH, 1912

My dearest Mother,

First of all while I think of it let me say that the mails are very irregular now, so if you do not hear I expect you will sometimes get two letters together. One of us will write each week but for the next few weeks the letters may not be so long. One of the boats has stopped running already so the mail only comes by car or wagon. We had letters yesterday but had not received any for ten days and have not yet received our papers, but one gets used to these things out here and I have given up worrying. One of the mails caught fire and they had to throw out the mailbags on the roadside one week, and the next week two cars collided and both were more or less smashed so this has caused the delay this week, but things will improve again when these cars are patched up. The boats will in all probability run until the end of October and so the Rainer box will get to Golden by then, but at present there are tons and tons of stuff waiting there and it is just chance whose stuff is put on the boat and whose has to be brought up by wagon and team. If the latter, the good Mr. Rainer will have to pay 10/- or 12/-, I expect. I am sure he is not a simpleton but a knave. . . . I have received the Woodman hair-wash, spendidly packed, for which many thanks. This shows that glass if packed properly travels well, even to B.C. Jack's hair is coming out, as well as Mrs. P's, but I think this will put matters straight. The portfolio, too, spendidly packed, as all the home things are, tell Freda, and also much credit to you for other parcels, papers, etc. The *rings* did come and I am so grateful, and thought I told you as I cannot get them here, but my mind brims over when I begin. Cards from Stanley and letter from Stewart. Please thank them for these.

Jack has had a terribly sad and heartrending letter from poor Ada this week. She was wrapped up in Kenny and the shock has been terrible. Jacky is seven years old and so cannot understand a bit. He is going to school, and her brother is taking her to the South of France. She is selling most of her furniture, and she has some of Jack's things and writes to know what she shall do. Shall she sell? I have advised Jack *not,* and so he has written to tell her to send anything to *you* and not to trouble to write, so if things turn up you will take care of them and store them for the present, I am sure. She may be short of money, so if things are C.O.D. you will understand and do anything to help her, I am sure. I cannot get her out of my mind.

I am writing this in our kitchen, as we have moved in thus far, and I cooked dinner on the stove tonight and it goes splendidly. I hope we shall be quite "in" by this time next week. It is most exciting and makes me wish you could see it all. We have had the hall and the bedroom floors done with stain, shellac, and then varnish, and the man begged us not to tread on them for a week, and I have to hold Jack back by force. He is so keen to see how it will all look (of course, I am not a bit anxious!). I have got some beeswax and turpentine from Eaton's, but cannot get furniture polish. They use liquid veneer here. I think it is horrid and 50 cents a bottle, so a small tin of Ronuk will be nice for a Christmas present! Jack's great amusement is an oily rag, as I have told you, and it is good for the wood.

I am sending you the programme of the Windermere district fair held last Saturday in Athalmer. A small printing press has just started there with this result, but I am sure it is Mr. Bruce's taste! The place it was held was a large wooden shed, I believe some day to be the Town Hall, and it was a great success. A sort of village flower show but much larger this year than last. I sent in some wood-carving and got a First, and my drawn thread cloth and got a Second. Jack said the First was a bedspread. I was horribly disappointed not to go, but my boil only burst on Friday, and Jack said the five mile walk would be too much so I had to obey. All the world and his wife went to the Fair in the morning, and there were some races in the afternoon on the wonderful racecourse that is still in its infancy! I got out my white coat and skirt hoping to look my best and brightest, but instead I helped Jack don his best, with regimental hatband and tie and grey suit, and saw him off with Mr. Bowden at ten o'clock. On the way there Jack picked up a two dollar bill, on the strength of which he treated Mr. Bowden to lunch, a small return for his various small kindnesses to us. Mrs. Poett, learning I had got a boil, came over on Sunday afternoon with her youngest daughter to look after me and brought me some books. Saw the house in its more complete stage and approved, and ordered me to take cod liver oil emulsion! I got some in Athalmer and am taking it to keep away any more, I hope. I am telling you this not because I feel very ill, but to show how well I am looked after. Mrs. Poett looked very charming in a pretty black dress and large tuscan hat turned up on one side, lined with black velvet, most becoming on white hair, and a beautiful black lace veil, diamond pendant, etc., but was delighted to drink tea out of an enamel cup and eat slices of bread and jam!

Friday night. We have been moving in all day and I feel rather tired but happy and pleased at the result. The hall will look awfully nice and cosy, the dresser looking specially nice, and Jack says he likes it all very much. He is most domesticated and quite an expert with a dustpan and broom already! He thinks the pillows are very special. He unpacked them and remarked on their niceness at once, so I told him to inwardly thank his mother-in-law. He keeps on saying "Mrs. Oxley has been awfully good." The paragraph you sent about Captain Fox we saw in the *Overseas Mail.* Jack knows him and all the country round well, and chuckled over it, as he says it must all have been written up from a cable of a few words by a man who knows not Africa! How strange you should have sent it. He loves the *Gazette.* His Colonel has just retired and MacAndrew has succeeded, and I know so many friends by name now.

Goodnight, dear Mother. I have got a letter from you and Freda but have no time to refer to contents.

Daisy

[25 SEPTEMBER 1912]

Dearest Mother,

If you do want to send J. N. P. a trifle you are quite right, a coloured silk handkerchief is the very thing. I hear continually of a wonderful silk bandana he had years ago—this because I made him get some red cotton handkerchiefs for working hours! I was going to ask you to get a couple as my Christmas present to him, but now I am going to get him a candlestick, don't smile, for use when he gets up early to light the fire or if he has to get up in the night to stoke the stove. A pair of white woollen gloves for best, size 11, as he only has one pair. I shall write to Freda re candlestick, which I see in Stores catalogue, and if it will run to it and you will spare the photo of his mother with her plush dress and lace collar, carte-de-visite, I should like to give him that in a little silver frame for his birthday. He has all Kipling's poems, *The Seven Seas, Five Nations, Departmental Ditties,* and loves them all and often reads them aloud in the evenings. He has not read *Just So Stories* but says the last book is bad. *The Light That Failed* he likes but has not got. We have not received the candlestick from Johnson after all, but I think you must not spend any more on us. Any little thing for the house we shall be delighted with. If Stanley sends Jack a diary for his writing table instead of a Christmas card—I mean a shilling one—it would be most useful to put what date we plant things, etc.

Much love, dear Mother, and make up your mind to come here some day.

Your affectionate child,

Daisy

PRIVATE

ATHALMER, B.C.,
OCTOBER 1ST, 1912

My dearest Freda,

I feel quite in a whirl as the mail has arrived today with so much and so many things. I want to write to Stanley, Mother, and you—and I owe Stewart a letter too—but as it is about your birthday time when this will arrive, accept the very best of all good wishes for the 27th. I hope next year I may be able to give you a kiss, and verbal instead of written good wishes. I had not answered yours and Mother's last letters properly before two more arrived and various parcels. The mail now comes in once a week on Monday and goes out Wednesday. I so often picture you writing to me in "our" bedroom though I should not know it in its new guise, I expect, and it will soon be getting too cold for you to write there, I am sure. Tonight I am writing this in our little smoking room and Jack is writing too. I hardly know myself in a house, it is almost like being in Heaven to be surrounded by pretty things and to tread on carpet once again, or I suppose I should say on rugs! But I must tell you all about this later. I am awfully glad you have seen so much of Toussa[1] as I am sure she is *good* for you, also as Jack likes and approves very much of Mrs. Rough and Toussa. He is always most interested in hearing of them. I have not found out yet if the Mrs. and General Poett we know are the same that they know, but we shall be going there to tea one Sunday soon, I expect. Not all the people here are married folk. There are Captain White and Mr. Bennett, who are together and who are carefree bachelors, and who I think will have an awfully nice house when done, much bigger then ours! But we always come to the conclusion that we like the shape of ours best as it is a bungalow pure and simple. . . . I am glad you are starting a B.C. fund and I wish I could help — anything to give you a push! But it is so lovely now to say, "I wonder how Freda will like this and that?" The other morning at breakfast I said, "We shall have to get breakfast in the hall when Freda comes. This table will not hold three." Jack remarked, "Oh, but when Freda comes she will be waiting on us, won't she?" with a merry twinkle and to tease me

I was so interested in hearing of all the soldiermen you have had about, as you say, as long as it is not *real,* and now more than ever I pray, "Give peace in our time." If it was not, you know what it would mean for me. Jack spoke of it once on our wedding day and told me that duty would come first, but said, "Now, never think about it any more, but understand I am still a soldier." I have learnt to be so much braver here, but at times the thought will jump up. You understand, don't you? And now let us change the subject. I am sure you will be able to write to Dr. Mollison and tell him you are much better when you get to B.C. This air is so dry and pure, and bright and crisp. I have lots to do all day and keep on the go all the time. Of course, at times I get a little tired, but I am sure I could not do it in England without being worn out. I liked to hear of your stroll across the Horse Guards and Westminster. I got to love that part of London after being there nearly every day when we paid our visits to Cox's Bank or to the C.P.R. I do hope you don't mind doing all our commissions re writing desk, etc. Jack has quite made up *his* mind that you enjoy it, but I know you did not love shopping and I feel it takes up a good bit of your time when in London. All the catalogues have now arrived from Maples and the Stores. J. N. P. digests them but he is very difficult to please! Anyhow, when you have no shops catalogues are most interesting, and we spend many evenings with them when washing up is finished at 7:30. Other evenings we patronize *Punch* and the *Overseas Mail,* and tonight it has been *Lady's Pictorial* in search of

1. Toussa Rough, one of Freda's friends from the Slade School of Art.

the hat. Not found yet! We will write to the Stores direct for lamp glasses and also a green cardboard collapsible shade and frame "to go on with" for the second lamp. I must begin to keep a list of all the things you will have to bring. Now I must write, my dear girl, and thank you ever so much, and Mother too, for the little box from Goodes. You seem to forestall and fulfil so many of my wishes, I "brim over" very often. The box came the very day we had got the dresser put in place, and I think all the contents are charming. . . .

One day when I have time I shall take you round each room and describe it, but this week there is not time. Thank Stanley for going to King William Street on his way to Newquay. What a thing it is to have a sister abroad! I hope he had a good holiday. Stewart sent me a *most* interesting letter too, bless him. How I wish the fare to Canada was cheaper so that you all could come by turns for your holiday. But you might find us dull with no amusements, only scenery and hard work! With regard to pickles, tell Mother, although we get it from T. Eaton it is Cross & Blackwell, and at present we think their marmalade is the best though we have tried Canadian makes. I think they cannot get real Seville oranges over here. . . . During the winter evenings Jack is going to write you a pamphlet, "Tips for the Journey," and I expect he will instruct you in what clothes to bring, which you may find amusing! . . .

We now have a box nailed to a tree by the side of the road where we turn in to Lot 22, and on it J. N. Phillips atop of one of the cards we had for our luggage. Mrs. Poett brings up mail. Any small commission is done by our placing a note in the box; she and her daughters always look to see if they are driving by. It was her idea and awfully kind. They have two horses and some of them drive by two or three times a week, and here there is no chance of anything being stolen. The idea of sending the bulbs is a simply lovely one and I shall plant them and hope for good results. I know they are grown in Eastern Canada but have not heard of any here. I am sure they will do better as it is not so cold. . . . How lovely it will be. Of course, we cannot get anything of the sort at the experimental farm, cabbages and potatoes are all you see there at present! I shall try planting a few in boxes and putting them in the dark in the root-cellar. I shall be greedy and keep them all for myself, I think. The wet has been bad here and worse than England, but the last few days have been glorious and bright, a fair frost in the morning and then mid-day beautiful and warm. In the house I wear my brown and blue cotton dresses and only have a fire in the kitchen. The Poetts have no nurse with them now, only a "Chink." One of the elder girls looks after "the babies." Oh, will you also please send the recipe of our *soda* cake. I have not got it in my book and used to have it at my fingertips, but other more exciting things have put it out of my head! How glad you will be to know we are *in* the house. It makes me long for you to see it, but I am sure you will highly approve. The Japanese prints look *awfully* nice on plaster and we have them hung low, just above the chair rail, very arty! We really want four more. If Mrs. Marley has any left will you pick them out and reserve them and you could bring them. . . . Your two pictures hang side by side and look magnifique! The gloves have come and are most cosy. Jack has some like them, but in thicker skin. Have not taken to my bed-socks yet! Tell Mother the lampshade looks delightful now it is lit, and the bead-fringe looks so pretty. The pillows and mattress are most comfortable and the blankets luxurious! I wonder if I shall ever wash them? Jack shot a grouse this week so more experience in plucking and trussing. Its heart got left inside by mistake, "But what matters, the feathers are so handy for cleaning my pipe. . . ."

If a small parcel arrives from the Stores you will know it is from B.C. Only a trifle with our best wishes and hope it will be useful in the studio. . . .

Best wishes from Jack and your affectionate sister,

Daisy

ATHALMER, B.C.
1ST OCTOBER 12

Dear Stanley,

Your present to Daisy from Newquay certainly struck the greatest of her wants and has given her tremendous pleasure — she has been trying it on most of this afternoon and evening and decided she must write and thank you for it at once. As she has only this morning given out the names of about six people to whom she owed a letter I put my foot down and said she must answer them first and I have taken the opportunity of writing you a letter which I feel has been owing for some time.

Our furniture has been out in the rain for some time, still packed up but covered only by a tent. We decided therefore about six weeks ago to unpack it and put it in the barn and since then I have been putting it together. It was packed most scientifically and carefully and hardly suffered a bit, but when it was all put together the muddle in the barn was indescribable: furniture, provisions, boxes of clothes, cooking utensils, agricultural implements, all jumbled together, which has made the move into the house all the more appreciated. The house was furnished twelve days ago but we had to wait till Thursday last before moving in to allow the floors time to dry. Everything seems to have been made for the house. The pictures just pan out for each room. There is just the right place for the sideboard, just the right place for the wardrobe and the dressing chest, the big carpet fits the hall floor to half an inch, and our smoking and writing room done in matchboarding makes the house. The walls may interest you. In winter at night the thermometer drops at times to 30° below zero and to keep out the frost an outer layer of boards are put up, then a layer of very thick paper about twice the thickness of elephant paper, then an inner layer of boards fitted together, so:

then a 4" air space, then the lathes and plaster. In the case of the match-boarded room an additional layer of paper is put behind the boards, and this arrangement will I hope keep us warm on the coldest nights. Both our doors have additional doors which go on in the cold weather only. Our cellar, which is, I'm told, necessary, contains all our winter provisions and is frostproof. Our house is so small and everything so much at hand, with so many labour-saving devices such as washing machines, bread-making machines, and wood-consuming stoves that I hope Daisy will find it quite easy as running a house at home with a limited number of servants. Of course, we are not quite settled into the house but most of the spade work is over, and as I see the large quantity of things Mrs. Oxley and you people have given us I feel we are very lucky and you very generous. I think Daisy looks twice as fit as when she first started and — at a rough estimate — twenty times as fit as when she finished the sea journey.

Was very interested in your centenary number and in your speech.

Many thanks for seeing off the Pandora box for us.

Yours,

J. N. Phillips

ATHALMER, BRITISH COLUMBIA,

OCTOBER 7TH, 1912

My dearest Mother,

Here I am sitting in the hall and writing to you on *the* table and under the light of the table lamp and the pretty shade with the bead fringe. You *cannot* imagine how happy I am to be surrounded by all our pretty things. The house really looks *awfully* nice. Jack is very pleased with the way the furniture fits in and the suitability of it all and I quite agree, although it was my own choice. If I had seen the house I should have chosen just the same things. This has been a most exciting week getting fairly straight, and then on Wednesday came the first washing day. It went off fairly well, but clothes that have not been boiled for five months will not come a good color all at once. Jack spent a whole morning helping me as emptying the water and filling the boiler (like a large fish-kettle) and the washing machine, and rinsing both, is a big business at first. The washing machine makes things much easier as you push a handle backwards and forwards and it works the dolly inside. Without the machine I am sure I could not tackle a big wash. Things dry very quickly if it is a sunny day so there is no bother on that account, but all the same they do not look as if they had been done by Mrs. Littlewood, but I suppose I must not be *too* particular. I asked Jack at lunch how he liked "wash day" and he said, "Not at all." However, he is going to help me again tomorrow.

You *all always* seem to be thinking of me and us at home, and it is very sweet of you. The pamphlet you sent Jack pleased him immensely and he thinks it is very good and *sound*. As usual, you have hit upon a *good* thing and "Mrs. Oxley's" opinion on various things is always approved! Freda's little linen parcels are marvels of neatness, the gloves are splendid and just what I shall want. Many thanks too for sending the Jay catalogue. I have not decided *which* yet and Jack rather fancies a Burberry, but nous verrons. Mr. Bowden came over on Wednesday to see the house with the furniture in and was surprised at the difference it made. He said the floors were too good to walk on. But you have to get used to nail marks. They cannot be helped and a house is more for use than ornament after all. With Mr. Bowden came Miss Colebrook, the friend who has come to keep house for him, an awfully nice girl of about thirty, and ready for anything. Their furniture has not come so at present she is our guest and the spare room is already occupied in true Canadian fashion. She sleeps here and goes over to their camp and house during the day, coming over here for tea and a rest in the afternoon and then back here to dinner and, of course, to spend the evening (she is writing at the same table as I am while Jack is fitting photos into frames). Miss Colebrook is very kind and helps me wash up, and can give me heaps of hints re washing and cooking, too, as she trained at Edinburgh in domestic economy and was at Reading too. She can make bread but finds it is quite different out here.

On Friday Mr. Bowden asked us to go down to Invermere to lunch with Mrs. Bowden and to be introduced. She had just arrived and was feeling a bit lonely, and it is hard lines their furniture has not come. It is at Golden, but the boats are packed just now and there will be tons of stuff to come by road later on and then you have to *pay*. Mrs. Bowden is rather charming, slight, with grey hair, a nice voice, and a rather sad expression. She writes a great deal, I think, but in what form I know not, and she told me she had had a terrible operation and cannot use the muscles round her waist so cannot do much hard work, which is the reason for Miss Colebrook coming, I expect. However, she will be nice to have for a neighbour and was to have come to tea today to see her house and ours, but she is in bed with a bad throat and temperature. Miss Colebrook has a Brownie camera and has promised to take a photograph of our house some day soon, so you may see it in a more finished state.

Jack has just said, "Ten minutes more," and the mail goes tomorrow. Has Freda got me the grey shirt braid? I forget if I asked for it or not—3 or 4 yards please. The black and white veils are *awfully* nice, *so* suitable. Where did you get them, I wonder? Stanley sent me an awfully nice jersey and cap, and I look fine in it. Just the thing for out here and the shape is charming, the size is right, and the colour I like, green. It was most good of him. My Christmas present in advance, but I can wear it now. We had 8° of frost yesterday morning. The water barrels outside are frozen over in the morning, but I still wear my cotton dresses in the house, and mid-day it is quite warm. Of course, later on we get 60° or more! Yesterday (Sunday) we took a bread and cheese lunch and went for a walk to show Miss Colebrook her way about. We called on the Poetts for tea, and there was so much talk about I forgot to ask about the Roughs! Thanks ever so much for sending the bulbs. I feel quite excited about them, and it will be another experiment. I believe I am becoming quite a good cook! Roast veal, our own cabbages and potatoes, orange jelly, and cheese and coffee for dinner tonight and the silver looks awfully nice, much better than plate, I am sure, and easier to keep clean.

You can declare things less than their value. Parcels are very seldom opened but at the London shops they always declare at *full* value, I suppose to protect themselves. There is bother about our silver. We have got it *free,* but the man at Golden has got into trouble from headquarters, but I think in the end all will be well. Re Christmas, I will let you know in a week or two if I may as Captain King is sending us candlesticks or oil and vinegar cruet, and at present I know not which!

I *must* go to bed. I am so sorry to stop. Dutiful wife!
Much love,

Daisy

ATHALMER, B.C.,
OCTOBER 15TH, 1912

My dearest Mother,

It is two o'clock on Sunday afternoon and having washed up the lunch things, swept up the kitchen, and changed, I am sitting on the verandah in the new Roorkee chair which Captain Richardson has sent us, clothed in my bright green skirt, white crêpe blouse with black and white Tennyson bow, black velvet waistband with Jack's regimental buckle, and Liza's combs in my hair! These I found put out on the dressing table by Jack, so I have taken the hint! Mr. and Mrs. Cuthbert are coming up to tea with us this afternoon (Jack went down there to buy some onions yesterday and asked him). Jack has just gone off for a stroll with his gun in case he meets a willow grouse, which are about just now. We have two hanging on a tree at present, one *we* shot on Friday, and one a present from Mr. Robinson as he got several brace being a man of more leisure! What a really wonderful mother you are. The parcels of clothes came this week and I am *absolutely* delighted with everything, they are all perfect. Both the blouses I like immensely and they fit me very well indeed and are just what I want. The veils are *exactly* the thing wanted, the hood is *perfect* and most becoming, the gloves are splendid, the woollen underclothes too are just what is wanted, and who told you I wanted those *mops* and had wished for them several times for lamp chimneys and washing up? You seem to think of everything. I was at the Poetts on Sunday last and one of the girls was using a mop for the teacups. It made me wish for one too, and then on Tuesday, lo and behold, you had sent them. The Italian Count I told you of who helped to build our house was over there. He is such a charming youth and speaks English quite well now. He is going round and getting experience in carpentering and gardening before buying a ranch of his own somewhere on the Prairie. Please thank Freda for her share in having the blouses tried on and, I expect, several visits to Miss Hutchinson, and much time given up when in London. I think we speak nearly every day of her coming out. Jack said today, "When Freda comes you will get the work finished at 10:30 every day." I hope, but I don't think for a minute, we shall.

I am perfectly delighted with the house and know that it looks very nice indeed, and people say, "How English! How artistic!" which is very amusing, I always think. I think one of the reasons is that we had our doors made with short panels at the top and deep ones below and we have the copper handles fitted very high up, which is unusual out here, and the *dull* oak stain with the plaster looks very nice too. Jack has been digging the potatoes this week and Mr. Robinson and their boy Smith have been over to help (paid, of course), and now they are all stored in the root cellar away from the frost. We only got ten sacks but we hope for better things next year, and we shall not have to buy any. I only wish I could send you some as they are most excellent, especially "Uncle Sam." Miss Colebrook is still with us, and as far as I can see may have to be with us for some time. Their furniture is at Golden but there are such crowds of provisions to come up I am afraid for their furniture as they have six tons. We had under *two*! Mrs. Bowden has been and is staying at Invermere Hotel and has been ill with a bad throat, so Mr. Bowden goes down every night and comes up in the morning to help with painting the house as they are colouring all their plaster walls with different colours in Hall's Distemper. I believe this is Mr. Robinson's choice.... Miss Colebrook has a cup of tea here in the morning and then goes off over to the camp and house (Hoodoo Ranch) and gives them their breakfast, does their washing and makes them savoury pottage for lunch;

helps with the painting of the house, prepares something for their evening meal and usually gets over here again at six o'clock. We have dinner at seven and change and make ourselves beautiful. It is so nice to use all our nice things, entrée dishes, etc. Tell Freda I keep thinking of Elsie's house and the washing up we used to do there. We have breakfast in the kitchen, usually cold bacon, eggs when we can get them, and marmalade. I like the plain white and gold breakfast things very much and the little marmalade jar with the gilt nob is very sweet. One day I shall get you to see if you can get a red and white kitchen cloth as it would keep clean and look cheerful. The table is long and rather narrow under the window and very nice for ironing. After breakfast *we* make the bed. Everyone remarks on and admires the eider-down and the bedspread. Jack likes this latter especially, and of course it looks nice with the white plaster. Then off he goes, I finish the bedroom washstand, etc. then wash up the breakfast things, clean the stove, brush up the kitchen. Then down on my hands and knees and sweep the hall carpet, and rub all over the polished boards. The door is always open so lots of dust comes in. Dust the hall, tidy up the smoking room, make the camp bed and tidy up the visitor's room, and do cooking to prepare for the evening or make cakes or scones! Lunch of bread and cheese and jam at twelve, then wash up, clean stove properly, and sweep out the kitchen. Then *lie down for an hour*. Then I write to you or darn until tea at 3:45 P.M., usually in the smoking room on carved tray, blow the whistle to fetch Jack from the po-tato patch or wherever he is — buttered toast or soda cake for tea as a rule — then I usually peel the potatoes, get the greens ready and the pots boil-ing for dinner, lay the cloth for dinner, see all is going well, and then change. My overalls that Nelly made me are treasures and cover me up. This week we have been living on veal, and I find I am quite a fair cook. I can boil bacon quite well and let it cook in the water! We had roast veal, cabbage and potatoes on Monday, *baked jam roly poly* (try it, it is very good with blackcurrant jam and looks nice in an entrée dish). Pea soup, cold veal and pickled onions, mashed potatoes. Next day, curry, blanc-mange and stewed apricots. Next, rissoles. Next, cottage pie. Next and tonight, some rather nice soup. As the joint cost about 6/- in the first place it is not so bad. Puddings are rather difficult as eggs are difficult to get. What about baked cake pudding? It is not called that in Mrs. Beeton. Do you know the proportion of suet? I don't want puddings with more than one egg at present, but I am going to try pastry this week and Freda has seen Jack eat jam tarts! It is just the same with scones and rock cakes. I find he begins on a piled-up dish I make to last three days and in a few minutes they have gone. Now I learn wisdom and put out a few at a time! But he is very easily satisfied.

The washing was better this week, I suppose because in a house things do not get so dirty. Kitchen cloths are rather difficult to get the stains from, though I boil them last in soda water. I am sure the laundress must use something, lime perhaps? Oh no, I usually "soap in" on Monday, wash on Tuesday (a horrid mess), and iron on Wednesday and perhaps Thursday as well. So Freda knows what is before her! Tell her to get all the hints and wrinkles she can. Nelly sent me a splendid letter of instructions I hope to answer soon, about pegging clothes on the line and washing flannel. So far I have not had to wash a tablecloth but that is coming next week. Jack was hugely delighted last night because he found a grease spot near my plate, as *I* always say, "You dare splash the cloth!" Miss Colebrook changes the plates (by request), and the hot box then comes in useful as the pudding and coffee keep just right while we eat the first course. After dinner I have been making little Madras curtains for the bedroom windows, two pairs at each and they look very nice. I have made them short and loop them back with a little frill along the top, but the cretonne in the hall will be like casement. I shall get them done by degrees and Jack reads while I work, usually *Punch*. The poetry by Evoe and Dum Dum is always popular, and we often have back numbers over again.

Another "want." I really must have some hessian aprons (like sacking) for cleaning the stove and washing. I expect Lizzie Bailey could make them. I think I had better have two, and if she washes the stuff first to get the dressing out they would not weigh much. At present I tie a potato sack round and it keeps the wet off my dress better than anything.

I left off yesterday overleaf as the Cuthberts arrived. They had not been here ten minutes when Dr. and Mrs. Turnor and three children (two girls and a little boy) turned up too. They had walked cross-country three miles, had a picnic lunch, and called here for a rest. Seven visitors to tea, but I had got an uncut cake and two dozen scones! Mrs. Cuthbert helped me butter and jam them and we soon had tea set in the hall, while the visitors basked in the sun on the verandah. Next time visitors come I wonder if I shall have cakes going! Mrs. Turnor brought me a marrow jam and she went off triumphant with six *Pictorials* which Mrs. Cuthbert had just returned, and the small children delighted at the thought of pictures for cutting out! Mrs. Cuthbert brought me a bag of parsley to dry for the winter. I hope next year we shall be able to give. We have really received so much.

The kitten flourishes, but *will* use the hearth in the hall when it wishes to put a penny in the slot, and this raises master's ire. But I think it so considerate not to prefer the carpet. Otherwise, it sleeps in the wood box and occasionally catches chip-monks or mice. I had got my blue cotton on just newly washed, and after lunch went to skim some bacon that was boiling and splashed myself with grease from top to toe. Serves me right for doing things without my overall. My brown and blue dresses I wear for all my work, and I shall have to think of something useful to take their place next year. Miss Colebrook wears navy and white stripe galatea with soft white collars, and one of her dresses she changes into is fine blue serge with blue and white spot sailor collar, roll-back cuffs and rather open neck, and bone buttons for trimming—very pretty. On Sunday she turned out in a Jay hat, like mine and Freda's, only green straw. Wasn't it funny? We have not got *Just So Stories* in our library, but we read a good bit of Kipling's poetry aloud, and Mrs. Poett has lent us two books. . . .

Thanks so much for the seeds. We plant them this week. At present we get about 6° of frost, but mid-day until five o'clock it is lovely and hot in the sun and I sit outside in a cotton dress. But in the shade it is very cold. The Durants are splendid with their cooking and washing. Tell Dorrie to learn to make bread and then she will be quite ready to come out and pay us a visit! I am so thankful you brought me up to be more or less useful in a house or I should find life here so much harder. Sunday is a lovely day when we try and forget work. Jack has brought some red and white cotton hankies for hard work, but they are Canadian and no quality when I think of the bandana cotton ones of the boys. I was so interested in Stanley's New-quay letter, and he sent me a most lovely jersey and cap (trés chic).

Hope you will enjoy a little jaunt to Malvern in Gloucester. Thanks for the velvet bows. We have ordered a green cardboard shade from the Stores for the second lamp. Oil is expensive like everything else!

Heaps of love,

Daisy

ATHALMER, B.C.
SUNDAY, OCTOBER 20TH, 1912

My dearest Freda,

It was nice to get a breath of the London Thames in your last letter. You seem to keep on the go fairly well, but I am sure it is good for you and will help the time to pass very quickly, until you get out on your big adventure to B.C. Miss Colebrook came out alone and got on quite well and I am sure you will, and will doubtless find another unattached female with whom to share a cabin. Miss Colebrook came out on a boat where there is no First Class but the top is Second, and so she came along on the train with the same two ladies as far as Winnipeg, Second Class as well. Of course, it is quite comfortable and there is a restaurant car where you can get meals, but I think you had better only have breakfast and dinner and the rest of the time live on heaps of fruit and biscuits, etc. As you get so little exercise it is quite enough. However, we will write and give you instructions and good advice in good time. You must come early in April, I think, or you will miss so much of the beauty. Yesterday we had our first fall of snow, and although it has melted this morning, it is right down on the foothills to the very bottom and leaves a distinct crispness in the air all day long, which up to the present we have only had until ten o'clock in the morning. By the way, before I forget, Jack went to Wilmer for the bread yesterday and came back triumphant with the chafing dish, so that has turned up alright at last. The only thing now I cannot find is the traycloth Annie Wellman sent me, but I expect it is in Pandora's Box. The last boat came up to Athalmer on Friday, so now it dumps the things down at a place six miles away, I believe.

We have begun the wood fires in our open hearth in the evening and they are great and look so lovely as we have great big logs. Jack has made a guard of a frame of light woodwork covered with mosquito wire netting, and this saves all dangers of sparks and is so fine you hardly notice it. We usually light it about five o'clock, for up to that time Jack is working outside and I am so busy in the house there is no need to be cold. The winter ploughing is now going on and this time it is very deep so they use a team of four horses to the plough. Jack thinks the five acres is about as much as he can manage so we shall have no more cleared at present, though of course next summer we shall have your extra help! I have been learning to truss grouse this week, a lesson being given by Miss Colebrook, and I managed it quite well! I did one and Jack the other. We went for a stroll one evening for half-an-hour and got one, and the other was given us. I kept the tail for you as the feathers were so pretty, but it has disappeared and I fear the kitten is to blame, so I can only send you a few feathers which are rather pretty. I roasted one bird and made a pie of the other. Tell Mother I find I am getting quite a good cook and find I can make most excellent flakey pastry among other things. I have tried the Madras curry with great success too. I have not made bread yet, only baking powder bread and this is quite good if eaten fresh — see Mrs. Beeton and tell Dorrie Durant to try it. Last night we had "dry curry and rice," followed by "baby carrots in sweet sauce" from the Mrs. Peel book, and then baked suet with apples inside. They were apple rings which had to soaked, but they seemed quite nice. I could not get the top sticky like the "Bottom Tosity" we used to eat at No. 4 High, but it was brown and Jack was pleased. He loves cakes, so I usually keep soda drop cakes going and they only use one egg, as that is the great difficulty with all my cooking, but I am getting to be very clever. I find that when we get meat and hang it a few days it is quite tender, but soon it will be frozen and cut with a saw and have to be thawed. Like everything else, Jack knows it should be thawed very gradually in cold water! He is most domesticated, and I expect you will be very amused. He always gets up and lights the kitchen fire, and after breakfast helps me make the bed. *Everyone* admired our bedspread and the eiderdown. Of course, it looks so nice in the plaster room. I have finished the Madras curtains, and put the little frills along the board last night. I have made a runner in the top and threaded a tape through and then drawn it up to size, so it will be easy for washing. Next I begin on the smoking room which will be plain blue casement, Jack's old curtains from his room at Aldershot. But I have to finish his overcoat and put in my grey skirt braid, and I only get about an hour in the evening after dinner, as when you wash you have also to iron. That takes time, but life cannot be perfect and otherwise I think it would be. I shall get quicker and better at it soon, I am sure. I find not the "colonial washerwoman" but the colonial work is very hard on underclothes, and the sleeves of my chemises and camisoles rub through so when my old ones of the former variety are worn out I shall discard them, I think. I always wear my best and ribbons on Sunday, and I should like you to send me several yards of Valencia lace and also of Torchon edging for mending. I think you can get imitation Torchon at Caley's or Milsum's. . . . Miss Colebrook wears galatea in different stripes for her work dresses, not the *very* good as it is too thick and clumsy but about 7 ¾d. a yard, and with a green belt and tie they look very nice. I still wear my blue and brown zephyrs[1] for working in the mornings. You see, we only have 6° of frost now and soon it will be ever so much more below zero. I must try and harden myself. Thanks ever so much for the hairnets.

Now for a walk round the hall! Open front door, green, with top panel glass divided into *four*. Copper handle high up, over door inside two hippo tusks. Window on left with deep sill, on it Benares pipe bowl and Jack's father in brown frame. Jack's armchair in corner. Behind it stands the teatray and above it the Greuze picture from Paris. Bedroom door, small mat left-hand side of fireplace. My carved table (silver and curio table) cram full both shelves. Silver box from Khartoum, old repeater watch, magnifying glass, Mr. W. Ruston's present, the barometer, and lots of little things. Fireplace. Broad marble shelf, dull brown wood, and it is divided into panels to take the Japanese prints. Quite an original idea. On mantelpiece three silver frames, Jack's clock in centre, Japanese cloisonné vase, two silver vases, and a baby elephant model. Swanzi, Spring, and "my nephew" in the frames. Iron dogs in the hearth by the Athalmer blacksmith (only $3 each for making them), but you *must* have them for the log fires so do not comment on the expense. Log box alias my oak chest the other side of the fireplace, and above, the two Greuze heads, one above the other. Kitchen door, then four ointment pot tops, then bookcase (Jack has left out the books in the plan). Window seat at present has a leopardskin rug on it and the four pillows. More bookshelves. The Angelus[2] and the two Japanese prints. The door of the spare room, dresser, brass ornaments and various china plates on shelves. I have mended some with seccotine and the new ones you sent. In centre, blue Japanese embroidery mat Mr. E. K. gave me long ago, silver

1. Torchon: a French lace; Galatea: a striped cotton material; Zephyr: a fine, lightweight cotton material used for a shawl or duster.
2. By the French artist François Millet.

kettle in centre, Mason's set in box one side and E. K. tea-caddy on other. One drawer fitted as a plate drawer and the other for table linen—the two cupboards for muffineers, etc. Underneath two entrée dishes and chafing dish on Archie Young's mat. Smoking room door. Your two paintings above and Japanese prints below. In the corner my armchair and behind it a corner shelf for the lamp. On each side Stanley and Stewart, and Gilbert at the back. Underneath shelf my work basket. Mother, Father, Mrs. Phillips and Daisy Mac are on the shelf along windowseat. Window.

Monday. I am writing against time as today has been washing day. I always try and forget Monday. It always seems to come round so quickly. Today I hung out the things in a biting wind and half-an-hour after they were frozen as hard as boards, the pillow cases stood by themselves. It is impossible to dry them outside any more, I suppose, as they freeze when the sun is shining. I suppose I must have a string across the kitchen. There is thick ice in the mornings on the water barrels and all day long as I dip in my jug a thin film has formed. I should shudder and grumble in England, but my camp training has been good for me. Will you please send me some *braid* hair curlers like Mother uses, and send me a bill for my various expenses some time. I think if the stencil Christmas cards are any way possible Jack would like to do our own and I think we could write in the greeting. I have sent Mother the Christmas pudding recipe. The red leaves are wild gooseberry I picked on Sunday. I went to Mr. Harley at the garden, and now I have planted some bulbs in the open, six inches down. Some in the root-cellar in boxes and some are to be put in the minute the ground thaws in the spring, so it is all excitement to see how they do as there are none about here, though they are grown in Eastern Canada. I cannot have rose trees sent, he says, because they have to be sent to the Coast to be fumigated and it is a great expense. They do not want to import English blight!

I love the drawings in the letters but I am sorry to see you have altered so much in the short time. Write and tell us what clothes you will be wearing at Golden so we can recognize you. Who is Goodman's fiancée, a friend of his or of the family? What an upset in the dovecot. Give my love to Dandy. Is Dolly Turner's fiancé the Baghdad railway man? Poor Madeline, it is hard lines for her. Get all the hints from Nellie you can re washing and ironing. I wish I could do some work for her but, alas, I have a husband and a house! Stanley's jersey and cap are awfully nice in shape and colour. I expect we shall get Stewart's lamp tomorrow, *and* letters. I love mail day and forget all about washing. I like the Debenham shirt immensely, open easy necks are the thing for *hard* work. Valencia lace, 1" wide, Torchon, ½". 6 yards of each, please.

Much love to all from both, and much to yourself, dear old girl,

Daisy

My dearest Mother,

After 8° of frost when Jack got up this morning, we are now (3 o'clock) sitting on the verandah basking in the sun, the advantage of facing south, and I have on a white muslin blouse! This is only possible until about four. When the sun gets low it at once gets cold. Last Monday (washing day) it was terribly cold and my poor fingers *hurt* when I was hanging out the washing. A sudden happy thought, and the mittens you sent saved the situation! There was *no* sun and a biting wind. The clothes froze in ten minutes and the pillow cases could stand by themselves. I had to bring all the things in, and then of course they melted and had to be dried in the kitchen, a foretaste of winter, I suppose. Jack could not see what there was to worry about, but clothes take up such a lot of room indoors and a hot, quick-drying sun has spoilt me. However, I learn now that all you do is to leave them out, day and night, and in about three days they get dry. So ironing day comes at the end and not the beginning of the week and the frost makes them a good colour. When we have more money saved I think we shall send some of the washing to the "Chink" as our first extravagance, but like everything else it comes easier by practice. I cannot get the stains out of kitchen rubber as I should like, but in this I cannot keep to English standard though I try hard in every other way. Jack says he would rather have a tidy wife than a well-cooked dinner, but I get on well with the cooking, I know, and like it very much indeed. I made my first batch of bread yesterday and am glad to say it was a great success, *more* than just eatable. The yeast cakes here are quite different from the English yeast. You have to dissolve them in lukewarm water, add flour to make a thin batter and leave them *all* night to rise. The great difficulty is to keep the batter warm. Even now you have to wrap it up in a blanket in the kitchen, and later on I believe the best way is to give it a hot-water bottle as well. Then in the morning you add more flour and knead, leave to rise until 12 o'clock, then make into loaves that have to prove for an hour, so you cannot bake until about 2 o'clock. I also had a marrow given me so tried some jam with the Eversley recipe. It wanted about ten minutes more and tasted very good, when a knock at the kitchen door, and a Mr. Newman called about the water, which had "gone wrong." Jack was out, and when I returned to the kitchen the jam had burnt, so it is dark and rather like treacle but quite eatable. We have planted some of the bulbs in the ground, some in a box in the root-cellar, and the others we shall put in directly the snow melts in the spring and see which is best. With regard to the eiderdown, it would be the very thing for the spare room bed. Everyone has their "comfort" out here, as eiderdowns are very sensibly called. Could Freda bring it? It would be heavy to post. At present I have done nothing in the spare room. There is a bed and a washstand, and the boxes that Jack's chest-of-drawers goes into, which is my linen cupboard. I must rig up a dressing-table and cover the cupboard with cretonne before Freda comes, but at present I have had no more time for curtains. I seem busy all day long and then in the evening I finish at 7:30 or 8:00, and mending must be done. I must try to start on the curtains for the smoking room this week. Jack always reads in the evening which is very nice, and I always find time to look at the *Lady's Pictorial* and, of course, devour the home letters. Auntie Louie has written me and I must try and answer soon, but my "home" letter is usually written against time so excuse shortcomings. I sent you the recipe for Christmas pudding about six weeks ago. I hope you got it. Miss Colebrook is still with us. Mr. Bowden's furniture has not come yet though it is at Golden, as of course supplies come up first and they are not all here by any means. Mrs. Bowden was ill at the hotel with a very bad throat, could not eat and got very weak, so they took her to the hospital at Wilmer to give her invalid cooking. Yesterday we heard she has erysipelas[1] and is seriously ill. It is a bad start but I think she is very delicate. Jack and I went to Church at Wilmer this morning and enquired, and she was a little better. Miss Colebrook is so thankful she can come to us. She is only 25 and very bright and cheerful, but it is a bad thing for her and she tries to make the best of it. She has been here three weeks now, and wanted to pay for board, but you can imagine Jack allowing that, can't you, if we hadn't a penny in the world? However, now it is settled that she gives me an hour's help in the evening, although she is willing to work or iron then, she is tired and it would not be fair.

The mountains look so lovely with their white caps, but when the Panama route is open I quite make up my mind you will come and lose all your catarrh. I am glad you had the little trip to Gloucester and Malvern, and that all are fit and well. I expect you enjoyed the description of the hall. Our bedroom is as follows. Enter door, on left Jack's chest-of-drawers. On top of this, bookshelves, now used for all his bottles and brushes (always very tidy)! I have no cover, so at present the "carving cloth" acts as such. Washstand under window. The chinaware is very pretty. Dressing table, cornerwise, then other window. Underneath, grey wooden box for stores, and the pretty table cover Freda bought at Liberty's comes in here as a cover. Chair, cupboard door, and bed, and the other chair. Then the wardrobe on same wall as door, so it all fits in perfectly. We have put all the rugs and mats in the hall, and we have the brown blankets as "runners" on the polished floor. Freda's lithographs of you and Arthur,[2] my watercolour, one of Ada, the family group, and Stewart's enlargement of Freda are the pictures. I find

---

1. An acute disease associated with vesicular and endematous local inflammation of the skin and subcutaneous tissues caused by hemolytic streptocococcus.
2. Arthur Oxley, another of Daisy's brothers.

silver only wants cleaning once a fortnight, and it is a sitting down job. So few things are, I find, but I am sure my back and arm muscles are getting very much stronger. Jack is awfully good at helping me, but of course there is such a lot to do outside. The wood cutting and filling the water barrels from the ditch is a work in itself every day.

Mrs. Marples and the three children have arrived and are very nice. Their furniture has not come either, so they have come up to the house to picnic. She is very cheerful and nice in spite of having lost her dressing bag with *all* her jewellery and papers to do with money en route. She gave it to her steward at Liverpool to put in her cabin as she had lots of friends to see her off, and it never appeared there or anywhere else on the boat! They want us to pay for our wedding presents at the head office at Ottawa, but we are *fighting* it!

Tell Stanley I am wearing his jersey and cap for my walks abroad and they are most comfortable. Stewart's lamp is lovely, too, and we seem surrounded by all your kind thoughts and gifts.

Much love, dear Mother, to you all from your very happy and lucky child,

Daisy

ATHALMER, BRITISH COLUMBIA,
NOVEMBER 2ND, 1912

My dear Freda,

How horribly near Christmas this looks. I hardly realize how far on we are, I suppose it is the lack of fog and mist in the early morning. All the same, it is getting very cold, in fact, has been freezing all today and we now have the water-barrel in the kitchen. It came in this morning with ice on the top, and only melted about five o'clock. That is, there was ice round the edges until then. I made a suet pudding yesterday and there was ice floating about in the jug in which I did the mixing. There was ice on our bedroom jug this morning, but that was just underneath the open window. In spite of all this I have not felt the cold *badly* and have not taken to my thick woollen underwear yet. Of course, when I am pegging out the washing I find the mittens Mother sent me most *comfy*. Thanks ever so much for all the parcels, the woollen gloves with fingers are most useful just now, and the lovely warm underbodice. I think it is really beautiful, and will be just the thing. Also the lampshade, which will do splendidly when we use the second lamp. Now Stewart's lamp has come we like it so much I find Jack always lights *it*. And it is so nice to write and work by after dinner and we find it burns less oil than the duplex, and no fear of chimneys smashing. My everyday garb, too, is the Harrods skirt and Stanley's jersey and cap. I find both so comfortable for walking and usually there is no wind so it does not feel too cool, though of course all the men look more or less like doormats when they are driving in their black skin coats. The Canadians seem to feel the cold so much more than we do, but they say, "Wait, and in a year or two you will feel it more as your blood gets thin!" I like the patterns of cloth you sent *immensely*. I like your overcoat so much. I am glad you have one something like it, and the other material I think is charming. It seems to me it is so close woven it will really be warm enough, and we always said *thick* coats and skirts were a mistake. Out here you will live in a *short* tweed skirt and golf jersey, I expect, until the cotton dress time, and a coat and skirt occasionally on Sunday. By the way, I think two useful aprons in blue or red and white, à la Nelly's shape or just with an ordinary bib and half sleeves, are more useful and not so heavy to wash; and cooler in summer as well. If you are making a clothing list, you can bring overalls as well for sketching and gardening. I think you had better keep a list and send it to me to revise. I wish you would send me a penny notebook, and two paper washing books if you are not tired of doing up parcels as I so often think of things and put them down on odd bits of paper. I hope I have acknowledged all the things you and Mother have sent. I am sure I have received them all, but when I begin to write I have such lots of things to say they may get crowded out. But they all give intense pleasure. *Punch*, the *Observer* and the *Express*. The last two as well as being interesting are *most* useful for the kitchen table and shelves as we get no other newspaper. I think the *Express* staff group is excellent. They all look as if they are very proud to be who they are! I love your account of Beresford and the photo taking. His patience is utterly exhausted in *five* minutes, and if he is not attended to in a shop he walks out! I am looking at your letter and will say now that Miss Colebrook came out White Star. I expect you could get an introduction to a "stable" companion at the C.P.R. Office if you interview the good lady up aloft, and I am sure you will write an amusing article on all your experiences and thoroughly enjoy yourself. I am sure you will not feel deaf here. I can always hear Jack speaking outside when I am in with doors and windows shut. This is not often, of course, only when I make bread! Don't worry about getting domesticated, you will learn more here in a month than you would in six months in England, but if you can get hints on washing from the Durants it will be a great help, as you will have to do your own! Finding out how to peg things out and *iron* will be the best help for you, I think. I *did* the damask dinner cloth today and it might have come from the steam laundry, but it took me over half-an-hour, a large amount of time when there is so much else to do. . . .

The last batch of bread was excellent but I find we eat an awful lot, at least Jack does. The kitten is to be called "Four-Paws" after the verses in

Punch. That is when she is good. When she is naughty, master shakes her (poor kitten) and will not call her anything to punish her. I like the way your new coat is made very much indeed. What chapeau goes with it, I wonder? Purple? I have had a letter from Alexina, also from Dorothy Durant. She is a kind little soul. Also a splendid book on washing. It will be a great help. I am glad the p.c.'s arrived for Mother's birthday. They really do not do little Wilmer justice. They were taken in winter or early spring. I am so looking forward to seeing your photo. The time simply flies along so it will soon be here. Miss Colebrook only comes here to sleep now, as Mr. Bowden has left the hotel and is up at the house, so she has to cook the dinner for them (and eat it too, of course) and she comes here after. Mrs. Bowden is in the hospital still but was to sit up today. I really wonder what will happen as I fear she is very delicate and the high altitude may be too much for her. If so, I expect they will have to go to the coast, but this is all surmise, I do not know. We have been reading a lovely book (lent by Mrs. Poett), *The Cheerful Day* by Reginald Lucas. Do get it. Jack reads while I work. I have tacked seven curtains of blue casement for the smoking room and have had one afternoon with the machine this week. It works very well, tell Mother. We shall soon be busy doing stencils, I expect. Old Jack will enjoy himself, I can tell you. I make a big batch of pastry every week and wonder we did not have more open jam tarts at home. I make open tarts with apricots and apples in the centre, which are très bon. I soak the dried fruit 48 hours and cook it with brown sugar, and it is very nice indeed. We have another hare hanging in the tree ready for the pot. I do hope Mother will decide to get the musquash[1] coat. I think she would have a fur coat of some kind if not *fur-lined*, plain ribbed dull silk with fur collar and cuffs, but I expect this would cost as much. "The Stage" is motor in summer and sleigh with team of four horses in winter, so if you do not get letters any time you will know it has broken down in some way. . . .

ATHALMER, B.C.,
NOVEMBER 8TH, 1912

My dearest Mother,

Like you I do not know where to begin. There is so much to say and so much to thank you for as usual, and so little time. First of all, Jack is awfully pleased with the articles by "Linesman," and the map which is pulled out and studied of an evening by the fireside with a pipe. Alas, no drink! Jack has not had a glass of beer or a whisky and soda since we have been

1. Muskrat.

Daisy as a little girl.

Daisy Oxley (r) was the elder
daughter of Frederick and Laura
Oxley (seated, centre). Daisy's sister Freda (l) and her four brothers
are also shown in this family
photograph taken in the early
1900's. The letters in this collection
were sent by Daisy to her mother
or sister. *Windsor Eton and Slough
Express.*

The Oxley residence in Windsor, where Daisy grew up and the destination of her Windermere letters.

Daisy (l) and Freda Oxley (c) at a picnic in Epping Forest, Essex. The picnic was organized by the Slade School of Art where Freda was a student. *University of London, Department of History of Art.*

Heston, the Phillips family estate in Middlesex where Jack spent most of his childhood. *Hounslow Public Library, Middlesex.*

Jack's parents, Thomas Edward Phillips II and Elizabeth Phillips, had three sons, Kenneth (l), born in 1877, Jack (c), born in 1875, and Francis (r), born in 1872. Jack's mother died in 1889 and his father caused a scandal by marrying the housekeeper. In the 1890's Jack enlisted as an ordinary soldier and received an officer's commission during the South African War. (left) Jack in the uniform of the Lincolnshire Regiment.

WINDERMERE
B·C

Clever advertising aimed at the English middle class—the cover of the pamphlet that brought the Phillipses to the Windermere.

The pamphlet presented a vision of prosperity and comfort. On their orchard lots settlers would establish homes surrounded by hollyhocks and other English flowers; in the valley people would drive on well-groomed roads with scenic views.

(above) Daisy and Jack with their kitten Four-paws on the porch of their bungalow (below) with Molly Gleave (l) and Miss Colebrook (r).

A portion of a painting in Ran
dolph Bruce's promotional pam
phlet on the Windermere show
ing a well-dressed woman pickir
apples.

The C.P.R. line from Golde
to Cranbrook, under constructic
when Jack and Daisy were in tl
Windermere Valley, was not con
pleted until 1917. *Provincial A
chives of British Columbia.*

Amelia Harris (holding the baby
Elizabeth), Daisy, and Jack outsic
"Heston," the Phillipses' bung
low overlooking Toby Creek. C
the back of the photograph Jac
wrote, "the source of all my wo
—the bacillus in white."

Athalmer, c. 1910. *Provincial Archives of British Columbia.*

(above) Bruce Avenue in Invermere, before the First World War.
(below) An early photograph of Windermere, showing the J. C. Pitts
general store. *Provincial Archives of British Columbia.*

A later photograph of the Windermere Valley looking north towards Invermere. Windermere Lake is in the foreground; the Phillipses' lot on Toby Creek is out of the picture on the left. *Provincial Archives of British Columbia.*

Jack Phillips and his daughter Elizabeth taken in January 1915 at Merton, Surrey, where his mother-in-law Mrs. Oxley and sister-in-law Freda were living. Shortly after this picture was taken, Jack left for the French front where, in April, he died of wounds suffered at Yprès.

here. He really is what Freda Dainty would call "a dear" as he never grumbles, even in fun, but just says he cannot afford. I think a bottle of beer is 25 cents. I really think the cuttings from the papers give him as much or more pleasures than the papers, as he likes to be thought of, and the *Gazette* always produces the same remark, "I really think I enjoy these more than anything else that comes from England." The mails come from Golden and also from Cranbrook. All the "winter comforts" have now come and I expect they will soon be in use as it has been snowing all day. We have had showers before which have partially melted but this has been very quiet and steady all day. However, I went outside without hat or jersey this morning and was not cold. Jack has not got sleeping socks, and I do not think he would scorn them later on when it is 30° below, as he feels the cold in his extremities. I have not begun my sleeping socks yet. My jersey is very much admired, and so is Stewart's lamp. We wrote to the Stores for a shade for the little brass lamp as we find it useful in the smoking room, and they have sent a very pretty one in *eau-de-nil,* like a very large candleshade and it clips onto the chimney. They really are splendid people, and always send just what we want and so well packed. Jack's tobacco from there has come this week, enough to last for three years, he says. Our daylight hours are much the same as England. Jack leaves off work now at 5:30 and we light up then. Jack is quite sure that the pudding *has* peel in it, he remembers that quite well. I did not mean the mincemeat as a hint for us, but thought you would like to have it, as Mrs. Bird wrote it on the recipe. I should like a length of the toilet-cover crochet some day if ever you have any to spare, for Jack's chest-of-drawers or the spare room, which we shall furnish and make gay, I hope, before Freda comes. I have so little time for work and there is so much I should like to make and do for the house, but it will come by degrees. I finished the blue casement curtains for the smoking room this afternoon and they are up, but the frills are not yet begun. The machine is going very well and is a huge help. There are eight curtains to each room except the spare room, and they are only short straight pieces, but I am making them properly in a way you would approve.

I wondered about the needlework guild and was going to suggest that during the winter you might like to knit your son-in-law a pair of cuffs! Not mittens, but long cuffs from the wrist to some way up the arm in khaki wool. You know he takes size 11 in gloves so his wrists would be bigger than Stanley's! . . . You are splendid, Mother, having a try at bread making. I have been quite successful so far, but today it is not quite so good as it got a little too hot when rising. How long do you "prove" your loaves after you put them in the tins before baking? . . . The bread here is different from English bread, it has more air holes in it. The lace for the broderie pillow has come today. I like it immensely, please do not send me any other. I shall make these things during winter and put them on when my "visitor" arrives.

I shall want her to bring various articles of clothing, but will let you know in good time, so that you can purchase them gradually and Freda could bring them all in a packingcase. . . . The cards do not do Wilmer justice. It is much nicer in the summer, but I am sure you will be much more interested in "Maisonette Phillips," sent last week. Balls Store is most imposing, isn't it?, but we never go there if we can help it. Things are a terrific price. They are trying to make, or I should say have made their fortunes before the railway comes. I went there the other day to get a pudding basin and a small dish, as I hate enamel and wanted china. They are the only people who keep china. They charged me 25 cents each, really worth ten cents. I can get them from Eaton's next year, but felt I could not wait until then, and I did not dare tell Jack how much I paid. Mr. Balls is a Canadian who does not like the new-comers on the benches, and nearly all the English folk shop at Athalmer. Mrs. Corby has a little general store. She is English and has been here three years. This is a wonderful mushroom place. Tumbledown stores when we came here now have imposing fronts and are as large as a big grocers in England, and they sell groceries, drapery, and "gent's" clothing of all sorts. . . . The Canadian Press is terrible. I suppose being so close to America they copy the ways and manners. The "fairs" out here are quite the usual thing—in the smallest places, the *only* event of the year. Grants are made by this wonderful Canadian Government for prizes and the rest is done by sub-scription and I should think every man and woman subscribes his dollar! And, of course, puts on his best bib and tucker for the occasion.

Thank you for the pillow cords and also for the charming mat from Gloucester. We shall use it as a table-centre as we have quite a small table when just alone. We are now looking forward to Freda's photo, a foretaste of Freda when she comes with the spring. I am afraid you will feel rather be-reft without either of your daughters. I only wish I could think of someone to come and stay with you, but we are so looking forward to her visit and what we shall do when she comes. J. N. P. thinks there will be no house-work for him then and I shall never be tired. I am feeling quite fit now and no sign of any more boils, so don't think any more about them.

Saturday. This was interrupted last night as usual by my *having* to go to bed. We woke this morning to find a perfectly white world, 4–5″ of snow everywhere. The sun came out about ten o'clock, and with the blue sky it all looked very beautiful. But Oh, the mess in the kitchen! Coming in and out you cannot help bringing in pools of water and they get trodden about the house. I love the bungalow house and could not run upstairs now if I tried, but stairs and passages do keep dirt and dust out of rooms, I am sure. Jack's work now chiefly consists of drawing water and chopping wood, but this is plenty of work. We have two large packing cases of wood in the kitchen and two on the verandah for the hall fire. The fires simply eat wood, and for the range the logs have to be split into the right lengths and size. Tonight I had laid the cloth for dinner and Jack and I were changing when a knock came at the door. Mr. Robinson had brought over a Captain Gordon to call, a friend of his who is on leave in Canada and had come from Golden to have a few days in the valley. They would not stay to dinner for fear of getting lost in the snow in the dark. Mr. and Mrs. Munsen came up to tea last Monday. They arrived on their wagon, she in her best bib and tucker, black feather hat and all! She is Irish and has kissed the Blarney stone, but dear little Mr. Munsen is like a little man out of Noah's Ark, and was rather subdued. However, they passed my bread as excellent. . . .

The "barn" chairs are now the kitchen chairs and the two Roorkee chairs are in the smoking room. They are such ripping chairs, with canvas seats and leather straps for arms. If you are at the Stores look at them. They are *most* comfortable, and I think they would be a splendid thing to give Gilbert if you are hard up for an idea. I wish we could afford to send him one, but wait until those apples grow. . . .

ATHALMER, B.C.,
NOVEMBER 22ND, 1912

Dearest Freda,

I have lots to say and don't quite know where to begin, but will try and answer various questions. The armchairs are superb in the way of comfort, and when the day's work is done we are truly grateful to have them. Also, the bed is splendid and the springs most satisfactory, tell Mother. So far we have only needed two blankets as being new I think they must be specially warm. The two books are much liked and will do well for reading aloud. I never get time to read myself, but I can work after dinner and Jack reads. Please thank Freda D. for "Owd Bob." Jack knows it and thinks it splendid, and will read it aloud next. The war maps have fetched up and are now pinned on the cupboard door of the smoking room, with black and white pins to mark advances, battles, etc., and have given much pleasure to him. Mr. Bowden and Mr. Robinson have dissolved partnership as they could not hit it off at all, Mr. Bowden being much older than Mr. Robinson, I should say. Mr. and Mrs. Bowden have left the valley, I think to go to the Coast for her health, as she was in hospital until they went out by the last motor until next spring. Miss Colebrook stayed with us until Monday and has now gone to Mrs. Young's. Jack got very sick and tired of her before she left, and now keeps on saying, "She has one very good point," (this when I stick up for her), "She is gone!" She is really very nice but talks a lot about herself and what she can do, and Jack thought her rather ungrateful, I think. But you may yet meet her next year. Mr. Robinson now has a China-man to run his house, and the Captain Gordon I spoke of has bought Mr.

Bowden's share. But I think Captain Gordon has returned pro tem to his regiment in South Africa. He came to call one day, a most chirpy little bird! The yeast I think I told you about is in compressed cakes, ¼" thick, rather bigger than a half-crown, and you buy them in boxes of six. The grey skirt braid has turned up and is now in my grey skirt. I wear this with my purple hat and scarf on cold days, and Stanley's "rig-out" when there is no wind. I have made up my mind to do without a new hat this winter unless my purple gets too shabby, and I shall repeat it exactly if so. I want you to bring out a good many things. The money will fly, and I must be economical if I can, where I can. I will enclose the beginning of a list, if I have time, as time flies so quickly and you will have to collect them. The storm doors will be very cosy. They are hung outside the others, one opening out and the other in. I cleaned the silver this morning. It had not been done for three weeks and was hardly tarnished. We have it all out. Jack likes it, of course. So do I, and an hour will clean the lot! Many thanks for the soda cake recipe. Jack eats cake as he eats jam tarts, and this is useful as I have so few eggs. I allow myself about three or four a week for cooking. Jack quite approves of the second lamp-shade, far better than crinkled paper, but at present old Stewart's is prime favourite. "Which lamp tonight, Jack?" "Oh, Stewart's. Don't you think so?" . . . Mother speaks of sending us out cards as games for the evenings. It is awfully kind of her. Between you, you seem to think of everything, but really we have no time. The two hours after dinner are very often the only time we have to sit down except mealtimes, and then Jack reads and smokes and I work, darning, or mending and patching my own or Jack's clothes. Everything wears out so quickly here. Today my fancy work has been mending and darning old trousers that are worn for wood cutting. My hall curtains are not done yet, but they will be by the time "my visitor" comes, also the spare room for which I want you to get me some cretonne. I *hate* sales, so do you, but I saw that Liberty's sold a lot of cretonne in the Summer Sale at ninepence a yard, or you might try D. H. Evans or somewhere like that in the early days of January and send it off at once, and I shall have till the second week of April, I expect. . . . I like your new hat immensely. Ribbon trimmings and Jay style are the best for this part of the world. A wreath of corn-poppies or cornflowers would not be out of place!

Last Thursday, which is now usually the day I take a walk to Athalmer with Jack and arrange for more or less cold dinner, as most other days I am too tired to walk far when all my work is done, we saw a printed notice (black on emerald green paper) in the hardware store, that a Dr. Hall, a dentist from Cranbrook, was in Athalmer for a few days. Jack has been having a good many twinges and had wondered what he should do. I also had once or twice "felt" a tooth. Saturday morning Jack started off to Wilmer, his lunch in his pocket, to see the doctor. He found out that Dr. Hall was no quack but a man with a large practice in Cranbrook. From Wilmer he walked to Athalmer, and when he returned and smiled I could see *gold* in his mouth, for which he paid five dollars. But no matter, no more toothache fears, and no dentist has been in the Valley for eighteen months. "Such a nice man. I made an appointment for you." Monday, two o'clock. On Monday morning I had to reach down all the washing and make bread as we only had one loaf left! "Never mind," says Jack, "I will bake the bread." I kneaded it, put it in the tins to prove for an hour as usual, and then started for Athalmer, three miles away, with very short time. The "Chinook" had brought mud, such mud, on the hill, far worse than ice. I thought I would fall down every minute. At the bottom of the hill, deep mud, and a strong wind in my face all the way, with the strange dentist looming in the distance. I arrived ten minutes late, had to wait half-an-hour outside the door of the surgery in full view of the previous victim! Dr. Hall was a very nice man, tall, with big gold spectacles, and clean shaven, a typical American to look at, but an Eastern Canadian. A wash-basin for his instruments and everything, of course, temporarily arranged on packing cases as the hotels in Athalmer are not luxurious, not places where they have many lady visitors! However, my tooth wanted painting with nitrate of silver, the very thing he had *not* got, but he told me if it ached again to go and ask the doctor to do it for me, as it was because the gum had shrunk from the tooth. There was no decay. On my return Jack met me with, "I am no baker. The bread ran all over the place." It had risen and run over all the tins. It was in the oven, some as black as cinders and some very underdone. He looked so helpless and hopeless I *nearly* laughed, but it was time to get dinner ready and then stencil Christmas cards. So you see, we have not much spare time. The bread eats better than it looks, so say no more about it.

Will you send me some more Belladonna. Jack has a nasty sore throat and cold and has been in bed. He is better tonight, so say no more about that either. He was so afraid someone would come today and find him in bed. The chickens have come and the very first day we had an egg, though they are not laying at present! The excitement of the journey, I expect. They are lovely birds, White Rocks, and I hope they will be a success. Jack has "chicken fever" very badly, and thinks of nothing else. They are fed on the tick of the clock at 12:00 and 4:00 and early morning. Goodnight.

Much love,

Daisy

ATHALMER, B.C.,
NOVEMBER 28TH, 1912.

My dearest Mother,

Your letter received yesterday and I feel I must write to you at once, as I feel the news contained must be the source of great worry and anxiety to you all and must be deeply serious. Eight hundred pounds! It seems to me such a tremendous amount to come off the yearly income.[1] I do feel so very sorry for the boys as they have always worked so splendidly and never spared themselves. It is not as if the work had been badly or carelessly done, but I suppose it is the "march of events." Motors have now made it possible for London firms to step in — or is it an enemy who has done this? Anyway, I do feel so deeply sorry for you all. Please tell the boys. I feel I owe such a lot to them for the past. As for poor old Stewart, I am writing to him, but it is very difficult to give advice without being able to discuss matters. I told Jack and he quite agrees with me, if possible do not go to a "black man's country." Even if pay is high, health and other things must suffer. I do hope he will not settle on anything in a great hurry until all sources have been tapped. Archie Young, it seems to me, could give information re Victoria, which from all accounts is a splendid place and going ahead, and where I should imagine he would have a good chance of something in his own line. You cannot go straight on to a farm here without experience. . . . On a farm you are more or less a labourer and that is hardly what Stewart wants at his time of life. *We* think, try and get a billet in an office of some sort, in town, where you can discuss matters and look round and see what you fancy. Things are so different out here from what they are in England. Victoria is *the* town here and the most English, but quite different from town life in England and much more free. I think it would be nice if he came to the *Far West*. We could then see something of him and be more or less in touch, and if at any time he was out of a job or did not like it, *there is always a home for him here with us* and plenty of work. Only at present Jack could not pay him enough to make it worth his while. If you employ help the wages are $3.00 a day. But we could put him up and give him a home. We are rather off the beaten track, and everyone here seems to have an income of about £200 to £500 a year. But the railway *is* coming and now I believe is only 43 miles off, and of course to go west all trains pass through Golden. Flora Nicholson might be able to help. As Flora says in her last letter, "If you get tired of B.C. sell up and come here," as mixed farming is *the* thing in the neighbourhood of Perth and I think there is a new irrigation scheme there. She also tells me of the Sparks, a whole family she knew in England who have just gone out and are doing well. Lemons fetch one pound a case, she says, from their own small fruit farm, so Stewart might write and also get information in London. J. N. P. thinks Canada is better than Australia, I know, as he gets on better with Canadians than with Australians or South Africans, and he likes the climate and the scenery. It does help even if you

---

1. The firm at Oxley had an important contract to do printing for the Ascot Races. In 1912 they were told that they would have to pay a franchise fee of £800 per year for the privilege of retaining it.

are poor. How will all this affect you and Freda? You must be sure to write and tell me all details as things begin to straighten out. If there is anything we can do or any proposal you have to make, do not hesitate to ask or let us know. I wish you could all come to B.C., but I suppose that is selfish. I am quite sure both the boys will come out of it well, though I suppose it is a thing that cannot be much talked about outside.... I think office work is the way to make some money and then buy land. I fear this is all vague and will not be much help or comfort to you. At present we have not been elsewhere in Canada or we could be more help. Stewart can get a lot of information as to likely work in Australia or Canada from the London offices. I am sure he will find his niche, Mother, and don't be afraid that you will be forgotten. I know how true it is that absence makes the heart grow fonder, and we talk and think of you all every day. God bless you.

Much love from

Your affectionate child,

Daisy

ATHALMER, B.C.,
NOVEMBER 28TH, 1912

My very dear Mother,

This is a line to send you the very best of good Christmas wishes, and this, of course, includes the others, and all from Jack and myself. It will be an unusual Christmas for us and for you, but the surest and best part will be to know we are all thinking of each other. We must try to look forward to the Christmas not far distant when we shall all meet again from Malvern[1] and Malaya and Canada, and join hands round a very large turkey and the largest Christmas pudding you have ever made! We shall spend the day very quietly by ourselves, I expect, go for a walk in the morning and come back in good time to boil the Christmas pudding. I am sure Jack will not be late!

Now for the little parcel. The "mocassins" are for you, made expressly for you by the Indians, and I expect they thought the "white" woman had the foot of a child! They will do to wear in your bedroom, and I hope the colour will not offend your eye. I have a pair and they are worked in bright green and scarlet, but now they are very dirty as I wore them in the barn days, that now seem so far off. The gloves are for old Stanley, real Canadian. J. N. P. has a pair and likes them immensely. All the men wear gloves like these out here, for cutting wood and, in fact, for any job. It is necessary when, like the last few days, we have had 23° of frost! Of course, they are

---

1. Arthur Oxley lived in Malvern near Worcester. Stewart had gone to Malaya.

made of rougher skin for hard work, but I thought for his bicycle they might be acceptable. There are some "button" hat pins for Freda, which I hope she will be very proud of.[2] It is a great honour, tell her, to have them, but I know she always liked the "volunteer" ones the boys gave me and these, of course, are far superior. I am sure she will like them though their value is small. The feathers are for her, too, the tail of a willow grouse that Jack shot on our estate about a week ago. We were going down to feed the chickens when this gentleman got up under our feet, and he was shortly in the pot. They are lovely to eat, something like a pheasant, but more delicate. I made Jack chop off the tail as he has got his winter petticoats on. I think they are so pretty. Jack has dressed it with some stuff of Rowland Ward's[3] so I hope there will be no scent. . . .

With regard to Jack's heads and trophies, I am afraid they will not come to Windsor after all. We had a letter from Ada this mail and in it she enclosed a cheque for £12. She said she let the house and had to get out of it by the 29th. She found it very painful going back, and decided to warehouse the best of her furniture and sold the rest. They would not warehouse Jack's heads because of moths, and she never thought of sending them to you so she sold them and sent the amounts. Some heads 15 shillings, some 12 shillings, and so on. . . . She kept the elephant foot and some rhino horns, and those we can have out later. Jack felt it very much, as he said he went through dangers to get them, and wonders that Ada's brothers did not write to him about them before the sale. But he says he cannot and will not blame her, and you cannot under the circumstances. This sort of thing has happened to him all his life, as there has never been anyone really interested in him. As usual, it is "out of sight, out of mind" so we say no more about it. I suppose they now decorate the bar parlour of some public house. We have got two hippo tusks over the front door in the hall, and the leopardskin rug, and a paper knife. Of course, his buffalo head he gave to the Depot at Lincoln, and I may see that some day. . . .

I am sure this will be in good time for Christmas, but Jack goes to Athalmer tomorrow and so thinks he had better post our cards. We have sent thirty-two stencil cards. J. N. P. did them all, *I* only held the paper still.

Much, much love to you all. With *every* good wish, and God bless you.

Your affectionate children,

Daisy and Jack

<hr />

2. The heads of these pins were regimental buttons, presumably of the Lincolnshire regiment in this case.
3. A taxidermist firm in London.

DECEMBER 5TH, 1912

My dearest Freda,

I have had a long day ironing with the kitchen window wide open, and blue sky, snow, and brilliant sunshine outside. About 20–22° of frost this morning. At 4:30 P.M. Jack called me out to get some air. I put on my snowboots and walked as far as our box on the tree and to my joy found two letters, one from you and one from Mother, so I was well repaid. I have not received the school magazine yet, but whatever the terrible contents are I shall not blame you, you may be sure.[1] I have not mentioned your coming out in my two letters as I felt it is best left alone. It hits us both hard, I know, you perhaps more than me, but I had so looked forward to it, and been counting the weeks almost until April. But we must just tuck it away, both of us, and you must try hard to be cheerful and full of courage. The clouds are very heavy just now but I am sure they will roll away again some day soon and show the sun shining brighter than ever. This is what happens to Mount Hammond every morning! Poor old girl, I feel if I were at home I could talk and discuss things just now and perhaps we could help each other to be cheerful. If you want to let off steam you could always scribble to me. There is always a ready ear, and sometimes lately a ready tear, when I think of you all and the splendid way you have all behaved to me. I feel now I had too much—and I have so much, I find, every day. Old Jack is always the same happy, even person he used to be when we saw him one day at a time, and I am a very lucky girl. Under the circumstances I expect Mother feels glad that I am married, although in Canada. Jack and I have been talking about you and I want you to feel there is always a home for you here with us, at any time if you can or feel you want to come, and although we are not rich we can always pay you £25 a year which may go a small way towards your passage, and you might be able to earn a few dollars as well. At present, of course, you will feel your place is at home to look after Mother, but later on things will again settle down. The £800 that Mother mentions seems to me such a terrific sum, and I wonder how it will affect you or what you think? You can always write me an enclosure if you want to tell me anything or discuss anything with me. I feel if only No. 4 High Street could be disposed of you could live on much less in a small house with one servant, say, and be much happier and more comfortable. But I feel as if even this is not possible or practical. Anyway, you could always come here and try it for a year if things point that way. I hated the thought of Malaya at first, but gradually it seems to be the thing that is right as there are the various introductions for Stewart to go to. He would be miserable if he were miles out of the world like Jack was in Uganda. With the local interest and so on it may help things. J. N. P. thinks it will very likely develop and strengthen him in every way as he will be more self-reliant. It is hard for Mother, but Provi-

1. Reference obscure. Freda and Daisy had attended St. Leonard's School in North London.

dence has brought it about and it must be for some good purpose for us all to be parted. It does not lessen affection, I am sure, but tends to bind us closer together.

I want you to get me some cretonne for the spare bedroom, and I think if you are in London during the January Sales you might be able to get me something fairly inexpensively.... The room has plaster walls so there is nothing to match, but it is small. So not a big pattern, quaint if possible and cheerful, and something that will not want washing at once, of course, and something you will like *when* you come, too! D. H. Evans, Liberty's, or anywhere. If you are busy with Stewart's affairs, don't worry about it but get it later on. Also, there is no hurry for the things I sent the list of the other day, and if they are posted I shall not have so much or so many but get you to send them by degrees. It will give you and Mother something to do when Stewart has left. I want a frill, 17″ deep, for the spare room bed (6′5″ long and 2′7″ broad), and I want a frill like an ottoman along the front and two sides of Jack's chest-of-drawers. I shall split it in the middle where the doors open, and have a cover for the top with a small frill on the edge. Another chest-of-drawers, 14½″ wide by 29″ long, otherwise a packing case with shelves. For this one, too, I want a curtain across the front and another cover for the top, and a small frill around it. There is a small canvas table and canvas chair. I shall cover the seat, if possible, so a few yards over three, say, will not come amiss. I have not allowed fullness for any of the curtains or frills, so perhaps Mother will have time to tell you roughly how much stuff she thinks and I shall not complain if it is too much. I think the cost might be about 12 shillings or so. If there is not enough stuff I could make the bed valance of white dimity. I ought to have found out how much stuff but I am pressed for time as I have written so much to you.

Heaps of love, old girl,

Your affectionate sister,

Daisy

ATHALMER, B.C.,
DECEMBER 5TH, 1912

My dearest Freda,

First of all, let me tell you how much, how very much I like your photographs. They are both on the mantlepiece, and the more I look at them the more I feel how much they are like you. It is lovely to have them. I like the dress, too, your Apsey, I suppose. Jack says, "They are awfully well done. Why didn't we go to Beresford?" Can't you hear him and see him looking at them closely? Thanks so much for the lace, too. It does very nicely indeed, and you bought it with my mind, I am sure. Tell Mother the mittens she sent are my great comfort. I can slip them on and off easily and they are so warm. I slip them on when I go to feed the chickens (this is one of my twice-daily walks—about 100 yards!) and also when I hang out the clothes and bring them in. Of course, they always freeze now as soon as they touch the line. Last night we had a fall of snow and this morning I had to go and shake it off as I leave the clothes out about three days. If not dry then I have to bring them in to finish, but they are such a nuisance in the kitchen. I am getting quite excited at the thought of the chair-backs. I do feel it is so awfully good of you to make them, and to give up the time. I have just finished and put up the curtains and the frills on the two little windows each side of the hall door. I like the cretonne very much. I must now start into the curtains for the long window at the other end and get them done for Christmas. Jack, of course, is deeply interested in it all and wonders when I am going to get the cushion cover finished, but the plain red and green do not look bad and I must be content to do things gradually. I find lots of mending and darning, and I have just turned the cuffs on some of Jack's flannel shirts so you know I am not often idle except on Sundays. It is so nice to sit down then and rest, enjoy the house, think of you all, and wonder what you are doing. I have worn my brown Fletcher's tweed and my brown hat and scarf *en suite* as it has been colder, but I have not had to put on any of my *extra* clothes yet. January and February are always the coldest times. Of course, I shall miss all my fresh air, having to be so much more in the house, but Jack sees that the kitchen window is *wide* open if he can possibly manage it! I shut it up for a few minutes when he is not looking! Getting up these cold, dark mornings is very difficult, I find. I am only *told* to get up once or I am in disgrace, so I am gradually improving in that direction. Jack is awfully kind and gets up and lights the kitchen fire for me so I am really very grateful. If I do not get up I cannot possibly get the day's work done. I find my blue woolly dressing-gown the greatest comfort when dressing, and all my things seem to be just what I want somehow. . . . I sweep up the floors and shake the rugs, sweep up the hearth and dust the hall every day as there is a good bit trodden in during the day. Jack helps me make the bed, then I clean the wash-stand and dust the bedroom. I wash up the breakfast things, clean the stove and sweep out the kitchen, and then as a rule do the cooking until lunchtime. Two days in the week I iron in the afternoon. Thursday I usually go to Athalmer. Then there is the silver to clean, one afternoon, say, for needlework, and Saturday is the big cleaning day. Jack helps me after breakfast. We turn back the carpets, take up the rugs and blankets, and sweep right through. Then down on all fours. I beeswax and Jack follows on and rubs, and this keeps the floors going fairly well. Then I cook for Saturday and Sunday in advance and, on Saturday after lunch give the stove its *big* clean until I can see my face in it, if possible. I find myself thinking of the old

Saturdays at Windsor, going to Budgens and Balls to order sausages, and Mrs. Grise and the market, and all sorts of funny things. The strange thing that happens to me out here are sounds. Suddenly I hear the Parish Church clock striking, or the bugles in the barracks, or a barrel-organ playing, and it is so real I have to stop whatever I am doing and actually listen, even though my thoughts at the time were not in England. . . .

The kitten (Four-Paws) flourishes and grows. When we shut her outside about six o'clock she is this size ◯ . We let her in again at 9:30 and she is this size ◯ , with at least I should say, three mice in her tummy. The wild mice ◯ are a nuisance when you have grain and so we encourage her to gorge. Tell Madeline not to worry about Dolly going to Nairobi. It is a very nice place and quite healthy. She will have servants there to do her work and I should say a very good time! Jack is now reading aloud Johnstone's book (II Vols) on Uganda, and it has most lovely illustrations. I think the ideas of Looker about the garden are splendid. I do love to hear all these details of things that are going on, and you tell them so well. I do hope you will get a nice girl to replace Harbour, but I am sure she will be a "Miss."[1] However, the new cook seems to be doing fairly well, I take it. The dried flowers have come and the lavender looks nice in the silver vases on the mantlepiece. The honesty is in a dark blue Chinese bottle we picked up. I believe it held brandy, but it is a lovely shape! It is on top of the sideboard with the Benares tray as background. You must not send me so many things or I shall be spoilt. Your letters are what I enjoy more than anything, and you describe everything so well to me. Mother's hat I am sure I should like very much and approve of, and yours too I *know* I like very much. However, I shall not order one just at present, and I shall not write about things I want until old Stewart's matters are quite settled. I shall not get the mail until Friday this week but just now I look forward to letters very much. I am glad you both enjoyed your day in London. It seems a terrific way off but it is really only a fortnight, and answers to letters seem to come so quickly. . . .

Jack does look in the glass, I assure you, and the result is he has never worn his overalls yet! He says the reason is that his clothes are so old they don't want saving, but he is much too fond of himself in khaki. Well-cut riding breeches and puttees or gaiters are more to his liking. Even though they *are* shabby they are well cut. . . . I hope you will like the stencil cards. We do very much indeed, and they gave J. N. P. so much pleasure in the doing. I went to see Mrs. Marples this afternoon — an hour's walk exactly. She is very nice and bright, tall and fair. Their house is further on, between the Youngs' and Poetts'. They cannot get their furniture from Golden until the snow is deeper but they have had enough lent to be fairly comfortable.

1. A young cook; older cooks, even if single, were often addressed as "Mrs."

There are two small boys and a little girl, and they have got a devoted nurse who has come out with them (elderly and plain but who seems to do all the work and is most superior). I have asked them here to tea on Sunday. The snow is about three inches deep and I had to wear snow-boots, but the blue sky and the white mountains looked lovely and I trudged along very happily. For dinner fish cakes (of tinned fresh herrings), curry, and baked apple suet pudding, and now coffee by the fire as we both write.

Much love to you all,

Daisy

DECEMBER 10TH, 1912

My dearest Mother,

Certainly when you last wrote (and in spite of all, so cheerfully) you were in what you call "a peck of trouble." Now I will say straight out, while there is so much going on and you all must have your minds full of important things near at hand, I shall not mind a bit if you do not write so often or such long letters as I know they take a great deal of time and thought. And too, poor old Stewart must have his share of home letters, and he will want them and appreciate them as much or more than I do (if that is possible). But I shall always be grateful to you and Freda for all the time you have given me in letters, which certainly helped to pull me through what was a trying time, though perhaps Jack does not know! So now perhaps either you *or* Freda will write not too long a letter once a week to say all's well until things have settled down. I do hope Stanley is better and that he will try and take things as easily as he can for a bit, but I know he is going through a frightfully worrying and anxious time and so are you all. I think of you all very much and wish I could do something to help. Lily Thruscott[1] told me Stanley was looking very poorly indeed when she wrote to me, and no wonder. I am sure he will come out of it well as he loves overcoming difficulties, though he has got a jolly big one this time and no mistake. I feel so much I have had a lion's share, as you and the boys were so awfully good in every way to me and Jack. I feel rather far away, but perhaps knowing I am married and safely tucked away in B.C. *is* a bit of help. I am most deeply interested in all you will or can tell me of arrangements. Gossip and scandal will not get round from here, as there is never anyone to gossip with except Jack, and you know *he* is safe. . . . The more I hear, and Jack too, of Malaya it does not seem so bad. After all, there seem to be so many friends who know friends there so Stewart will have a good many introductions. After all, that is a great asset in a new land and saves you from getting lonely. . . . As for

1. A friend in Windsor.

cutting down expenses, I can see it would be much easier and perhaps more comfortable for you as a smaller family to have a small house, but at present there is no getting rid of "No. 4 High," as John N. P. calls it. We talk over and suggest all sorts of plans for you all. . . . Of course, under present and altered circumstances we shall not expect to see Freda here this spring. You cannot, for one thing, spare another of us I am sure just yet, and it will be something to look forward to "some day." We have been looking forward to it, but "man proposes. . . . " and perhaps now, with a smaller family, you will be able to come and leave Freda in charge. Who knows, but it is nice to build castles in the air.

I am glad you like our hall. It is a very cosy room, far nicer than I ever thought we could have out here. The idea of the prints over the mantlepiece was mine, and the two bookshelves Jack's. He has got a good many books one way and the other so the shelves do not look very empty. We had Kipling last night for a change, and now he is reading pamphlets on chickens while I write. The two armchairs stand under the two small windows next the front door. This door has the top half of glass with a crossbar of wood, and I cannot make up my mind which is best to have, a brise curtain without fullness over the whole, or green silk curtains drawn back each side. I think, perhaps, the green silk would be more stylish. Of course, everything gets very hard wear, there is no denying that, and of course dust is everywhere but I just have to shut my eyes. Mr. and Mrs. Marples came to tea on Sunday afternoon. She is very nice, tall and fair, and talked away sixteen to the dozen and made J. N. P. knit his eyebrows! Everything was "charming, delightful, etc." but you see she, poor woman, is living in her house with furniture lent them by various people. Theirs is all at Golden and at present the snow is only an inch thick and sleighs cannot go to Golden, but the big fall is expected any day and then probably it will be 8 inches or so. We have had heavy clouds on the mountains and no sun for four days, so I expect it is coming soon. Our kitchen is very small and very compact, and on Sunday *very* tidy. Mrs. Marples, on entering, called out to her husband, "Oh, do come here, Norman. The kitchen is exactly like a doll's house! So nice and so tidy, a place for everything." This because there are two bars of wood along the wall, and on cup hooks hang sieve, chopper, grater, measure, etc. The enamel saucepans are on a shelf all in a row in graduated sizes. There really is plenty of room for Jack in the kitchen, though there is *not* in the pantry! But I find with a small house you *must* be tidy except, of course, on washing day! We used the silver teapot, had scones (like tall hats) butter and jam, gingerbread in the cake basket, and some Shrewsbury biscuits with jam between and icing on top! We don't always go in for such teas, though on Sunday if at home we do as tin soup or pork and beans on a tray save cooking and *washing up*. I seem to have to wash up every hour of the day. Jack always helps me wipe after dinner, which we have now at 6:30, and then hurry to get that two hours *sitting down* before bed. It is lovely to sit, and also I never knew the meaning of Sunday as a day of rest before. But if I get a bit tired and can manage it the best thing is to get out into the air. I washed the flannels yesterday—Jack's vest, pants, pyjamas, flannel shirts, three collars, two pairs of socks and stockings—and then put the white washing in soak. I rub in the soap on a washing board and find this loosens the dirt. I also made a pudding and a stewed steak for the evening besides tidying the house. I also kneaded the bread. It was ready to knead about two o'clock and make into loaves. I baked it (ten loaves) in the afternoon, and about four o'clock the kitchen was hot so I went out and helped Jack saw logs for three-quarters of an hour. Then in to lay the cloth, peel potatoes, etc. Dinner 6:30, to bed 9:30, but I always feel I have earned a night's repose. Today, washing. We have water hauled to us now, once a week, one barrel in the kitchen and the rest in a barrel and various baths outside. This means the ice has to be melted in boilers and saucepans before we commence! I often say to Jack, "The boiler wants filling." He brings in a huge slab of ice tucked under his arm, and this ice takes a deal of thawing. However, it seems to come quite naturally somehow. I had a sheet, two pillow cases, camisole, chemise, blue apron, brown cotton dress, handkerchiefs (six coloured and six white), three kitchen towels (round towels, most useful—Jack has made a roller on the kitchen door), and three chamber towels. I find I cannot make it less and be decent. Next week, tablecloth and table napkins, and starched things. You must not think I am overworked and am making difficulties but I sometimes blink and think, "Is it me?" After lunch I had a rest and did a little sewing. We had roast beef for dinner, two vegetables, boiled rice, and maple syrup. I had just put the beef in the oven when Jack called out, "Visitors." One of the Company's cars with *five* women. I have not seen so many women together for eight months: Mrs. Hamilton, wife of the Secretary to the Company. Mrs. Bennett, the engineer's wife. Mrs. Stark from the hotel in Invermere. Mrs. Smith, wife of Mr. Bruce's secretary. And Mrs. Dunn, wife of the man in charge of the fruit trees and also irrigation expert. It was getting dark so they only stayed 15 to 20 minutes. They had been to two other houses so would not have tea. We do not often get callers but they had evidently got the car for the afternoon (Invermere Society calling on the Benches). Mrs. Dunn remarked it was a dandy little cottage! A Canadian trying to use English words, I suppose.

Later. I am feeling very sad as I have just broken a teacup, but it can't be helped. Three glasses have gone too, but I shall get some strong ones from Eaton's in the spring. It is very cold today and the snow is beginning to fall. I find my Fletcher's coat and skirt very cosy and warm, and the brown and white silk veils you sent me are awfully comfortable. But even these cannot keep my face warm and where I breathe gets quite stiff. The baby mitts are splendid and I hardly ever use a muff, but it is going to be much colder yet.

Even now the ink freezes in the smoking room if we shut the door and the warm air from the hall does not get in. My warm dressing-gown is very cosy. This and warm bedroom slippers I appreciate in the early hours when I go into the kitchen to fetch the warm water. Jack gets up at 6:30 and lights the kitchen fire. I rise at 7:00 when the water is warm and we usually have breakfast before 8:00, when it is quite dark and the pilgrimage to the "Sentry Box" is rather fresh. We always wear snow boots for pottering about and they keep our feet fairly warm. The mincemeat and the Christmas pudding have arrived and Jack will bring them up from Athalmer tomorrow. It is good of you to send them off. I wish I could send you a loaf of bread and I wonder if yeast cakes would travel without breaking.

Much love to all,

Your affectionate child,

Daisy

P.S. I am so glad you liked the photos. I should like to get an enlargement done for Mother some day, as I have the films but there was not time for Xmas!

ATHALMER, B.C.
DECEMBER 15TH, 1912

My dearest Freda,

First of all I must confess and say how sorry I am. Jack started off on Thursday to the post, and when he had gone about ten minutes I found Mother's letter had not gone too. It was no good trying to run after him and I could not face the six miles there and back, and so it must go down tomorrow, Monday, when Mr. Hanley comes with the water. Meanwhile, I will begin one to you ready for the usual mail. We are sitting by a blazing log fire at 7:30 on Sunday evening. Jack is reading the new numbers of the *World's Work*. I have just finished looking at the pictures. I am so interested in all your home doings just now and I expect you are interested in all the latest doings of ours, though there is nothing especially fresh. This morning being Sunday we were late getting up and did not have breakfast until nine o'clock, which I enjoyed very much. I always like Sunday as we clean up everything on Saturday and everything looks so well-kept and in order, quite English in fact. It is such a day of rest, both of mind and body. You put on your best clothes and it makes a landmark!

It felt rather "fresh" on getting out and the thermometer was down to 8°. I think that means 25° or 26° of frost. It was *perfectly* still and very clear as it always is on these very cold days, and the snow has a *blue* look about it. We have had another fall of snow, but it is still only 3 or 4 inches deep. It does not snow in large flakes but very small and slowly, and always for a good many hours, but when down the crystals look very coarse in comparison to English ones. While we have breakfast the chicken food has to boil up (tea-leaves, coffee grounds, crumbs of bread, peel of potatoes, carrots, turnips, etc.) and this is mixed with meal called "shorts" and made into a crumbly mash in a bowl and given to the chickens hot. We have to take hot water down as when it is put into their drinking tin it soon freezes. They live in the inner house. The "scratching" shed is in front, and their two other meals of grain are given them there and put into deep straw so as to make them work for their living. They have a curtain which is let down over their window on cold nights. Jack is trying the open-air cure for the fowls as well as for his wife, but the latter finds she cannot stand too much when the temperature is low! However, I still wear my blue and brown cotton dresses when working, and when going in and out as on washing day to empty water my old drab golf jersey is my greatest joy.

Well, after putting out clean towels and having half-an-hour by the fire to manicure my nails (my hands are *very* clean on Sunday), we got ready to go out. I wore ordinary thick stockings, glacé walking shoes, and over them a pair of very thick worsted stockings without heels from Eaton's, very long in the leg, and then over these snowboots! I find at present this is warm enough! Puttees will come when it is below zero. I wore my grey crêpe-de-chine blouse and my snowflake tweed, my black hat with the green band, and my furs, and felt quite smart! The snow was fairly deep until we got on the main road and walked in the direction of General Poett's. We had lunch by the lake, cocoa in Mrs. Rough's flask, and jam turnovers, gingerbread, and bread and cheese. There was no sun and we sat for half-an-hour and did not get really cold. We then walked on to the next lake, Saw Mill Lake, and here Captain White and Mr. Bennett dwell. Captain White is about forty, was in the Warwickshire Regiment, but has lived on the west coast of Africa. He has rheumatism very badly as a result, which may be why he has come out here, and he evidently has lots of money. His house is large and quite the nicest out here, and he must be a man of taste, I should say. The house is grey, with green door and windows, and a red roof and chimneys. It sounds gaudy but it is not as the red is of a dull, rather terra, shade and the walls soft grey. The pines for a background in summer, and now the roof is white with snow and beautiful sparkling "Christmas trees" everywhere. It is an ideal situation near the lake. You enter not into the room but into a passage and on the right you then enter a large and lofty room called, I suppose, a drawing room but more like a luxurious smoking room, with stone fireplace like ours, large table in the centre, and lots of easy chairs and bookcases. In one corner, an angle with deep bow windows and writing table, I notice a nice column brass lamp and pretty shade. I sat on a sort of

oak settee, upholstered in green. Then there is an arch and you walk into
the dining room (there will be curtains over the arch later on, I should say).
He took us into the kitchen, presided over by a Chinaman, and then into
various bedrooms all very nice indeed, with a lovely bathroom, lavatory basin and proper W.C. You can have all these things if you have money! He
dug a well and was lucky finding water, but Captain Young and others dug
wells and spent hundreds of dollars, and were not lucky! We have got it below us, but so many hundred feet it is impossible to get without a motor engine or something of that sort! He also has a furnace in the cellar under the
house and this has huge shafts which
go up into a grating in each room, so
he and his friend are living in luxury,
an ideal bachelor establishment. They
have a cow, three horses, chickens,
etc. For Jack's sake, I wish they were
nearer as he likes Captain White, but
there is little time for social intercourse except on Sunday. The Poetts have
skating on their lake and we may buy skates later on and try, but it is a long
walk there and back when you have to do the work yourself. If we both go
out for more than an hour we have to come back and light the kitchen and
hall fire before we can get tea or coffee to drink. I think all the youth of the
district gathers around Mrs. Poett's doors and are made welcome, but I
have not seen them for some time as we have not been to town on the same
day.

When we got back about five o'clock Miss Colebrook drove up in Captain Young's "cutter" and pony lent her for the afternoon. It was getting
dark so she did not stay long, but she seems happy at the Youngs. Jack cannot bear her as she talks such a lot and "such silly nonsense" so he retired to
the smoking room to write while she talked. "Two new photographs of
your sister, I am sure. What a delightful looking girl! The curtains are up at
the big window now, finished on Saturday. How Waringesque, or is it Gil-
loway?!"[1] I told her it was neither, but Phillipsy! She is quite alright, but
"gusty," and J. N. P. still contends her one good point is that she has gone!
We had potato soup, herrings and bread and butter, caramel blanc-mange,
and tea for our evening meal. Caramel blanc-mange I can recommend (half
a cup of brown sugar and a teaspoon of butter melted until it begins to
brown, and stir into the blanc-mange before you put it into the mould). The
great excitement is that the mincemeat and the plum pudding have arrived
quite safely, but if anything else comes I promise we will not open until the
25th. . . . .

Jack came back from Athalmer on Thursday and said the butcher was

---

1. A reference to Waring and Gillow, Limited, a furniture store in Oxford Street, London.

having turkeys from Calgary, and although a great extravagance he ordered a small one. Of course it will be frozen! The meat looks like a piece of stone now-a-days, and I have to thaw it slowly in cold water and keep it in the cellar a couple of days. I find "stewed steak" suits it well as it is cooked slowly. Roasting it is not bad, but the meat is so lean I have to use a lot of lard. As you say, we may be living all wrong, but when you have lived in a camp and barn for many months, a damask cloth and silver and glass are things you love and they are worth preparing. We breakfast and lunch in the kitchen, but our evening meal is a great feature and we have it in style, entrée dishes and all, and we change always. It means washing up after. That is the worst part but it is worth it, and then the hour-and-a-half for reading and work before bedtime. In the same way I make bed-linen last a fortnight and woollen underclothes, but other things, if left longer and if they get very soiled, are doubly hard to wash, and scrubbing things on the washing board is really hard work. The washing machine takes out general dirt but is no good for soils and deep dirt like the bottom of a petticoat, or soils on pillow case and sheet. These must be rubbed hard, but I am getting used to it by degrees and if I had time, could do it all as well as Mrs. Littlewood. When I have a lucky day my table linen beats hers! That's conceit.

Later. I went to Athalmer on Tuesday with Jack and was amply rewarded. A letter from you, from Mother, and from Stanley with his interesting photos. A letter from Kitty Wall[1] (the blind one). She writes with a Braille typewriter, and says Mr. Ruston was going the next day with Ida and his nurse to see a specialist in Harley Street. Also a letter from Tottie Mason, and a card and a letter from each of the Vidlers. I do think it is so awfully kind of them to trouble to write as well. Please thank them *very much* from me and say I will write some day, I hope soon. It is so nice to think your old friends have not forgotten you, and it is nice to have a chat with another female although so far away. Tottie and Jennie and Edith say there is nothing fresh in the way of Windsor gossip. *The* great excitement is Stewart going to Malaya, and no wonder! I feel so excited and interested in it all myself and can imagine he is getting quite excited, but you will find it a bit quiet with the "bubble" out of the house. Give him my love and tell him to keep a level head! Be sure you let me have his address. Jack keeps on saying, "I am sure he is doing the right thing under the circumstances," and you feel that an ever kind and watchful providence has brought it about. In time things will work out for the best, though at present you all feel you cannot see very far and things are rather perplexing. We have always been so happy together and there are no regrets in that way to look back upon. How differently things have worked out in the last year to what we expected. I don't know how it will all end, but if you and mother were to leave

1. A cousin of Jack's.

4 High, where would you go? Jack and I talk it over, and he very strongly thinks *London* for Mrs. Oxley, even if you have a small income! Mother need not go to the rush of Piccadilly unless she likes and you would be in easy reach of Windsor and the folk that are left there. The neighbourhood and your chief friends and interests could easily be followed, and all your friends come up to London sometimes, Daisy Mac, Toussa, Elfreda, and *us* when we come home! Battersea does not sound inviting but *we* know the charms of the Park, and I can imagine mother enjoying her strolls there. There are some awfully nice flats on the west and south sides, close to the Park. Jack knows or knew some people who lived there. The flats are well appointed and most comfortable, *and* the rental *quite* low. Do go and look one day. You go straight down Sloane Street, but there is no need to tell you the way, so when Mother wanted shops she could always stroll to Knightsbridge. I know you would like the Park, it is so quiet. I never liked the thought of "flats," tell Mother, but after calling several times on the Birds and the Snellies, I began to think for a small family they are ideal, and you need only keep one servant! You will laugh at my little ideas for you, but *if* you ever leave No. 4 *don't* go on living in Windsor.

I suppose Stewart will be on his way when this reaches you. (Things seem to us to move so quickly as we live in such a quiet spot so far out of the world.) But it is best for him to start at once and I feel sure he will get on alright. Jack tells Mother not to worry about it being the "tropics" as you can keep quite healthy even there. I suppose by this time too, *we* are Aunts! I wonder whether to a niece or nephew, and what colour *its* hair is—red? I hope I have got a niece *not* a nephew!

A long parcel addressed on both sides by Mother has come for Jack. He fingers the string lovingly, but I say *no,* not until the 25th! With regard to presents of any kind, I do want you and Mother to feel that a letter or a paper (and in Jack's case I am sure the *Gazette* and cuttings by Linesman) have given more pleasure than the most costly gifts. So please do not think anything about it. We know you think of us often and we think and talk of you, I am sure, every day. It was most awfully kind of old Stanley to write me such a long and interesting letter about himself and matters generally, and although doing without smoking and drink is rather a hard task at present the added benefit to his health in many ways will compensate. Jack has never had *anything* except water, tea, or coffee since we left the boat. He cannot afford them for one thing, and all the men *say* the beer and whiskey are not worth paying for. As for tobacco, he calculated it yesterday and it worked out at less than half-a-pound per month! He had some sent out from the Stores, and at this rate says he has enough for three years! Of course, we always have tea or coffee after dinner as we sit by the fire, and Stanley may adopt this plan too! I do hope the new doctor will do you good.

It is scarcely the right thing for you and Mother to have Dr. Hathaway, but I know it must make you feel sad about the poor old doctor. I sent him a Christmas card, by the way! Has Dr. Hathaway put you on brown bread? I find it most excellent for the liver, not Hovis but the coarser sort. I will send my recipe. Get the "little cook" to make some for you and try it. You will be an accomplished domestic person when next we meet, but when things have settled again I hope you will not quite give up art. What comes next to the transition period in architecture. I forget. I only know about wooden houses nowadays! . . . Please remember me to Mr. Lightfoot and tell him there is plenty of room in Canada if he makes reporting his baby. The Canadian press is rotten, much too American and they like a murder much more than *News of the World.*[2] I shall have to stop soon, but I could go on for hours! I, like you, take you about with me and can never write all I want to say. We read about the Goat Farm in the *World's Work* but came to the conclusion it would not do out here. I am sure I could not stand the smell of a Billy. . . .

Our front bit of land would make an awfully pretty garden, with winding path on the slope and a rustic seat on top to sit on and look at the view. A dream of the future! A small flower bed on each side of the verandah will be all this coming year as Jack will be so busy on the land and I am not strong enough to dig virgin soil though I can cut down trees with a cross-cut saw! There! The bulbs in the root-cellar are just peeping, so soon they must come inside out of the dark. Captain White has planted in boxes too, so nous verrons! I do hope Stanley enjoyed his big Christmas cigar and that things went off well on the 25th. What a good job we did not know last year.

Hooray, the Pandora Box is in Athalmer! Jack heard yesterday that a sleigh had brought it up from Golden with many other Settler's Effects for various people. I don't know yet what it cost, and I do hope it will come up by Christmas Day. I feel very excited to think it is here. I am going down on Monday to bring up the turkey—frozen of course—and shall go to the Livery Stables and look at it!

P.S. Now when you are in London some time, I want some green ninon for making a curtain for the glass part of the front door. The cretonne is too heavy for the middle windows of the window-seat so I shall have curtains there too. I have cretonne on each side and the frill the same as the small windows. I have tried my old green scarf and the effect is very good—at least, it is J. N. P.'s idea so must be carried out. On the door I shall run it on a rod and pull it to one side with a green cord, so, and on the small window, so, to keep out as little light as possible and also to give colour. I have tried the grey motor veil I bought at Harries and that is the *right* thickness. It

---

2. A still surviving Sunday tabloid that goes in for sensational news.

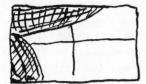

must be *thin* but firm so as not to exclude light. I think at Harries or at Bourne & Hollingsworth they keep ninon at 2/11d. per yard, 40 inches wide, at least that was the price I gave for the grey, and if at this price 3 yards please, a reel of sewing silk to match, and 2 yards of 1d. cord to loop back with. I enclose the pattern of the cretonne so please get a nice green to go with it. What should I do without you to shop for me? Another reason if you move that you must go to London! How goes my bank balance? We shall not get any money for some time as the estate is not cleared and death duties are so high. But we live on very little and a simple life is a very happy one. The old cockerel has hurt his foot and is quite an invalid so J. N. P. spends his day making bread and milk and savoury messes of boiled oats and wheat.

I really must stop. Ever so much love.

Your affectionate sister,

Daisy

ATHALMER

25 DEC 12

Dear Mrs. Oxley

It must have been very annoying to you when on questioning Rainer about his first misdeed you found the Pandora's Box was still waiting, five weeks after its packing, in his yard. It arrived at our house on the 23rd inst. and we decided to reserve its opening until Christmas Eve and turn it into a Christmas present from you. If you had seen Daisy's face as all the useful and well-thought-out things came one after another out of the box you would more than forgive Rainer and perhaps thank him for his stupid negligence. All the parcels have arrived safely and were kept till Christmas Eve. We stopped work at 4:15, had an early dinner at 5:15, washed up, and then settled down to opening our presents. I can't express my thanks sufficiently to you for all your generosity and kind thoughtfulness in sending such appropriate things. First one of my parcels was opened—the handkerchiefs and pictures—then two of Daisy's, Freda's book, and the breadboard, then one of mine—my mother's photograph (very many thanks for that)—then

Daisy's lamp from Mrs. Dainty, and my picture (the glass unfortunately broken). Only the Stores, I'm afraid, realize the importance of strong packing for glass. Then my gloves, the chocolates, the cake, the bread knife, and the eiderdown. Then we went to the window-seat and unpacked the Pandora's Box. As Daisy recognized old friends and new, she was more and more thankful to you, but I really think the baking dish, pattypans and cake tins made her realize most how much thought as well as treasures had been put into the box. Needless to say, I have never enjoyed a Christmas so much before.

It is now 3:15 P.M. The turkey is all ready, and is on the point of being put into the oven. Potatoes and cabbages grown on our own land are awaiting a saucepan which is already on the stove. Your Christmas pudding, safely received, is patiently awaiting another saucepan likewise on the stove. Daisy has already made six splendid-looking mince pies from your mincemeat, two fine apples kindly given by Mrs. Munsen are on the sideboard with several of Mrs. Tull's chocolates, and both of us have good appetites.

Thanking you and all the others ever so much for all the presents,
I remain,

Yours sincerely

John N. Phillips

ATHALMER, B.C.,
CHRISTMAS DAY, 1912

My dearest Mother,

I really do not know how to begin as I feel brimming over. You really are the most wonderful person and Freda is a wonderful person too! All the parcels and letters arrived on Monday. Being Christmas time we did not have Washing Day on Monday but took a holiday, and I walked down to Athalmer with Jack directly after breakfast. The letter mail was in, one from you, and one from Freda, and one from Stewart. An awfully nice letter from Auntie Kate Ormsby! She is evidently most excited and interested in what she calls my "story-bookey" romance, but so sweet and nice in the way she expresses herself. A letter and card from Eileen, a very nice letter indeed from Amy Lee, and one from Mrs. Wall. I felt surrounded with thoughts and good wishes on all sides. The parcel mail did not come in until noon, so I sat in "the Store" beside the stove and read my Christmas letters. It did not seem like Christmas otherwise, except the "Hardware Store" had skates and wool and sparkling powder in the window. Presently the mail came in on a sleigh with two horses and we waited while the bags were sorted, about an hour, and were rewarded with a lovely haul of parcels! Then we marched home laden, and arrived home to find Pandora's Box on the back door-step and the butcher with his sleigh delivering our winter supply of meat (83 lbs. of beef, a ham, a large piece of bacon, 2 lbs. of sausages, and last but not least the "turkey gobbler" — such a weird-looking creature frozen hard, with a long stiff neck! Then it really seemed like Christmas. We were very good, put all the parcels in the spare room and shut the door quickly to avoid temptation, and put out the turkey on a dish to thaw. Then I cleaned the silver and chopped some suet ready for the stuffing. Then came Tuesday, and I kept on trying to picture you all, eight hours in advance of us, wondered what my nephew was like (and what a young-looking grandmother he has got), and if Freda was going the usual round. I made mince pies, the first I had ever made! Not very extravagant pastry as I had not pattypans (then!), so I made them in drop tins that I make my soda buns in and cut out the tops with one of the large tumblers and they rose and behaved nicely. Then for the stuffing, which I composed of suet and bread-crumbs and mixed dried herbs and a little onion as Mrs. Beeton talked about chopped veal and fat bacon. Then we discovered the turkey when thawed was not drawn so Jack came to the rescue. I held it while he drew out the sinews in the legs with pinchers, and we had to laugh over it all, even over the innards, as this process is usually a Company job! The other day Mr. Peak at the hardware store gave Jack a wild duck as a Christmas offering. The difficulty was to pluck it, as under the feathers it had got a coat of down as thick as a blanket! We picked until our fingers were sore, and then Jack got a newspaper and singed the brute. I often laugh at myself when doing these jobs and see Mr. Barnes busy in his shop doing the same thing! We decided to have dinner early on Christmas Eve and directly after to open our parcels by the fire. I wish you could have seen us both. It was absolutely lovely, all the kind thoughts kept tumbling out one after the other and I was overwhelmed! I even saw a glisten in Jack's eye when the silver frame was undone. It was quite a surprise, which pleased him very much. . . . How did you know that a bread board and knife have been some of the things I think we have wished for most, as cutting bread on a china plate is difficult. It is such a nice design too, and we shall use it tonight for the first time. And those sweet, charming Sandby drawings![1] I love them, they are so dainty, and we shall passe-partout[2] them and hang them up. Jack hugs the chocolates and says they are *his,* and I should say he has never been so much thought about at Christmas for many years. He is delighted with his presents and also with Freda's letter. Freda's present has quite knocked me over. She is a brick. The chair backs are very beautiful and represent many hours of giving up and unselfishness. The colours are so beautiful, and I love the design. They are on the chairs today, and J. N. P. keeps walking away and admiring them

---

1. Prints of watercolours of Windsor by Paul Sandby, an 18th-century artist.
2. A cheap method of framing pictures using a sticky backed paper tape that is stuck around the edge of the glass.

afresh. Then we opened Pandora's Box, and my cup brimmed over. After waiting for it so long it was lovely to get it for Christmas. I cannot thank you enough for the contents. It was splendidly packed and, Oh, one thing after another that I had wished for—if you and Freda only knew half of what I felt and do feel inside! Indeed, it was a Christmas to be remembered. I thought you would not mind Christmas Eve for the presents as we did not have breakfast until nine o'clock, and when there are fires to light, beds to make and breakfast things to wash up, we felt we could enjoy presents more fully in the evening, and we wanted to write to you on Christmas Day.

This morning it was snowing but we thought we would go out for a walk and take our lunch (It may seem strange to you, with the thermometer at 12°!) as this is Jack's great idea of a holiday for me, no meal to get ready and no washing up. So we strolled (!) in fairly deep snow across country to the other side of the main road and up a steep clearing to look at two new houses that are being built for a Mr. Pope[3] and a Mr. Sinclair. Wealthy Scottish lawyers from Edinburgh, I believe. They bought the land some time ago and crops have been sown this summer and it has been ploughed. The houses are about 500 yards away from each other, with barns and engine-room and cottages (I suppose, for employees). They must be investing a huge sum of money. They and their wives come out in the spring. One has a daughter of 19, we hear. But we hear *most* extraordinary things out here and we cannot believe half. We are now writing in our "Sunday clothes." I have on my black velvet and it is so nice to feel so respectable! I must leave this shortly to put the turkey in the oven and the pudding in the pot. I could write a dozen sheets more. . . .

Please tell Stanley I am awfully glad he is better—but he is always a good patient. His Christmas gift I appreciate as much as any of the others, and coming when it did I could wear it.

Much love to you all, and *many, many* loving thanks,

Your affectionate child,

Daisy

WEDNESDAY,
[AFTER CHRISTMAS 1912]

My dearest Freda,

I am writing this on the spinning-chair with my toes in the fire as they are very cold. It is really a letter to Mother and you of deep thanks for the Pandora Box. I think it has given me more real pleasure than any present I have

3. Mr. Pope was English and had been a magistrate in India. He had two sons who joined up early in the First World War; one was killed and the other returned to the Windermere.

ever received. I deeply appreciate and value all the thoughts and work that must have been expended on getting the things together and packing them so wonderfully. *Everything* seems to be just what was wanted. My two pairs of brown shoes—just the thing! The muslin curtains I have already begun to cut up for the spare room windows. The water softener (I feel like a lady of fashion with all the cosmetics, but it is necessary to put grease on your face before you go out these cold days). The old sheets, *lovely* to wash this cold weather. The butter traycloths are breakfast cloths for the kitchen, so easy to wash. The stationery Jack keeps and looks at with loving eyes at the bottom of his cupboard. Your old overcoat, splendid for feeding chickens in and hanging out washing. I have covered the long pillow, and I love the material and cords. It is in the centre of the window-seat, and the piece left over will do for a mat on the table when the Japanese embroidery is worn out. Jack came in to fetch the American cloth bag this morning to sit on. He was sawing up a tree on a sloping bank and had to sit. (It is the *very* thing to prevent the snow soaking through the seat of his trousers!) The Maggi soups and *sardines*. We had a Sunday night supper of sardines and bread-and-butter, such a treat! We do miss fish very much. The chocolate will come in for our picnic lunches out-of-doors, and the butterscotch, if Jack does not eat it all, will please Dr. Turnor's kids or the little Marples when they come. The Lux too for flannels, and the Wright's coal-tar soap. In fact, all give the greatest pleasure. The box of odds and ends, the skewers, the little moulds and pattypans (we can have jam tarts now which Jack loves). I do feel so grateful and think when I come across these things in various places, "England fair, dear England. There is no place like it." Even Jack who has been abroad and has no home on the other side finds his heart strings tugged at times. He is so domesticated, I am sure you would both smile! He tries so hard to help me and gives such funny suggestions. He has pulled me through so many occasions when my courage was oozing out at every pore. I shall always feel grateful.

Many, many thanks for all you do and have done,

Daisy

NEW YEAR'S DAY, 1913

My dearest Freda,

My dear girl, I really don't know how to thank you for your lovely Christmas gift. There is nothing you could have sent me that I could prize or value more, and they give such a "home" touch to the armchairs. I quite expected them to be unmounted but they are *perfect* for size, and I love the colour of the blue satin and the beautiful way they are finished off. I deeply appreciate every stitch you have put into them and they seem to me quite a bond. I look at them and then at you on the mantlepiece and the tears will come up—not sad ones but from an overflowing heart, and always looking forward to when I shall see you again. I love your photo more and more and it is one of my greatest treasures. (Jack has just come in and said, "An egg. Mine." You see, we take it in turns to have them for breakfast as they come along.) Well, Christmas is over and it is hard to realize that we have begun a new year. This last has brought so many changes for us all, but I hope for you and for Stanley that business things will take a good turn and that he will be rewarded for taking courage and going forward....

The bulbs are beginning to peep above ground in the cellar so I shall soon be able to bring them into the house, I hope, and watch them there. You ask about the snow. Well, it falls onto the trees and freezes on the branches so that you can see the shape of them outlined in white and they all look like lovely decorated Christmas trees. I so often wish I could send you a baby one, they look so sweet. The cart that brings the water makes a track for us out onto the main road. The sleighs soon make good deep ruts, and the two heavy horses keep it beaten down. The snow is loose like powder and very little clings to our clothes or snow boots if it is freezing hard. We sleep with our bedroom window open. If we leave the jugs in the basin the water freezes but if we put them on the floor they are alright. For this reason I never fill the water bottle as it is our only one and I do not want it to burst! As a rule I do not use the hot-water bottle but luckily for us it is an *exceptionally* mild season, they say. The cold must come, but it cannot now last more than 8 or 10 weeks. Invermere has had the coldest temperature, 10° below zero, but I take it that is because of the lake. As a rule I think the "benches" are not quite so cold as the valleys and lower land. Our log fire in the hall and the kitchen stove keep the house warm enough. It is not as *hot* as other houses out here as J. N. P. keeps the windows open most days, and although I do not always like it I get used to it.

We heard from Uncle William Wall this week that Mr. Ruston[1] died on, I think, December 5th. It seems awfully sad, and Jack feels that now Kenny and he have gone his two tightest links with England have gone too....

I wonder what Mother thinks of the Christmas pudding? We think ours is the very best, and it saved me making a pudding so many evenings that I especially bless it. The turkey is in its last stages of being "re-chauffed," and as Jack says we shall not relish our beef very much after it. The beef is not like English beef. I suppose it has not the quality and it has hardly any fat. But last year there was not a proper butcher even, so things advance. Did I tell you that milk is 7d. or 8d. a quart? We use evaporated milk. It is just like thin cream and pours (not thick like Nestlés), and it makes quite nice pud-

1. An uncle of Jack's by marriage.

dings and blanc-manges. I do not think you can tell the difference, and the saving for people with small incomes is immense.

Well, we had a most festive time at Mrs. Poett's last night, I can assure you. I feel so unsettled today as the result, and so does Jack, that not much work has been done by either of us. The invitation was for eight o'clock, so we started at 6:30 in our best and brightest, Jack having made me rest in the afternoon for a couple of hours. I wrapped up in my lovely fur coat and my dress pinned up round my waist out of harm's way as the snow was up to the top of my boots very often when off the main road. We had had some wind and it had drifted. The electric lamp Mrs. Dainty sent me for Christmas being a new treasure, we decided to take it instead of the storm lantern. Alas, it caused *me* much woe! We kept it alight until we got to Captain Young's and, then feeling we were on the main road and could see the track, Jack switched it off! A little further on we wanted to know the time and it would *not* light. Jack pulled the back off and tried to put it right, but it was too cold for fingers to do much so we walked on and a little out of our way to the Marple's house to see if they could lend us a light. They were highly excited and busy as the first lot of their furniture had come the day before: china (lovely china jugs and moulds and basins!) and glasses, linen and blankets (which were all *frozen* and being aired) and, among other things, a great big sofa and a piano! Mrs. Marples said she does not play or sing but leaves it all for her husband. I just touched the keys to see what it felt like. It was lovely, but the children were asleep and we were in a hurry! They gave us a Japanese lantern and a candle as their storm lanterns were not unpacked, and we had directions given us to go across the lake, it being shorter! We had just got down the bank and onto the lake when the lantern caught fire and we were in the dark. We knew it was straight across, but it takes twenty minutes to cross the lake and we could not see the friendly light on the other side. About half-way across I thought I saw black marks that looked like water, and in fact got in a bit of a funk as for two days it had not been freezing hard and, of course, it was pitch dark, remember. Jack did not get cross, but said we must go on, and finally we saw the lights and fetched up safely.

All the youth of the district were there and various other married folk. Mrs. Poett informed me we were going to have "a frolic," as they always make a great feature of seeing the New Year in. All I can say is they are the most wonderful people, Mrs. Poett is a wonderful woman. Gowned in a deep red velvet teagown, with real lace turned back on a crossover bodice (that Mother would love) and just a fold of chiffon to fill up the bare neck V; with her pretty grey hair and diamonds, I could not imagine that they live seven miles from a town in the depths of Canada and have no servant, not even a Chinaman at present. The drawing-room rugs were up and the floor polished for dancing. At one end the biggest Christmas tree, from floor to ceiling, all decorated with silver bells, balls, and tinsel, the real German things, sent from Dresden. They had a children's party on Christmas Eve, and Mrs. Marples said the tree was laden with things sent out for the occasion. Mrs. Poett's mother, I think, lives in Dresden and Mrs. Poett has lived there with her a good bit while General Poett was in India. They have a gramophone and soon dancing began. The girls, who are all beauties in various ways, in charming white frocks with transparent necks. Oh, how I did enjoy it all and so did Jack—alternately minding the gramophone records and dancing. Then in to supper—*such* a supper: prawns in aspic, salmon (frozen), rice (but fresh, not tinned), chicken mashed in white sauce, veal cake, lemon sponge, creams, mince-pies, scones . . . and on the sideboard a huge iced cake made by Babs, the second girl. They took me into the dining room before supper and showed me the good things, all made by "Mummy." They simply adore "Mummy" and, of course, help her, but she is the leading spirit as the girls had never done any cooking before they came out here. Mrs. Poett has lived in India all her life and been waited on hand and foot, but she is one of those wonderful hostesses and managers, and really I feel they are too good and charming to look at to be out here at all! Of course, they have ample means and are able to have salmon from the Coast and prawns in bottles, and all those luxuries that cost double what they do in England. After supper, back to the drawing room, and all the lamps put out and we played Snapdragon. How I thought of you with the weird light playing on the faces! Then a fortune-telling game. A box was handed round, and with eyes shut you selected a lump of lead, each a different shape—mine was a heart, Jack's a riding boot. Mrs. Poett sat at a table with a little spirit lamp and a ladle. We each in turn melted our lump of lead and poured it into a basin of water where it took weird shapes which Mrs. Poett explained, and each lump of lead had a motto in German attached to it. It is a Twelfth Night game they always indulge in. The bonbons on the supper table were the biggest and most lovely I had ever seen, and had such things as penknives and brooches in rolled gold. I got a curbbangle. These were all sent out by a very rich uncle. General Poett said they had three crates of Christmas presents between them! At 11:45 the tree was lighted and the "babies," Angela and Nigel, appeared with rosy cheeks, pale-blue dressing-gowns and scarlet slippers, and a teddy bear and a golliwog. Nigel handed bon-bons on a tray and Angela had a huge snowball with baby bon-bons, while Mrs. Poett distributed punch. At twelve o'clock we drank to Absent Friends, the babies drinking lemonade out of their little silver mugs in a most serious fashion. Then we all crossed hands and sang Auld Lang Syne, and the girls banged down the windows to let the new Year in. Such a time I have never had in England! The eldest girl is just engaged and this makes them want to sell their place, and also the other two girls in England will be "Out."[2] They only came for five years, just for the experience and to get braced up, I imagine, so as soon as they can sell I expect they will go. We do not see much of them, but they are always so delightful it will be a great loss to the Valley if they go. We walked home with a storm lantern and were in bed soon after two o'clock, but I did not get up until nine this morning and have had a lazy day for Canada as I have only done some ironing.

I must write more later.

Much love, dear old girl, and every good wish for the New Year.

Your always affectionate sister,

Daisy

ATHALMER, B.C.
JANUARY 8TH, 1913

My dearest Freda,

The "cold snap" has come at last and, to tell you the truth, I do not like it the least little bit in the world. Zero feels very cool and I can endure it and go out with more or less comfort, but 18° and 19° below are horrible! The fire did not make the room warm enough so we had to bring up the stove, which is an iron thing on four legs, 2 feet long and about 18 inches high and 18 inches broad. The beautiful thing stands on a mat in the centre of the room and a stove pipe rises from it into a hole above the mantlepiece that leads into the chimney. This means you cannot have a fire as already the kitchen stove smoke is taken off by the chim  ney. The result is most depressing. I may say the brute stands on an iron mat! Can you imagine what a room looks like with this ornament? All the Canadian houses have them, of course, and often one in each room, but the Canadian houses proper have no fireplace. I think the cold touched my liver and I had horrible flatulence and felt most horribly depressed. I went out a *little* way each day and blessed you for giving me the fur coat. I wore my white woolly hood and the white shetland shawl *double* over my face. How thankful I was of those long flannel nighties, too. However, these low temperatures only come in snaps of a few days or a week, and I must be

---

2. "Coming out." Daughters of wealthy or titled families were presented at Buckingham Palace, and balls launched the social season. More generally, middle-class girls could be considered to be "out" (that is, adults) when they left school, put up their hair, and wore long skirts and adult clothes. A Coming Out dance might emphasize the transition.

thankful we have not had it so cold before. I keep telling myself I shall get used to it, and I have got to live out here. Of course, Jack never grumbles. He never grumbles at anything, he can always remember something worse! I said, "Next time there is a cold snap Mrs. P. will remain in bed," and he remarked, "If Mrs. P. does I shall call her a coward!" So don't pity me too much when you write.

Miss Colebrook sent us a charming New Year's gift of a pair of bellows, plain stained oak with rough leather and brass nails. She had sent to England for them and I think it awfully kind of her. She also sent me a saucepan scraper, just a ball of brass wire shavings but it is a splendid help. Both things she noticed we wanted when she was here. I suppose a return thanks for her lodging, but it is very kind of her. I have only seen her twice since she left, as I have not been to Mrs. Young's for some time. The snow is so deep now, about 7 inches, I find walking any distance is hard work and I plough along like an old woman! It is hard to find time to make calls in the afternoon when I have had a busy morning. It requires energy to go and change and walk for three-quarters of an hour, stay 30 minutes, and get back to prepare the evening meal. I usually take Thursdays "off" as I told you, as Jack likes me to go out with him to Athalmer and I am lured by the mail. Other days I usually get blown up for not going out enough, though I often go as far as the box to see if there are any papers or letters, as the Poetts often bring them up for us. This morning we were rather short of water so had to melt snow, a boilerful and a big pot on the fire. The result with so much cold was it dampened the fire in the stove and I could not get my irons hot. I made rissoles and a blanc-mange for this evening, about noon began some ironing, lunch at one o'clock, then washing up, and I ironed until four o'clock. I then sat down before the fire and *read* the *Vailima Letters,*[1] the first time I have done such a thing since I have been in the house. How I love the book! I read and forget all my troubles and difficulties, reading about those other people. In many ways it reminds me of us, cleaning the house and clearing, only they had Paul to do the cooking. Thanks ever so much for sending it. I must try and get some more half-hours and read. I think it does me good. I cannot always be washing and ironing and cooking. I always look forward to the evening when we have dinner and change and Jack helps with the washing up. I have been wearing my black velvet dress as it is so cosy and there is no use in saving it. Jack always wears his khaki undress uniform in the evening as he can wear soft collars and he has leather buttons put in place of the brass ones. These are silly little details that may interest you. It is 6° above zero tonight and we have a fire. My spirits have revived owing to Nux-Vomica,[2] I think. We had soup, rissoles, and canned corn as a vegetable, blanc-mange and a tinned pine-

1. By Robert Louis Stevenson.
2. A homeopathic remedy.

apple (the latter a great luxury). We ordered several tins from Eaton's, as Mrs. P's ideas on pudding had run dry! All the puddings have two eggs. I can allow myself about two eggs a week for cooking purposes, and J. N. P. likes a cake! By and by when the hens are laying we shall be better off. At present I have only got those I put down in Waterglass. The poor old cock is dead! Our first great misfortune with livestock. We nursed him in the kitchen for a fortnight but he got no better. Two days ago he departed and several dollars with him! Now we shall have to get another. . . .

Amie Wellman has written to me again. She says she will make me a duchess set for my dressing-table, and will I send measurements by you. I shall not say no to such a kind offer. Such lots of letters to answer. Tell the Vidlers and Maud I really will write soon. Alexina Caley hears Stewart is going to the Himalayas. Did you know? All the Windsor folk seem very excited at Dora Bois' wedding! Tottie Mason tells me she is to be married in the spring, but she does not seem very much excited about it or very much in love—just that she feels so old. Thank goodness I have never felt that yet, although the high altitude is bringing grey hair! Mrs. Woodman's tonic has quite stopped my hair falling, if she wants a testimonial from B.C. . . . Thanks ever so much for the transfers and the scraps. Funnily enough I never thought of any shop but the "fancy" one on King's Road. The drawing books are splendid and they will give great joy to Gerald Turnor, also to his mother! Those snapshots are lovely. I look at them each day. *You* look very indignant, and I love Mother's hand over her tummy or heart. Which is it? I have seen her do it so often. I do hope the few days at Hunstanton[3] did old Stanley good and that he will get on well and not find his treatment too hard. I do wish I could write you a description like Stevenson. I really believe I could if I only had more time. I never write half what is in my mind, as I make mental comments all day, "I will tell them this and that," and when I write it all goes for something else. Oh, I forgot to mention the Ronuk. It is *quarter* the work of beeswax, and the floor looks so nice.

The best of all good things for you all in 1913 and much love in which Jack joins. Always thinking of you.

Your affectionate sister,

Daisy

ATHALMER
JANUARY 20, 1913

My dearest Freda,

I am feeling very sad this evening as I know there are some letters for me

---

3. A resort town on the Norfolk coast.

at Athalmer and I have not received them, which is always tantalizing. The Poetts always go down for the mail on Monday, and lately have brought ours up and put in the box. Jack walked across at five o'clock, but came back with no letters. However, I shall have them on Thursday, I hope. It has been snowing all day today and I have been down only as far as the chicken house to see the new cockerel, who came up this morning from Wilmer with Mr. Hanley and the water. Mr. Hanley is an Irishman who is in charge of the Company's garden in summer. He hauls the water during these winter months. It comes up now on a large sleigh with a strong team of horses. Mr. Hanley is the only visitor we see nowadays, as nobody else has been for a long time and I find it too hard work to walk as far as Athalmer and Wilmer in the deep snow. I hope to get as far as Mrs. Young's one afternoon soon. I arranged to go on Thursday (that is soup and cold meat for dinner) and then it snowed too heavily. Friday afternoon there was bread to bake and Saturday afernoon is always the kitchen, and so time goes along with me and with others too. But, as Jack says, they have horses and a cutter and we have not. I shall be awfully glad when the winter has gone. It will be over, I expect, in six week's time, though the Poetts say there was a little snow left at Easter last year. I remember the date, don't you, April 5th on the *Empress of Ireland*? I wonder if we shall come home on the same boat and when it will be, but I expect there will be more Empresses by then! Did I tell you that Mr. and Mrs. Bowden are at the Coast, and Mr. Robinson and Smith the ploughboy are living in luxury for bachelors, though they only have camp furniture at present. Mr. Robinson evidently has plenty of money. I think he was at Eton and is late of the Yorkshire Light Infantry. His friend, Captain Gordon, who came here for a few days and who I believe bought out Mr. Bowden, is a bachelor, but still in the Service, and I believe is now in South Africa. We do not see much of Mr. Robinson. Jack went over and had a chat with him yesterday morning, but Mr. Robinson does not care to turn out these cold nights when the day's work is done, nor does Jack. He loves his armchair and felt slippers (How are the mighty fallen!) and has just remarked, "Bring me some butterscotch before you sit down again."

I like the look of the black velvet hat you bought, so comfortable. I have some pictures of them, or similar shape, and thought I should like one, but I have got heaps at present and only need my woolly hood. The Poetts have got hoods with wool strings. They come from Dickens & Jones, I think, and are rather nice. Never mind about the things from the Stores. We will send back the ink-stand. They got hung up at Golden, but I expect they will be at Athalmer this week. I think perhaps you could get my stockings at the Stores, but wherever you go and get your clothes will do equally well for me, and if you cannot get things I expect Daisy Mac would. The list I sent for you to bring with you, but as you are not coming I shall only have a little at a time, and I will send a list some time later on. I think I told you in my last letter how much cretonne I should want for the spareroom. I hope all my wants do not bother you very much.

You love the postcards of the scenery and say it is grand, and it is. *I* love to look at the postcards you sent me of the garden, and think of green grass and flowers, the privet hedge and the lilac, and all the soft green. I admire the mountains but I shall never love them. My heart, or really my true love, is and will be England! In fact, in some ways I envy old Stewart his sunshine and warmth. I was talking to Mrs. Poett the other Sunday. She has lived abroad in India and she says, although the warm Colonies have many drawbacks, from a woman's point of view they have many advantages. The doing without green vegetables and fresh fruit, and in many cases fresh milk, and the hard work that must be done because there is no help, makes Canada chiefly a land for men and a very hard one for women. In hot countries the women as a rule thrive better than the men. Without a doubt *all* the men here love the life, but I think when any two women get together and talk from the bottom of their hearts the tears always shine in their eyes and they long for a "general" and a washerwoman. An old, or elderly woman could not live here unless she was as hard as nails! It would not suit you and Mother. You would enjoy a visit of a few months, I am sure, but you could not live here. Of course, this is just between you and me.

The Poetts are leaving in the spring. The eldest girl is to be married soon and comes to England for her honeymoon. She is going to live in Vancouver, which is a town and very much like England, I believe. The flowers and foliage must be very beautiful—and the sea—and no snow! They intended to stay for five years when they came, but I think Mrs. Poett finds it a bit hard. The other two girls are just grown up and "the babies" are big enough to go to school. I think it would be absolutely wicked to send such charming mites to hob-nob with the school children at Athalmer—No, I am not a democrat! We don't see the Poetts often, but they are so awfully kind and always help me with kind words. "We don't see you óften, Mrs. Phillips, but if ever you are ill or need somebody, one of us will come. We all admire your pluck, and the General admires your courage." A handshake and tears in her eyes, and you know she means it and is being tested too.

I like your Christmas card very much indeed. Auntie Louie comments on the pretty card (ours, I mean) and Mr. Wall says, "We wonder if it is Daisy's handwork, as none of us are artists." But they would have had a shock if they could have seen Jack with the brush and a serious face! After all, the credit is due to my good little sister at home!

Well, as luck would have it I opened Stanley's letter first. Of course, it was a terrific shock,[1] and Jack had to wait long for his dinner that evening,

1. The "terrific shock" was probably news of Stanley's engagement, which would mean a move for Daisy's mother and sister, since Stanley and his wife would take over the house.

but I am awfully glad as it really is the best thing that could happen to him. All the same, the two people that my thoughts are chiefly fixed on now are you and Mother, for you will be my home on the other side. I wonder so much what you will do. Your studio dresser, the grandfather clock, the blue china and the oak music cupboard in the drawing room the schoolroom chairs, and I have furnished on room in "the flat" for you. How I should love to be near and help and go through all the stores with Mother. What a business it will be. But I believe your inside will be better for a change, and Mother's general health too, I am sure. I have had a letter from Sissie. They seem in a terrible muddle as to plans, but they always were.

No more time this week. So sorry. Much love,

Daisy

SUNDAY, FEBRUARY 2ND (1913)

My dearest Freda,

Your most interesting budget I received on Thursday. As usual, it did me a power of good. I seem sometimes to get replies so quickly I feel very close. I think the tie and waistband are awfully nice and quite my colour. I had a blue tie on last Sunday and spilt something on it (dirty girl, as ever), and then remarked to Jack, "I cannot buy a new one!" I think it so awfully good of you to go on shopping expeditions for me as I know you do not love to very much. I am sure I shall like the cretonne very much indeed. Are Liberty's sending it direct, I wonder? Sometimes you can avoid duty in sending lengths of material by cutting it in half and sending two parcels. Mrs. Cuthbert told me the other day that her sister does this. In fact, now I am here I find what *useful* things sisters are. Everybody seems to have a kind sister in England. . . .

The *very* cold weather has gone and in consequence my spirits have risen with the thermometer. The midday sun is getting warm enough for me to put on your fur coat and hood and to sit on the verandah for an hour wrapped up in rugs when I take my rest. We may get another cold snap but it cannot last long so I do not mind. It is only the below zeros which are rather trying, and this has been a very *mild* winter! . . .

I suppose old Stewart is nearing his destination, and the more I hear of it I think it is the best place he can have gone. There evidently are openings and a chance of getting on, and there are so many English there it cannot be so very dreadful. If you have got any literature or pamphlets about the Malay States will you send them along sometime, though I often feel what a lot of yours and Mother's time and thoughts are spent on us, even in doing up papers! But old Jack does enjoy them so much. I think he more often walks down to Athalmer on the chance of getting fresh papers rather than for my letters. I do hope George Ling will rise to the occasion and be a help to Stanley . . . [and that] Gilbert will buck up and work hard now so as to get through his exam and realize that "life is earnest. . . ."

This has been a week full of excitement. On Wednesday after lunch I had just put the bread in the oven and was sitting on the verandah for a few minutes with the *Vailima Letters* when Mrs. Cuthbert turned up. She does not often brave the hill. She said, "I have come to show you my Christmas present. I am dressed in them!" A very charming duck-egg green knitted coat and a dutch bonnet to match. Round this a golden syrup colour chiffon scarf tied under one ear in a big bow, a rather bold herringbone tweed skirt, and a pretty blouse. She looked so pretty, you would have liked her for a model. I then discovered that her eyes were the colour of her jersey, which made it most becoming. Jack was busy so we chatted *hard,* as we always do when our husbands are not there, silly nonsense, and laugh together at various difficulties, until we both felt 17 instead of 57! I had made some rolls out of the left-over dough. They were hot for tea, and a soda cake was also on hand. We had just begun when I heard voices outside, and Jack came in with Captain White and Mr. Robinson. Captain White could not come on Sunday and had been to lunch with Mr. Robinson, our neighbour. Both had come to call, and made themselves most charming. They brought two dogs, and Mrs. Cuthbert had brought her retriever, so we had an exciting five minutes in the dog world. Mr. Cuthbert was away at the Coast as he is secretary for the Fair this year and they were all meeting at Vancouver.

I went down to tea with Mrs. Cuthbert on Friday and took her a few bulbs as she was "green" when she saw mine. I took the hill slowly coming back and was not very tired. Jack went to Wilmer yesterday to a lecture given in the schoolroom on apple trees by a Mr. Dunn. There were about fifteen people present. Dr. Turnor and a few other settlers have started a Wilmer Improvement Society. All it is is to get a few local people to give small lectures every month on subjects like fruit growing, chickens, etc. to try and help newcomers. Jack is loath to go to any of these things but I tell him he *must,* as one makes enough mistakes as it is, goodness knows. He really enjoys having a talk with other men sometimes, though he dearly loves his own company and shutting himself up tight in his shell.

We heard the sad news that poor Mr. Bowden is in hospital at Vancouver, suffering from loss of memory, and now hear that it is an abcess on the brain and he cannot live more than a week. The poor man has had such heaps of worry, and as nothing has gone right since he came it is no wonder. His wife was a charming woman but she evidently liked social life and *hated* Canada, and was not really strong enough to face it. Jack is rather apt to judge her, but she was over fifty, I should say, and she found Canada very hard and "unsympathetic" so could not be transplanted. Their furniture is still at Golden, and she cannot sell it to raise money as it is marked Settlers Effects, which cannot be sold until they have been in the country for twelve months. To me it seems a terrible tragedy. I am not sure, but I think Miss Colebrook quite parted company with him. However, I know lots of her possessions and clothes were packed with their things.

Mr. Marples was in Wilmer on Saturday and asked us to go over on Sunday afternoon. It was much warmer, and the road is fairly level so we walked there in an hour. All their things have come now, although it must have cost them a tremendous lot to bring them by road it is evidently nothing to worry about as they must have ample means. Everything is awfully nice, a real, English home, with good big solid sofa, armchairs, dining table, carpet, piano, and lovely sideboard. Their bedroom *quite* English, even to goffered frills and monogram on the pillow shams! They had been practising at home for Canada for some time, I should say—Mrs. Marples and the wonderful nurse, who is quite the old retainer and calls Mr. Marples "Mr. Norman"—and have bought out mangles, washers, plateracks, patent cooking pots and steamers, and some wonderful portable corner cupboards with curtains in front. The spare room is quite a nice room; the boy's room with all their own pictures, Cecil Alden style,[1] and two little beds; and then the nurse's room, where the little girl has her cot, her dolls, and her toy cupboard. Molly is her name. She is 2½, like a rosy-cheeked apple and *very* friendly, in a brown velvet Liberty dress with blue embroidery, very short to show very pretty unders. Nurse grieves and says she always wore white in England! They have a Bissel sweeper and say carpets are no trouble. Jack says two women in a house out here can do three times the work of one, as the nurse scrubs, cleans fire-irons, washes kitchen cloths and all the filthy dirty jobs, while Mrs. Marples does the needlework and lays the meals, and they divide the cooking. We had lovely scones and seedcake for tea, made by the nurse! . . .

ATHALMER, B.C.
FEBRUARY 11TH, 1913

My dearest Freda,

I believe somehow I have got two letters of yours unanswered, but you will understand it is not a slight. I was so interested in hearing of old Stewart's departure, and yesterday a letter from you and one from him at Malta. Quite cheery and bright, and very much looking forward. This keenness certainly will be a great help in keeping him going at first. He is great in

---

1. Cecil Alden was a popular artist who illustrated scenes of country life.

his praise of Mother and the way she kept up. It was such a *huge* help to me that I know exactly what he felt too. It made it seem more like au revoir than goodbye. Won't it be lovely if some day we can both come back at the same time and see you and Mother, not much quieter and older but having taken a fresh lease of life, being free from so much worry and anxiety? Don't let me find you or Mother much older when I come back, will you? Stewart says it will only cost £10 more to come back this way via San Francisco. Lovely to dream of! Dreams, idle dreams, and lately I realize how much £10 means. But even if you are poor you can be awfully happy, and I am sure I have learned to be most economical without knowing it. There are never any scraps for the chickens except vegetable peelings, and mince makes potato pie, and potato pie makes rissoles! I shall teach you all about it one of these days.

Poor old Stanley. I do hope he will soon get quite fit and be able to keep on his golf and out-of-doors exercise in some form, though I realize at times he will find he has much to do and doubtless much to give up, but Connie will be a great help, I am sure. Do you know the whole time we have been out here Jack has never even seen a glass of beer, whisky or brandy, but drinks water, and coffee after dinner, and even very much limits his tobacco. He took to smoking a long slim pipe after dinner for a week and then said, "I must give this chap up! It makes me smoke too much tobacco." He has cut himself down to a very fine limit, as his supply has to last for three years. He never grumbles at his food and says he can live on the same thing every day of the week and enjoy it. "Men who went through the South African war seldom grumble at food." The only thing he doesn't like is food in tins so we never have it, except tinned tomatoes as a treat for me sometimes. You can get tinned beetroot, shrimps, spaghetti, lobster, beans, peas—in fact, everything in tins—and most people have them. They are usually three tins for 50 cents (2/-), and that is not cheap, I know as *I* do the housekeeping, so it is just as well to do without. The hens now give us an egg every other day. We take our turns to have them for breakfast and they really are a treat. In spite of plain living, I have lately had a bitter taste in my mouth and a rather yellow tongue, but I think it is the result of the cold. However, the last two days are warmer and I have wrapped up in your lovely coat, for which I bless you, and then an army blanket on the boards of the verandah, and with a coconut mat for my shoulders and blankets and coat on top I have rested for an hour with the sun on me and been warm. It will be lovely when the snow goes (the end of March). I heard a little bird twittering today. . . .

I am afraid dinner has been late once or twice on mail day, so now the rule is, I may look at my letters before but not read them until I have washed up. I am quick those evenings, Jack finds. Amie Wellman has promised to make me a Duchess set for a dressing table, or anything else I like if I will send measurements. The offer is too good to refuse, so I will try and send measurements, though I have no time to write to her for a bit. I have written to Elsie this mail, and so I gradually go on. The *Windsor & Eton Expresses* have been very interesting to me lately: the Parish day, the reception, and the two weddings!

Yesterday I had a note from Mr. Bennett saying Miss Colebrook had a day off today and he was driving to Windermere. Might they call and have tea on their way back? It was washing day, but luckily no big things or starching, mostly flannels. We got water boiling early and Jack helped me all the time so that I was not tired. The "affianced pair" arrived at four and stayed until 6:15, and made themselves most charming. Jack behaved *very* nicely to her, though he *says* he dislikes her. Her father seems pleased about her engagement so she feels happier, and she hopes her father and sister will come out at the end of the summer and see her place and him. She will return with him, and they are to be married about Christmas time and come back here. She finds plenty to do at Mrs. Young's as they have two men and three children, and many animals, but she sees him nearly every day! Captain and Mrs. Young come to tea on Sunday. Mrs. Young and Miss Colebrook take alternate Sundays off. They paid "the help" they brought out with them £40 per year, but I do not know what Miss Colebrook gets—not *nearly* as much as Mr. and Mrs. Bowden were giving her, she told me, but she had to get in somewhere for the winter. I wanted to write a line to Mother this mail but it must wait as Jack goes down tomorrow early to try and catch this mail. I enjoyed your description of the Mayor's and *Mayoresses'* reception and am glad you wore the dress....

Ada may be taking a flat in London at Easter and if so Jack has asked her to send his elephant foot, some horns, and a box of curios to Mother to look after for the present. These are all the things that remain. He also wrote to Vivian to know if any of his books and things are still in Mrs. Phillips[1] possession. His father's sword and his own Mausers she says she will send to the solicitor, so these may come too later. Make no comment at present. That wretched woman has the lion's share of money and the capital is hers too, so we shall never see any. I do hope the estate will be settled soon, but all the Wall property is being sold this month. Under Jack's mother's will it has to be realized, and therefore £70 we ought to have received in October did not come and another £70 is due in April which I expect will not come either. But we shall be alright next year. It is just a tight corner at an awkward time. This is quite entre you and Mother, so don't mention it. We shall be alright I know and trust.

Much love,

Daisy

---

1. Jack's step-mother, a former housekeeper whom his father married against the family's wide disapproval.

My dear Girl,

Here I am at three o'clock just finished work and, instead of sleeping, sitting down in a Roorkee chair (very restful) to write you a line. I find lately if I sleep in the afternoon I sleep so heavily that I can hardly wake up, and instead of being fresh I am as heavy as lead although the bedroom window is *wide* open, of course! So I am sure though rest is good for me, such sleep is not. I have got both your photos in view, so here goes. Yesterday morning Jack started off at ten o'clock, taking beef sandwiches, jam sandwiches, gingerbread, and coffee in the Thermos. He went to Athalmer for the mail and some shopping, then to Invermere to the Company offices on various items of business. There was a "Farmer's meeting" at Athalmer at two o'clock so I did not expect him back until five. After he had gone I started on a big iron— such a big wash this week, but of course a small one the week before. I worked hard until one o'clock, and got my damask cloth and table napkins better and almost straight at the corners, but I do wish I could find out what laundresses use to take stains out of table linen. They tell me in my books to soak tea, etc., in cold water and borax, and pour boiling water through. It certainly improves them, but does not take out tea stains, which are the most difficult.

When Jack had gone I began to think he would not be back for hours. Mr. Robinson and Smith were away on the Poett's Lake cutting ice, I knew, and so I suppose the nearest soul was three-quarters of an hour away! I did not mind a bit, but this time last year I should have felt funny. I fed the chickens and had my lunch. I have taken to drinking cocoa midday, as we always have a very simple meal, cheese and potted meat, toast and jam and sometimes potato salad. And *when* there is an egg I sometimes have a boiled egg. Cold boiled bacon and marmalade for breakfast every morning, tea at 3:45 (usually tea and scones), and dinner at 6:30. Tonight roast beef, turnips and potatoes, and jam tart, so you see we live the simple life! However, at three o'clock J. N. P. turned up. He had not stayed for the "Farmers' meeting," found there was no important topic, and they always begin late (three-quarters of an hour is nothing), and that always annoys him! He brought up a 9-lb. ham and the mail, such a fine one. A letter from you, a card from old Stewart at Port Said, the *Lady's Pictorial, World's Work, Observer,* and the *Punch Annual.* It was much appreciated, and J. N. P. was pipe and smiles the whole evening. He does not read *Punch* once, you must know. The pile is always handy and back numbers with favourite pieces by Evoe are often pulled out and read again and again until he can almost say them by heart! I read the *Lady's Pic.* and the article on Kim in the *World's Work* until bedtime, so no darning last night. Also many thanks for the book on Malaya and Letts seed catalogue. I sent you a list of seeds last mail so I will not alter it as I see you can get them there. What I want are hardy, quick-growing annuals that like sun! Godetia I think do very well, also poppies of various sorts, and cornflowers. The garden proper will not be much again this year but must be a gradual growth, I suppose. We have been storing piles of paper in the barn, a pile of tissue, brown and yellow, and it is most useful. However, we found that a squirrel had discovered it and had torn up an immense quantity, all alike, in long twisted pieces! It could not have been for a nest as it would have made hundreds, and when we also discovered horsehair Jack began to wonder about his saddles which are there, and although usually very tender-hearted he set a trap, and yesterday he was caught and skinned. There are hundreds of squirrels about so I am afraid he will not be missed. I helped Jack scrape and powder the skin yesterday, and now it is inside and drying on the verandah! The warm spell I spoke about only lasted three days and then we had another light fall of snow and it is normally cold again now. Still, it was a big promise of spring and a help on. I keep thinking now, only a month more and the snow will begin to melt. And then *what* mud. You have never seen the like. On the road to Golden feet deep, I believe! But no matter. It would be funny to get wet in a fog once again, but the colder it is here, the clearer. I love to see a little mist hanging round Mount Hammond in the mornings. The days are drawing out now. No lamp until 6:30 last evening, and what a saving in coal-oil! All the pamphlets on Canada are very clever, I think, and don't say much about the winter. Jack does not mind, of course, but Miss Colebrook is the only Englishwoman I have found at present who likes below zero. But she hates the summer!

The parson called the other morning and stayed an hour! I was busy and wished him anywhere else, the clotheshorse was round the hall fire, but I did not apologize and tried to tell him he should come in the afternoon. He is a youngish man, rather frowsy, and I think him very boring. He is a Canadian to the backbone and knows nothing of England. He cannot think what Englishwomen do all day long when they keep servants. I told him they do not sit in armchairs and twiddle their thumbs all day long as he supposed, but are excellent housewives although they do not scrub their kitchen floors and wash their husbands' shirts. Jack was outside, so I had my innings without being reproved! I said the *very* cold weather made me feel rather depressed, and he informed me it was not so much the *cold* as the altitude. The air becomes so very rarefied in the very cold weather. I think perhaps he is right in this, as directly it gets a little warmer my spirits rise! I shall always endure the winter, looking forward to spring and summer. All one's difficulties are increased so much in the cold! I am sure Jack does not realize how brave I am sometimes. I tell him so and he can't make it out at all! Mrs. Marples, Nurse, and Molly came over on Tuesday afternoon and I enjoyed it ever so much. I wrote and asked them to fix their own afternoon about a week before. Molly now has a sledge and the nurse dragged her all the way. It took them an hour and twenty minutes from their house. This gives an idea of distance.

Mrs. Marples was in a coat and skirt, made exactly like my Fletcher one in a green shade, and a pretty moss-green stretched velvet hat with cockade at the side, and a pretty lace jâbot. Nurse, who is elderly but a lady, in black, with a musquash toque. She is a perfect treasure as she is so nice and superior and yet does not mind doing all the dirty and hard work, and corrects and trains the children just as she did in England. Molly was in a blue bonnet and a lovely Jaeger camel hair coat, a brown velvet dress with lovely lace frills underneath, and blue ribbons in her hair. She played with the bellows and helped me bring in cakes for tea. All went well until in stirring her milk too violently with the "baby" spoon the whole lot went over. You should have seen her face! We have St. Charles milk which is like cream and you dilute it with water. After a scone, a small voice remarked, "Mummy, this is *skim* milk." Mother and Nurse exchanged glances and smiles but said nothing. Then Molly tackled gingerbread, her "favourite cake," but it made her thirsty! "Now, you drink up your milk," said Nurse. "Molly don't like 'bedensed' milk," was the only remark, and the host and hostess felt they had failed! The word created great surprise to Mrs. Marples as she had only used it once before. They use St. Charles for themselves, but Molly has milk from Captain Young's cow. Did I tell you milk is 7d. a quart here, so we nearly all use the other, it is such a saving. Then Molly forgot all as she went down to feed the chickens out of a tin cup she held herself. I walked to the mailbox with them, and they have asked me to go over and practise on the piano one afternoon in a week or two. These little outings are great rests and pleasure to hostesses and guests, and they seem to come every month or so. Mrs. Marples is rather like Grace Walker but much more vivacious. In fact she talks all the time, and she and Nurse borrowed books. I love all your small details so hope you like mine!

Mrs. Dainty has never written me on the subject but the *Life of Faith* comes every week now and I presume it is from her.[1] I am so glad you feel a little stronger, so just go on and prosper. I believe the changes and plans in the coming months will do both Mother and you good, and then some day B.C. must complete the cure! I still dream and hope. It is not yet but it is not dead, and I love to look forward to it. I am so glad you are going to the dance at the Trails, and have got to stay a young aunt, do you hear! . . .

Give my love to Maud and tell her the knocker looks awfully nice! The

1. The Oxley family were members of the Brethren, an evangelical sect that had gained a considerable following in late 19th century England. She, herself, was not very involved with any church, and this is one of the few oblique references to her sectarian religious background.

only one here at present. Mrs. Marples has a gong, but I tell her the knocker is more English than that. I much prefer writing home letters than any others. Many thanks for getting the bits, and for all you do. When the mail and the papers come I realize how much time it means and thank you deeply always. It makes a very strong bond, if one is needed.

Much love,

Ever your affectionate sister,

Daisy

ATHALMER, B.C.,
TUESDAY, [MARCH ? 1913]

My dearest Freda,

What do you think! I am actually writing this sitting on the verandah in the sun and quite warm too! It is too lovely and I know it will not last, but it is good to be alive. In England crocuses and primroses are flowering, I hear, but it is lovely here to see patches of Mother Earth showing under the trees, and to see drips falling from the verandah and a small pool outside the back door. I have got my two bowls of bulbs at my feet and they are enjoying the sun too. One pot is showing four buds. Four-Paws nibbled some of the tops in the other pot so they are more backward. The cold was responsible for my dyspepsia and low spirits, I am sure, for the last few days I have been feeling quite myself and very cheerful again. I don't like to say too much about the cold to Jack but I do feel it. Anyway, it is really healthier than heat, I suppose. The Canadian heats his house so much that he does not feel the cold, I should imagine, and the women all wear thin blouses, but this does not suit J. N. P. as you can imagine! However, I try and endure open windows. Next year I am told the house must be kept warmer as the cold depresses me. I think Mother must have put in a good word for me. Dear old Jack is awfully good and kind. Don't think I am complaining of him, but he is unused to "women-folk." I sometimes find he does not realize they are different flesh and blood, and that hardships, if one may call them that, are more difficult for them to bear. I find it better to say nothing as after a bit he sees for himself, or a chance word from Mrs. Poett or some other female does it! I feel this is about the last letter to be of much good before M. G.[1] has to pack so it must be for you and Mother too. I am so glad she is coming, but sometimes I feel I should have braved it out by myself and then gone to the hospital a month before. But I did not know *how* I should feel later on

1. This paragraph contains the first explicit reference to Daisy's pregnancy. Molly Gleave (M. G.), a former nurse with hospital training, is being sent out to assist Daisy before the arrival of the "little Colonial." See the Introduction.

or how Jack could manage for two months. Of course, he helps me now lifting things, but later he will be working on the land all day and some way from the house. I do hope terms can be fixed up quite satisfactorily. M. G. wrote me a line and said she could earn 2½–3 guineas a week constantly in England, and thought therefore she was dealing fairly in what she asked. I feel she is doing that, and I would rather she did not come then be a little dissatisfied after. If she has any small expenses I feel I could perhaps pay them out of my own money. I hoped this would bring me home one day, but now it will largely go towards the "little Colonial" and bringing you out here one of these days.

I had an awfully nice letter from Connie, and in it she speaks very sweetly of you and Mother and how much she appreciates your kindness in getting her through the somewhat difficult time and introducing her to so many friends. She seems to be really and truly fond of old Stanley, and I like the tone of her letters very much indeed. The photo has not come yet, but I expect it by any post now. I expect it is at Golden as papers sometimes get stuck there, but I do not mind as long as I get my letters. Mother and you are too good. Later on I shall insist on only having one letter a week as I feel it occupies such a large part of your time now there is Stewart as well. I wrote him a good long letter on Sunday. My great idea of a flat was so that you should not be dull, but if you were able to get to Cheltenham or some such place for a concert, shopping, or little amusements, I expect it would be quite alright. I hope you will not settle down this winter, and if Fanny's house is comfortable and her terms not excessive you could have a month or two there, perhaps. My thoughts are always wandering off in odd directions about you too. There has been a lot of interesting items in the *Windsor & Eton Express* lately, and I usually read it through. I saw about Mary Bickland and various letters from Canada. I also study the advertisements for "generals," and this week see what a lot is required for a girl of 16 or 17 for £10! Poor little soul, she could get treble the money in Canada if she did but know! I would willingly have her for £20!

I am awfully glad to hear of Auntie Louie's bravery (I call it that, for she must have needed pluck!). . . . Since I have been over here away from everything I seem to see many things in a very different light and that arrangement has struck me as being very unnatural and unjust.[2] I must try to write again to Auntie Louie and Auntie Kate Ormsby too, the "The High" letters must come first and I never write all I want to. Please thank Dorrie Durant for the seeds, and such a nice letter. I must write a line soon on *small* notepaper! Mother asks about bread. I bake three or four loaves in tins, very similar to cake tins, and I use for bread and butter for tea. The others I

2. An obscure reference that is probably to a maiden aunt's decision to leave home where, in effect, she was an unpaid servant.

form into four long rolls and bake them side by side in a tin like one used for baking meat, and they join up in one slab that is broken apart. This is Canadian fashion. I have never seen a cottage loaf or tried to bake one. My dough would be a little loose, I think, though I really am very proud of my bread as I have never had a failure. Does Lillie use tins?

....I really am awfully glad that you really *do* feel a little better, you cannot get strong all at once, but it comes by degrees, I am sure, if you get a really good start. The green ninon has come by the last mail, sent while you were away, I think, and is just right. Nothing thicker would do, and draped across the front door window it will look very "arty." The verandah keeps out brilliant sun so hope it will not fade much, but it pleased Jack as it was his idea. Later on I must get a flat lace brise panel to hang flat.... The chickens excelled themselves yesterday by laying two eggs, but today only one again. You can picture me at one o'clock now lunching from cocoa, boiled egg (they are delicious things after five months without), blackcurrant jam, and stewed prunes! The beef was getting near the neck end of the beast and very coarse, so I put some through the mincer, and with breadcrumbs, seasoning and egg, make it into a roll like mock galantine! It is quite good and we cannot always eat "Brazilian stew," though it is the best way for very tough meat. Please thank Mother for all the cuttings she sends, I always enjoy them. The Willbank boilerette is what I hope to get some day. The Youngs and Turnors both have one and say the results are good. I do dodge about, but it is best to write as things crop up or I forget to mention them. This week Jack has had a nasty boil on his right forearm. It was a spot that got scratched and dirt in, I think, but for two days he could only sit by the fire and read and be miserable! However, fomentations and boracic got things to a head, and today he is carpentering and putting a new perch in the chicken house. I have used all my bandages and boracic lint, so M. G. might bring more, though I can get them by writing to T. Eaton's in Winnipeg. Mother's roll of old pillow linen has therefore come in useful too. We could get some in Athalmer, I expect, but Jack was not fit to walk and I am not allowed to walk up that steep hill any more so cannot go down. Mrs. Lance, the nurse at the Hospital, called the other day, not on *business,* purely social. She is very nice, about 45, an old London nurse though she has been in Canada some time and recently married. She is a newcomer at the Hospital and she and her husband share the work. The doctor[3] lives with them at present as his wife is at the Coast on holiday. Mrs. Lance hopes to go home to England in the autumn, and when she returns they are going to start a Nursing Home of sorts in the Okanagan Valley. She thinks it would pay. At present she has a lady patient and a baby, the chambermaid at the Hotel. Nothing disgraceful! They are nearly

3. Dr. Darryl P. Hannington who later would delivery Daisy's daughter.

always married women out here, and this one's husband is the barman. The Columbia Valley paper gave a *paragraph* announcing the arrival of a son and *heir* to Mr. and Mrs. C.! No time for more.

Lots of love,

Daisy

My dearest Freda,

Jack had to go to Invermere today instead of Thursday and I hoped to have written to you last night, but truth to tell I was very tired and so instead of writing I went to bed directly after dinner instead. We had been having comparatively mild weather for a fortnight and the snow was rapidly disappearing. I had enjoyed walking on terra firma once more, but on Monday it snowed all day and all night and never ceased. Tuesday morning we awoke to 8° below once more, and of course the barrels were outside and frozen and the wood all wet and would not burn so this made washing day a nasty one, especially as we had sheets. I make them last three weeks but after that they are impossible. I find the best way to make work easy is not to let them accumulate. I am feeling awfully fit and well in myself now and believe I look very well indeed, with plenty of freckles. I sleep well, eat well, and enjoy my work, but find I must rest in the afternoon and put my legs up or I get back-ache. Jack looks after me well and devoted the whole of Tuesday morning to me, fetching and emptying water, and while the boiler boils and I wash out handkerchiefs, reads silly nonsense from *Punch* or recites it. . . . My bulbs look simply lovely. They are up and out, and in a brass bowl in the centre of the table, with lavender in the silver vases! Everyone has admired the lavender. It would look horrid in glass vases, but in silver quite nice, especially on the blue Chinese mat Mr. E. K. gave me. I have the china bowl in the window but only two bulbs are out at present, and I have tulips coming up in the cellar but they are very slow. I am so glad the flowers will be out for Easter Sunday and I hope this fall of snow will not stop the Turnors coming to dinner.

Did you remember, we had been married a year last Sunday? I expect you did. How the time flies. I had an awfully nice letter from Nellie sending me elastic stay-laces which will be comfortable, I am sure. At present I only need to put my skirt hooks into the first eye or use a safety pin! The skirts are nice and round, but I have put elastic in my black skirt ready for the next move. I hope Mother is sending me a soft, cheap pair of corsets. A splendid time for wearing old ones if you have them, but these I am wearing are on their last legs as I find "light" household work is very telling on these garments. I have utterly done for one pair, and besides these I only have a pair of brand-new ones and waistbands! A tube of lip-salve, Vinolia, can come in some parcel as lips get very dry as well as skin, but my skin is getting much tougher. Sunday we walked over to the Poetts, taking coffee and sandwiches to eat en route. The doctor ordered me not to go to Athalmer or Wilmer because of coming up the steep hill, but on the level I do not get tired or out of breath. We walked on muddy roads, just imagine, and arrived at West Lake at 2:45. The General was in his room with a bad cold, and Jack marched off with Phyllis, the bride-elect, to see chicken houses. I was left alone to tell Mrs. Poett (by Jack's request) that I should come to the wedding on April 15th if possible. He thought that, as the Brigadier's wife, she would expect to know. She evidently did. "I hoped you would tell me, but I should never have asked." At once, she was full of practical suggestions and advice. She has a splendid pattern of nighties as worn by the twins, the running string only at neck and waist, so easy to wash. Also a flannel one, all made in one piece with two strings on the shoulders. She will look them out and let me have them. Jack must make a stand, like a luggage stool, for the washing basket to bring it level with the bed! I must order cakes of White Castile soap and permanganate of potash crystals in my next Eaton's order. She was forty when the twins were born, and so she rattled on. The people that do what other people call impossible things get on well. She took *impossible* railway journeys in India. I am so healthy and Jack is so healthy, I shall manage splendidly, and soon get used to the extra. I expect when Phyllis is married she will be over to see me, as I must not walk so far again. The General came down to tea, and the twins (Nigel in pale blue tunic, and Angela in a white muslin dress, white socks, and lots of leg!) recited poetry, walking over to the hearth rug to take up this position. R. L. Stevenson's *Garden of Verse*[1] selections and "If no-one ever marries me" from Angela, and Nigel finished the programme with "A jolly old sow." The second girl, Babs, teaches them and they do her great credit as they are only five. Jack has lost his heart to Angela, I can see. She is a most fascinating little girl.

I have finished the valences for the spare-room bed, bound them with dimity binding quite properly, tell Mother, so I progress slowly. I was cutting out the cupboard curtain on Monday afternoon when Captain White called to see Jack, or rather get a subscription to the Board of Trade, and he remarked what charming cretonne it is. I shall get no more done this week as I have silver to clean and ironing to finish, and I want to get ahead for Sunday. . . . Am so glad you have had cheerful news from Stewart also. Hope your visit to Fanny[2] has added a little polish to "the cure," though you

---

1. *A Child's Garden of Verses.*
2. The Oxley family's former nurse, then living near Bournemouth.

evidently do not think Bournemouth neighbourhood is *the* place. Anyway, I think somewhere *warm* for this winter would suit you both, if possible. Have you seen anything of Toussa or Elfreda lately? I wish I had more time for letter-writing, but I hope friends understand my limitations. I think Miss Hutchinson[3] is a "good egg" for my clothes! Jack would be cross if he could see this expression. He is so particular about my personal appearance and figure, I am afraid he will not approve of the new order of things. Still, I must try and look nice under adverse circumstances! You are a dear kind girl to work for me. I am so very grateful but it makes me want to see you, and I am sure if things go well you will *have* to come by and by....

I left off last night as I fell asleep and then Jack said I argued with him that I had not done so! I may as well remark, I am not usually allowed to argue. Well, in the night it dropped to 16° below so it was fairly chilly this morning and I again wear my flannel petticoat. The flowers were slightly touched with frost in the hall and drooped their heads but I soaked them in warm water and put them near the fire, poor things, and gradually they revived! Still, I have managed to keep cheerful in spite of it all, as I feel it cannot last long. The roof, of course, is deep in snow again and I loved to see it green. The good chickens gave us four eggs yesterday so, on the strength of it, we had an omelette last night and it was fairly successful. Not as good as Mother's though I tried to make it her way, but I hope to improve. Tonight, mince and poached eggs, and baked roly-poly jam. You cannot know how lovely it is to have new-laid eggs again. The first one or two were like nectar of the Gods! Our supply of meat ran out, so Jack had to get a joint from the butcher's. It had not been frozen hard, only kept in cold storage, and it was more like English beef than any we have had. There was a little fat, so we have been having dripping for lunch, and a lovely piece of kidney suet, so J. N. P. can have some of his beloved suet puddings. They never had such things in the Mess, and now he enjoys them as things he had when a boy! The candlestick has come at last and gives great satisfaction as it is exactly the shape he wanted and likes—so it was worth waiting for it. He is now smoking and is reading the *Cornhill!* Thank Mother for all the papers about Scott. We shall keep them. All your and Mother's letters are cut up and folded into spills! Nothing is wasted in this house you will perceive! A year tomorrow since we sailed! I shall hope to hear from M. G. next week, if she can come for the sum we can afford. If she cannot, I shall quite understand, as she says she has regular employment now at 3½ guineas a week. If Jack had not come into more money it would have been quite out of the question. I *can* go down to Wilmer and be quite well looked after, I am sure, so don't you and Mother worry. I am just waiting and hoping, but *not* worrying in the least as I am getting used to the idea. Jack is thinking of having

---

3. A dressmaker in Windsor.

Amelia[4] out later if she cares to come and, if so, I shall not be a bit hard worked but I do not think of it yet.

Much love to you and Mother, and ever so many thanks for *all* you do and are doing to help me.

Your very affectionate sister,

Daisy

HESTON, ATHALMER,
MARCH 25TH, 1913

My dearest Freda,

Once more the thaw has commenced so I feel very happy. A Chinook has been blowing all day, with the result that Mother Earth is again showing in patches and a little stream of water is flowing at the back door. 7:35 P.M.: Jack has just been to put the chickens to bed and reports it is just freezing, but that is nothing. At zero I am quite comfortable, but below that I do not like it very much. I tell people I go out when it is "below," and Jack says, "Like a cuckoo in a clock, just out and in again!" But today all the windows have been open. It was house-cleaning this morning. I only Ronuk the floors once a fortnight. The other week a sweep and rub with the duster keeps things going. Then a stewed steak to prepare for dinner (I always cook in the mornings and warm up about an hour before dinner), and a baked suet pudding—"bottom tosity," Mother used to call it—as apple rings seem to cook so nicely this way and Jack adores suet puddings! Our frozen winter supply of meat has all gone so Jack brought up a piece of steak from the butcher last week that has only been in cold storage. It thaws in a few hours in the warm, and with lots of nice gravy is more like English meat to look at and taste. I shall not have to use the mincing machine quite so often now, which will make things quicker. I have taken lately to putting the suet through the mincer. It is so much quicker than chopping and the result is quite good. I also made brown bread this week instead of white. It makes a change. I find I am slower over my cooking than anything else. The pastry tastes very nice but it always seems to take a long time. I am still progressing with the cretonne for the spare room and like the stuff more and more, you will be glad to know. As there is not much proper furniture it makes things look cheerful. I have this week made the two curtains for the cupboards that stand on top of each other and hold Jack's chest-of-drawers when travelling. These stand under the window and the top must be the dressing-table! I find a white cover will be best for the top, as the sun shines in during the morn-

---

4. Amelia Harris, the Phillips family nurse from Heston days, who at 57 years of age would come to look after Daisy and the baby.

ing. I have plenty of "old bleach" to make it, but will you please get me 6 yards of B. B. Loreton, 1½ inches wide and a coarse make. I see in Harrods' catalogue it is 5¾d. per yard, but I am sure Caleys keep it. It is machine made, but a Loreton pattern. I shall never come to an end of things I want, but at Pryce-Jones exactly the same lace is 25 cents (1/-) per yard, so even with postage it is better to get it in England. I would send direct but it means getting a money order, and Jack has so many little shopping errands to do already it only fidgets him. When I can go down to Athalmer again I shall try and do this and not worry you so often. If you are in the depths of the country, do you think Daisy Mac, Nellie, or Connie would be any good for a little shopping? Also, I suppose if I write to Miss Hutchinson or Apsey for a blouse or anything of that sort, they would trust me for the money. I am so awfully glad Apsey is making my coat and skirt. I know I shall fancy it more. I think I shall be able to go to Phyllis Poett's wedding in my white coat and skirt, as it is in three weeks time and my figure is only nice and round at present (more like Freda Dainty at her normal)! I cannot walk so far, of course, but I hope someone will be able to give me a lift on the road. I shall write to M. G. in Montreal and also at Halifax. If the season is not an open one I expect the boat will come in at the latter place. Only imagine if you were coming I should be standing on my head in excitement, but I shall look past the next twelve months and try and imagine it then. I am sure just now your inside wants strengthening up, and later you will enjoy the whole thing the more. Elsie writes and says she will start and embroider two petticoats for the short coating for her ladyship or his lordship, whichever it is. I am afraid I shall have no choice in the matter, but I am sure it will have heaps of clothes to start with and later things will be most acceptable to save stitches. I shall love to have Mother's "old things" as she calls them, and value them all the more. I think all the arrangements about everything that you and Mother have made are splendid. Thank you from the bottom of my heart! I am feeling very fit and well, and try and rest in the afternoon as much as I can and put my feet up on the "spinning chair." I lie in my bed every other day as that mode of rest makes me so sleepy. . . .

I am glad old Stewart's letters are cheery. A welcome at the start is a great thing and will help him a lot. I have written again but told him not to worry about writing much to me. I would much rather that Mother had all his spare time, and I know how few they are for the pen. I must write to Dorrie Durant, Nellie, and Edie Bird this week if I can, so perhaps you will go a little short and you will not mind. I have *twelve* letters unanswered, people are so kind at writing! Nellie has sent me a book by the author of *The Wee MacGregor,* but I have had no time to read it yet. Jack is busy studying your book on the rotation of crops and he finds it most useful as he has no book on farming. I have not used the Pandora box pillow yet, luckily, so it will come in for the "Colonial." Where everything extra will go in this small house I know not. I fear our lovely tidy rooms will be a thing of the past for a good many months. I shall put everything I can away in trunks in the barn. Jack has put doors on the front of the window-seat and that will make a storage place for some of the things, but at present when I bring in the washing, before I iron I throw it on the spare room bed! The clothes horse, etc., all live in there at present. It is like a big cupboard! But I shall soon learn how to manage fairly well, I expect. . . .

The chickens have given four eggs today and three yesterday. They were lovely, just new laid and best plain boiled, I think. With cold bacon, egg and marmalade my breakfast is a large meal nowadays, but my hardest work time is the morning and I find it helps! I enclose a cheque for £6 to pay Miss Hutchinson and Tina.

No time for more. Heaps of love.

Your affectionate sister,
Daisy

HESTON
ATHALMER, B.C.
APRIL 4TH, 1913

My dearest Freda,

The last letter I had was from Mother written on March 5th and I expect there is one from you down at Athalmer, but I shall not get it until Monday, I expect, so must answer beforehand. Thanks ever so much for the parcel that came this week. I like the overall very much. The shape is good and easy to wash as there is not a great deal of stuff in it, and it is thin, another advantage for washing and coolness point of view too! The corsets are excellent, and just the thing. I wonder where you bought them. Flora Nicholson asked for them one day at Selfridges, I remember, but they did not keep them. Just to ease your mind I am keeping very fit and well, and rejoicing in the milder weather! The snow is slowly disappearing, and Oh, the mud in consequence! But I still don't mind that though it gets trodden into the house, of course, the only disadvantage to a bungalow, it has no hall! The next we build!! will have a small porch or something of the sort. I have quite made up my mind! Yesterday I cleaned down the verandah with mop and pail of water — just the job you would like, I know, as it is fun! This afternoon Mr. Dunn, the new man the Company have brought in from the Okanagan Valley to advise and plant apple trees came up to see Jack, and with him came a huge dog like a Newfoundland, and although his master left his muddy overshoes by the steps the dog walked all over the place, with such huge paw marks it must be done again, as the Cuthberts are coming to tea on Sunday. I have not been able to see them for some time as they live at the bottom of the hill. I could walk down but must not walk up. It is so steep all the way. I expect she will wonder why I have not been. Jack told her it was because of the mud! With regard to M. G. coming into the Valley, Jack saw Mr. Malandane on Monday and told him we had a friend coming. He says the Company are starting a passenger boat of their own this year and it will be running by then as it is made to go in quite shallow water, and they will bring her up here in one of their motors. We will write to the C.V.I. representative at Golden to meet her and tell her which Hotel, if she has to stay there one night. It would not be more. I hope she does, as it will give me time to undo my boxes and get clean clothes, as the luggage does not come up at once. I have written to her c/o the C.P.R. at Halifax and St. Johns with "Please forward," so she will be sure to get a letter when she lands as well as at Golden. It sounds complicated to you but it is quite easy. There is no rush and bustle in our part of the world, and plenty of time to find out things. I am afraid I have asked for a lot of things and made you very busy, but it will save you bringing a lot when you come, and I always look beyond to that time.

I expect you enjoyed your afternoon at the Opera with Mrs. Curtis. All this sort of thing seems so far away from us except in the illustrated papers. We get various ones handed on to us which we, in turn, again hand on. Jack has "chicken fever" very badly and thinks and dreams of them all day long, with the result we had 31 eggs last week. They have all gone so I ought to get fat. We have them always for breakfast and lunch as boiled new-laid eggs take a lot of beating. I try omlettes, but they are not like the French ones! The whites always seem to cook too much but I have tasted worse! Connie's photo has not turned up yet, but I expect old Stanley is very busy and it will come some day. Fancy the Daintys selling Dulverton. Wherever will they go now? Come back to Windsor, I suppose! You and Mother must have a nice holiday time without a house during the winter, I think, and have a small round of visits. . . . I feel it will be rather a tax for you both to write every week. I love to have the letters, but I know there is Stewart as well, so if I have one letter a week I will be perfectly happy. I have written to Nellie this week, and Elsie must be the next. I wonder if you have been to West Hyde yet. It must be a difficult place to get to, I should think. When is Tottie Mason to be married? Do you ever see Dorothy, and what is her daughter like?

I have been able to get on a bit with the spare room hangings this week and have covered the chest of drawers, a packing case put on end with shelves fixed in by my "head carpenter"! He is improving very much, entre nous, as I make him do things more neatly and plane the wood. I have covered the sides quite tightly, with just a narrow frill along the top, a rod across the front, and a curtain to draw backwards and forwards on rings. I have done the bed valences and two curtains for Jack's cupboards, and this week I hope to stain the floor. I shall write to Pryce-Jones by and by for two

Japanese straw mats for the floor, also for some washstand ware, plain white if I can get it. All the china out here looks such common style in the catalogue, and is so expensive when one knows the pretty but cheap things you can get at home. I must wait until the boat runs, however, before I can get them, so M. G. must start with an enamel basin and no jug like Miss Colebrook did. The only thing I have broken much at present is glasses, so I shall get some of the kitchen variety in my next order to Eaton's. I have been baking bread today, besides polishing the floors and clearing up generally. I like Friday for this better than Saturday. Then omelette, rissoles, and open apricot tart for dinner. We have bacon for breakfast, and cheese and eggs for lunch. Our meat bill is about 7/- a week. I often wonder how much it ought to be, for two on a small income. I must ask Nellie one of these days. I made jumbles last Saturday, but if Jack smells cake it is gone in two days. Tomorrow a big soda cake must be the order of things. You would smile to see him peeping into the larder to see what there is in the way of pastry and cakes. You would think he was twelve and not a white-haired old gentleman, I tell him! He is now busy making frames to fit in all the windows and these are covered with wire gauze to keep out the mosquitoes when they arrive. Things are waking up, and I saw a squirrel today.

Must close now for bed.

Very much love and God bless you. You go about with me every day and I talk to you very often and ask your advice.

Your affectionate sister,

Daisy

HESTON,
ATHALMER, B.C.
APRIL 11TH, 1913

My dear Girl,

I can hardly believe that by now (7:30 P.M.) M. G. is tossing about on the "briney" on her way to the Columbia Valley. Just fancy if it was you! I should be nearly off my head with joy but... we still have it to look forward to if Providence wills next year. The thought is with me constantly now it is warm, and I feel how you would enjoy the freedom and the sunshine. I am sorry you will not see things in their pristine freshness and we shall not be quite so tidy, I expect, when you come, but I hope there will be added interest and you will hear M. G.'s impressions. I saw the first bluebird yesterday, and the robins as big as starlings are about again. All the birds have piping notes but they do not sing. The woodpeckers are always tapping away, and yesterday I saw a hawk hovering over Toby Creek and thought of our precious chickens. Jack must show me how to shoot. I could not bring anything down, of course, but I could frighten it away, and J. N. P.'s gun will fit M. G. better than me, anyway.

The snow has nearly all gone on the flat land and things are drying up. It is so lovely. The waterbarrel stands outside the kitchen door, which means that the door is always more or less open and that it does not freeze! We washed outside on Tuesday. Jack *insisted.* It was 70°, but round the corner was a cool breeze! When we are alone we have breakfast cups of tea made with the infuser and a piece of cake. Bread and butter for tea is not the rule out here, where we bake our own bread, cake or scones. Sunday is the only big tea day. You see, we have dinner at 6:30, directly Jack has changed, and that gives us a longer evening as we retire at 9:30. He is now very happy reading the latest *Cornhill.* I must also thank Mother for sending the *Gazette* so regularly. It is certainly the breath of one of his nostrils! Lately, in the evening while I darn, he has been reading Military biography to me, and then usually he has to read a "Bab Ballad"[1] or an old favourite from *Punch* as a nightcap! He really is a perfect baby about some things. Today he finds he has got the noise made by the hens perfectly and can puzzle them, which pleases him immensely. I am feeling very fit and well, and Jack declares I have a double chin coming. I can't see that—but many freckles! If he teases I can always retaliate by, "A little thin on top, Sir." This is a very sore point, and it is, "Am I really?" and I find him struggling with the back glass shortly afterwards.

The second lot of bulbs are out, and they are very pretty pale yellow with deep orange centres. They are narcissi, star-like but not those with big trumpets, and I love them dearly. Everyone says, "Bulbs! I never thought of them. How lovely. How do you grow them? I shall have some next year!" Anyway, Mrs. Captain Phillips (as the Canadians call me) has set the fashion. There is no such thing as a democrat, I am quite sure. They love a title and put them in where they are not. I put a few bulbs in the ground and planted them deeply. Yesterday, like a small child, I dug some up to see how they are getting on. They are just beginning to sprout and are not dead. However, about six inches down you come to frozen earth, so I suppose in some way the snow keeps them warm. I now have a large box of tulips coming on in the spare room and I hope they will flower too! What shall I do without the spare room? The stores of linen, the sewing machine, various chicken foods, the unironed washing, in fact, everything that had not a place lived in the spare room. We stained the floor this week and now the bed valances are on, and the one cupboard quite finished. I have put the front curtain on a thin brass rod, so with the rings it draws quite easily. The little washstand is mahogany, but it has a hole for the basin and I have no basin. You see, it was Kenny's and of course they used their own china in it.

---

1. Numerous poems by W. S. Gilbert.

M. G. must have an enamel basin to start, and I think I shall order a perfectly plain white one from Eaton's, like servants use in England. It is such a simple little room it will be best and safe, as the Canadian loves everything decorated with bright pink roses, etc., very common style, and of course not cheap. The white costs double what it does in England, so you must not turn up your nose. My Eaton's order goes in on May 1st as the boats will not be bringing big loads until the end of May, and we cannot get things in until then.

My groceries have lasted very well, but the next order looks such a big one — about £15 worth, I suppose. We make out the list ready for when we have enough money, as Jack has to pay the first instalment on the land on Monday. I do hope he will be able to buy the land outright when he gets his capital as then we shall always know what is left is what we have got to live on without wondering if we have got the £130 every April. Mr. Wall[2] is awfully kind at managing his affairs, but of course writes to say the property has not realized at all what it should or he thought! But never mind, we shall not starve, and I really do not mind being rather poor. It does not make a bit of difference socially to us, which is a great thing out here (this, of course, entre-nous).

Many thanks for the p.c. of Fanny's house. How perfectly charming it looks. It puts Heston in the shade, only she has no view! I picture you and Mother in something about this size. Only do have a nice holiday first, and try Newlyn or somewhere warm for the winter, and from there you can get to Penzance,[3] which is quite a nice little town, and buy cakes for tea. How really thankful you and Mother must be that those boxes of mine are really shut at last. I know it has caused you both trouble and anxiety as well as great pleasure, and I am so really and deeply thankful I have you both to help me so much. I love the sound of all you have chosen and done and soon you must picture me very busy at needlework — though of course I am always busy, but very happy even if I go to bed tired. Jack seems so perfectly happy and content I do not mind, and I always wake up fresh and ready to go again. I now wear my black coat and skirt and I have put on an elastic band, measuring 30 inches at the top and let out the two side-seams, so at present I am quite presentable. I have had to do the same to my white skirt, as I could not get into it otherwise. I wish I could have worn my blue silk, but with my Angrave hat, and your feather boa, I think I shall look quite smart! Thanks ever so much for sending the flower seeds, and the rings which are now on the curtains, as usual just what I needed. I wonder if perennials will stand the winter? I shall try, anyway. Our garden proper will not be made this year, I am afraid. I hope to fence off a small piece each side

2. Jack's maternal uncle.
3. Newlyn and Penzance: Cornish seaside towns popular with artists.

of the house, but to grow things properly the land must be ploughed up, and now that must wait until the autumn or next spring. I shall plant the seeds in the beds Jack dug last year just beyond the house, but we cannot make a garden there as in digging the hole for the pipe from the cistern to the house our plans were all upset and they will be working at it again, of course. What will happen I do not know. None of the cisterns put in were satisfactory and I do not know if we can run to one made of cement. I say, let them experiment on somebody else and if successful we can follow.

It is difficult to explain about the soil here. With water one can grow anything, without nothing is successful. Watering with a can is no use as it is fine and sinks through. The sun cracks the earth and it all evaporates, hence cultivation and running the water along in little trenches or ditches about once a week to thoroughly soak into the earth. I should love clumps of flowers on our bank as you suggest but the soil is covered everywhere with the creeper I enclose, and it is a frightful business to get it up as it has clinging roots, and of course there is very little grass. Grass is not the close croppy sort, but grows lank and coarse and very quickly, and turns brown. It is not even green yet! I shall plant nasturtiums in boxes on the verandah, I think, and try and keep them moist. At the corner there are two holes left by tree stumps, and if I fill these up shall try poppies here as they love sun and heat. The others I shall plant on the cultivated patch and they will be watered and cultivated with the vegetables. I can pick them and have them in the house and find out what really does best.

I like the sound of my cotton dresses, and also my Apsey. It sounds just right, quiet and cool! Today it was 70° on the verandah! This will not last but I do love it, although I have killed five mosquitoes! Of course, it is very cool with frost first thing, and it gets hot only about noon. This is why we cannot plant seeds until May. I believe now this letter should have been Mother's turn. I have got mixed up but I am sure you will share it and she will not mind. The basket sounds most lovely and will help me to keep tidy. That is what worries me a little, where shall I put all the extra things? But it must gradually arrange itself. "The Colonial" will have heaps to start with, and of course "it" must have flannel later on. I am sure you have sent what I shall like. I wonder how much it will cost a year? I have had two letters from M. G., quite cheerful, and I should say quite pleased and excited at coming. I am so glad as her other letters worried me a bit, but I suppose it was re the money matter. I feel it *is* great extravagance, but I think it would cost nearly as much to get a nurse from Calgary for two months if all the things were sent out from England and Jack would have had to board *somewhere*. M. G. says, "I am bringing a cradle, my dear, but it is mine, not yours, so don't get excited!" and a lot of other silly nonsense.

The enclosed photo I have sneaked out of Jack's treasures, as I thought you would like to have it. If you want to remark on it, put in an enclosure, as he does not know. I should like to have him taken out of the group and slightly enlarged. Do you think it possible? Don't have it done but let me know what you think. In all his photos in uniform his helmet or cap is always worn right over his eyes, but if you cover it up you will see *him*. We have done nearly all this group in passe-partout, and they look so nice in his room on matchboarded walls. The two guards of honour are at Gibraltar and at Portsmouth, where I tell him he looks very serious and he says, "It is not an occasion when you grin." I shall never teach him sarcasm or the meaning of it but I do tease him now and he does not mind! No-one had ever dared do that before, I am thinking.

Much love, dear old girl, to you and Mother. I am really glad you are feeling better. . . .

Ever your loving sister,

Daisy

HESTON
ATHALMER, B.C.
APRIL 26TH, 1913

My dearest Freda,

Here I am, Saturday, and no writing done at all. I have been striving all the week, but I have seemed so busy at every odd moment getting the spare room done and now it is finished. Quite à la Home Chatelaine, but it looks a very pretty little box! thanks to your good taste in cretonne, the old school room curtains at the window and little bands of cretonne to hold them back. I have tried to make it all proper and complete as if Mother were coming for inspection and I think it would pass. . . . I have made the window seat into my linen cupboard and Jack has fixed pull-down doors below each of the supports and the rug falls down in front, but I have to be very tidy. The grey box in our bedroom is a good store place too, but I have to dive down in a hurry sometimes and you can guess the result! The recess by the side of my wardrobe is fitted with shelves—four, but on these are Jack's boots and shoes. Nine pairs, I think, and two pairs of riding boots by the washstand—they are his idols! I long to put a curtain in front of the boot shelves! and shall do so some day when I have time to make bed valences, and later on I may or "it" may require the shelves and the boots must find a place in the writing room! But I must let my poor John down gently about a lot of changes I see must come. . . .

I had a letter from M. G. to say her boat was postponed, so she would not be here on May 1st. That won't make any difference to her pay as it is not her fault. I expect we shall not know the exact day of her arrival, but Jack will leave instructions at the C.V.I. offices that directly she comes, either by boat or motor, they bring her direct up here. Jack goes down on Monday and may hear more, and she can telephone from Golden to the C.V.I. offices, and we have written to the representative at Golden and asked him to look after her. Mrs. Marples' sister, coming by the other line, arrives at Golden May 1st. Mr. M. has gone to meet her and if M. G. happens to be there she may come back with them.

I am keeping very well, but of course I shall be glad to have her help. I get tired in the evening sometimes, but if I am I go to bed directly after we have washed up the dinner things and Jack comes into the bedroom for his read and smoke, so I am well looked after. I often wonder at myself, especially on Sunday when everything is spick and span, and think how clever I am to keep it all going! The housework I love and the cooking, but the kitchen work is rather the horrid part—pots and pans and stoves, and greasy pudding cloths, and bread tins to keep nice, and the tin we roast the meat in. Even ovens, I find, require cleaning. I never let Jack know or even guess that I am tired as he gets so worried and says, "I wish I had never brought you out here" or something stupid. . . .

Thanks awfully for Ryders seeds. I hope to plant the mustard and cress in boxes tomorrow, but we still get night frosts and lately lots of wind. The tulips are nearly in bloom in the two bowls, and those I planted in a bed outside are all coming up well so I feel very happy. The mauve anemones I told you of last year are now springing up everywhere. The four silver vases and the little bowl with a cock-a-doodle are on the table full. It is lovely to have flowers again, though everyone has admired the lavender I have had all the winter, thanks to you again. Miss Colebrook commented on the green ninon curtains the other day and said "Of course your kind sister in England must have bought the stuff and sent it to you." You are known as my kind sister! (I have curried eggs to cook for dinner so will return to you later!)

Last Sunday we set out at 12 o'clock and took our lunch with us—hard boiled eggs, bread and butter and cake—and sat down on a log in the sunshine and were quite warm. I live in my black and had on my big hat with royal blue bow, white silk shirt and collar outside coat and blue tie. Of course, the skirt gets very spotted and dusty but I clean it up with ammonia occasionally. When you come, khaki drill is the best for everyday hard wear, remember! While at lunch Mr. Bennett and Miss Colebrook passed on the road, riding, but did not see us. He was leading her and she rides quite well. If only Amelia comes I feel I shall be doing the same next year. Jack is always looking forward to next year and promises me if all is well I shall ride then and I can go about with him more again. He does not like stride riding very much so I shall begin "side" anyway. Perhaps you will learn too and it would do the both of us good. We then went on to Marples and Molly came running down to meet us, a vision in pale blue satin Liberty dress, very short, and pale blue satin knickers to match, and a pale blue silk hat with a wreath of daisies round! English clothes are worn on Sunday out here. Mr. and Mrs. were out, had gone to "Jim Johnson's" where we went last summer, but "Nan" asked us to stay to tea. I went inside, indulged in the chesterfield and Nan talked to me and gave me lots of good advice and was very kind. She is a sweet woman. The two boys took Jack to show him their new chicken house, and the motor pump which they have to pump their water. They have a well as they are near the lake, and of course have bathroom and W.C. in the house. Molly said, "I am not to call him Jack any more, only Capt. Phillips!" We had tea on the verandah, Jack cutting bread and butter for the family like a man of 50, and then we walked slowly back — and as usual I rested when we got in! . . .

With regard to my clothes, never think I shall not approve. I am sure you know what is nice as well as I do, and you must be my fashion guide as I am out of it now. I believe if my new clothes are *very* big I shall have to take them in! but I expect I shall soon fit them. I told Jack my new clothes were very big and he looked grave and wondered if I could wear two pair of corsets to fill them out! This is entre nous, but he is a frightful fad about women's dress and also figures! Who would have thought it. "Mrs. Wilson (wife of one of his brother officers) always wore white, and when she was like you I used to go to tea on Sunday and she always looked very nice, although expecting." But I guess Mrs. Wilson did not do her own washing. This, of course, entre nous to amuse you. . . .

I am so glad to hear Mother is better. I hope it was not the worry of my box. You will both be better when you can get away now, I am sure. . . . I can see it would be nice for you to be in touch with Gilbert, and if you keep chickens, we can have egg laying competitions! Our hens are doing very well, I think. One day this week 6 eggs from 7 hens, and the other days 5 is not bad for a start. I do hope Gilbert will pass his exam this time as otherwise it will be bad for him finally, but he is hopeful. Everyone writes and says Connie is a dear and is so sweet and Stanley is a lucky man, which is nice to hear. I feel we must come to some arrangement about postage and your railway and bus fares to London on our behalf! "We are poor but we are honest," and "honest John" is worried about his sister-in-law's pocket. How much will honestly cover your railway and bus fares lately, 15/ or £1? Tell me, and what about postage? Have you heard anything of the Rustons or Walkers lately. Grace wrote and told me they had let Denham Lodge but were living in Ealing still. I suppose I must write to Aunt Mary Wall soon and tell her of the coming event. . . . Am glad there is good news of old Stewart. I must write him again soon. Had a letter from Auntie Kate, which was very kind. I wish I had more time to write, but I like to give all my spare moments to you and Mother.

Please give much love to Stanley, and Connie, and Dandy, and remember me to all my old "pals," and with much for yourself and Mother.

Always your affect: sister.

Daisy

My dearest Freda,

My last told you of M. G.'s safe arrival on Sunday afternoon. We gave her a good tea, then a hot bath, and put her to bed as she had a bad cold. Monday her cold was so bad I kept her in bed all day as I know how glad one is to rest after the journey. Still, it was nice to feel she was in the house. Tuesday, washing day, her cough was bad so we told her to stay in bed and Jack helped me with the washing. In the middle M. G. turned up but felt very weak, so she sat in a chair in the sun and enjoyed the air and has gradually revived, and todays seems quite herself. I heard you were as "smart as paint" when you saw her off. I eagerly asked for every detail of you and Mother. It is so nice to hear all about you from one who has seen you so recently. I think M. G. will fit in very nicely indeed and I am so glad to see that Jack seems to like her and thinks she is *not* like Miss Colebrook! Of course, her boxes have not come up yet but the river is open now so I expect they will not be long.

Today we thoroughly cleaned the house and Ronuked the floors, then M. G. made shortbread for tea while I dusted, after lunch cleared up the kitchen and then each had three-quarters of an hour in our beds. Tea at 3:15 on the verandah, then down to the barn to pack away my coat and skirts, and after peeling potatoes we went for a walk to the box! On our way back a sharp shower wetted us through so now M. G. has on a white blouse of mine, muslin collar and black and white bow and looks very nice. The black rather suits her and the way she does her hair looks charming. This week Jack is back on the land. The disc and harrow have been at work and next week we shall plant the "small fruits" which came yesterday and are now buried to keep them fresh. Then I expect we shall be planting potatoes next week, which will take two days. We are planting not ploughing in this year, but M. G. seems "game" for anything, and I think likes the place and says I am looking very fit and well. At present my arms and legs are eaten up by mosquitoes, which have been about again the last day or two. I thought they would have left me alone this year, but I suppose my flesh is still tender, although my arms have developed *such* muscles! We made bread today which I am glad to say was a great success, as I know she would be critical. I find she does not talk but quietly does things, which is a great relief. Even to eat cake someone else has made is a great treat! I am working with her all the time just now but when the packing cases come I shall have to sew hard, and then she will be able to carry on by herself with numerous jobs. Our patient sitting hen is still sitting and just comes off the eggs each day to feed, but I hope the heavy blasting that has been going on near us will not upset the results of all her patience. Several new settlers have come into the Valley, we hear. They are not near us but in the direction of the Poetts and Captain White. Dr. Barber has bought land *near* us but he is not here yet and may not be coming this year. The pink tulips are now out in the china bowl and look so pretty on the table and the mauve anemones are springing up once more, so we have flowers and I do love them so. I have sown a box of mustard and cress too, and some cabbage and celery seed, and they are on the verandah. Soon, I think next week, we shall be planting the vegetable garden.

Sunday. Today Jack set off to walk to Windermere at nine o'clock (it is nine miles) to see a man about a horse! Sounds nice, doesn't it? So M. G. and I took our lunch out and walked to where we had a good view of the Lake and took the glasses. She cannot walk far yet as she has no boots, but luckily can wear my snow boots! When we got back we had just changed and got the kitchen fire going when Mr. Hanley turned up (the man who had charge of the nursery last year). So we had tea and did not wait for Jack, who has just turned up after his long walk. He has seen a horse but not bought it as he is to see two others on Tuesday. Mr. Hanley says he has news of the fruit trees and they will be here this week, so things progress. . . .

It was good of you to open Jack's box and send the mosquito curtain as it will be useful if we sleep out. My arms and legs are badly bitten again this spring and have come up in little blisters, which shows my flesh is tender although I have developed muscle. M. G. does not think me the slightest bit Colonial, and I have not the faintest accent! I am glad your paper was such a success and so thoroughly appreciated within the Castle precincts! I was quite sure it would be the best of the series. . . .

Thank Mother for the Salvation Army pamphlet. It is most interesting and may be helpful. We must just wait and see about Amelia. If she does not come I shall be able to manage somehow, I am sure. I am writing to Calgary this mail for a "washing basket." The Daintys seem to be doing things in their own funny way as usual, but Oxford and Cambridge Terrace does not sound exciting, to say the least. I wonder who will be the new Vicar of Windsor, and who the new Dean? M. G. seems to have made lots of friends on the boat and quite enjoyed her journey. Won't it be lovely when those packing cases come and I can begin work! In the meantime, I am working her in to my ways in the house. I have made up the yellow and blue Dutch stuff into cushions and tablecloths for the verandah, and they look very fine. Of course they will fade but that cannot be helped. My pink tulips look so sweet in their bowl. I must close as it is supper time.

With ever so much love from us both.

Always your affectionate sister,

Daisy

HESTON,
ATHALMER, B.C.,
THURSDAY
[ABOUT MID-MAY, 1913]

My dearest Freda,

A grilling afternoon, but will start a line to you while M. G. sits on the step and does her crotchet! I wrote last on Sunday morning. Well, in the afternoon Jack had not returned so in spite of the heat M. G. and I walked up to the Sinclairs to tea. I say up because their little white house is on a good rise and I feel every inch of uphill nowadays. They were reclining on the verandah and gave us a very cordial welcome. Mrs. Sinclair is a very warm-hearted genial soul and I was given the biggest armchair and lots of cushions and very kindly looked after. It really was a treat as I make a practice of never coddling myself. M. G. is good and practical but never errs on the side of sympathy, which of course is a splendid thing, I know. Why should I have sympathy?, I am told, I am not ill! Nor am I. But do you know, I sometimes look forward to September and breakfast in bed! Miss Sinclair, an adopted daughter, is a very pretty girl, tall and very goodlooking. She does not seem to go about much, but I take it she had a nervous breakdown before she came out. She had a rest-cure and the doctor ordered an outdoor life. She has over 200 chickens and lots of little houses, beautifully arranged, and looks after them herself and spends all day at the work. She is like Lily Thruscott only younger, and in a pretty tussore dress[1] and big milkmaid leghorn hat I thought you would like to paint her!

On Wednesday afternoon Miss Phillips came to tea. She is Mrs. Pope's sister and lives with them, and I think does most of the work. Mrs. Pope is rather pretty, and I think perhaps a little spoilt by her husband who is a good bit older than she is. Miss Phillips was a nurse in Bombay and gave up work to come out here and help as her sister was not very strong! M. G. got on well, I suppose being "brother brushes," and she likes any excuse to walk over there of an evening. I expect she gets tired of Jack and me. We let her have the horse whenever possible and on the whole she goes out a good deal. Mrs. Pope brought me over some butter they had made it was most delicious. They have only a small hand-churn, but they keep a cow which Kenneth, the son of sixteen, milks and looks after. They have a pony called Dick. They could not make pastry. Mrs. Pope said it was always tough. M. G. could not when she came but I taught her and now she is very proud of the accomplishment. So she asked might she go over and give Mrs. Pope a lesson. I said, Yes, certainly. So M. G. started off at nine o'clock and came back to lunch at 12:15, quite pleased with herself. She rested from 1:30 to four o'clock in her room. I spent the morning having a good hustle and get-

---

1. A coarse brown silk made in India.

ting rid of the dust. M. G. thinks B.C. folk too particular, I know, but High River form would not suit the Benches I can see. She always keeps her person so nice but her bedroom is not our style, I mean Mother's, yours and mine. It rather surprises me, but you never know a person until they live with you. We get on very well but she is always surprising me in various ways of not being particular. Also, she is not nearly the mountain of strength I thought her, but she is a great comfort if only she would not break things. I do hope Amelia will not be heavy-handed. I see now that doing without help is cheap in many ways. I suppose Jack and I were specially careful owing to our small income and knowing we could not replace. But don't mention this. It makes a difference when things are one's own, Mother will quite agree. We had high tea at five, as in the heat of the afternoon I cannot do much but rest, and the cabbages wanted transplanting badly. After washing up Jack and I went down to the patch and worked until eight o'clock and M. G. wrote letters on the verandah. By this you will see she is not overworked. If she thinks she has too much she does it but does not speak to me, which is more than I can stand! This has only happened twice, but never again (quite entre nous)! Madelaine Turnor rode over in the evening to see us. She has just learned to ride and M. G. went out with her one evening. She came to the patch with M. G. and watched us work and talked. She is such a nice child and getting so capable.

Mr. Horsley came over later to fetch her home (he was in the Company garden last year but now has work near the Turnors). He is the nice Irishman. He looked over the patch and seemed to say all was going well. He showed us how to fertilize the marrow blossoms as there are no bees here yet and they are just in bud. The apple trees have nearly all budded, and Jack has planted a cover crop of clover underneath which is about an inch high. It helps to keep the roots warm during the snow and will grow after the snow melts. We shall hope to sell it next year. The oats and wheat are doing very well now as we had two terrific thunderstorms last week, both in the night, and now the hot sun acts like magic. The potatoes look well and are all in flower. Jack has hoed them twice and is now busy cultivating to conserve the moisture. Lettuce, cabbage, beetroot, and spinach all doing well and we have one or other every day. It is lovely, I can tell you, but we are three weeks late, I think. Never mind, next year I hope I shall be fit and well and able to do my share. I am afraid I love the outside work too well in summer, but then I love my house too and cannot bear to let things go. They will soon get shabby, I can see, and I cannot allow that until you have been!

My dear girl, I love the sketch Mother sent for my birthday, and it makes me feel happy to see your fingers have not lost their cunning. Go on and prosper in the future, after having done your duty so nobly and splendidly. I do feel so proud of you, when I know so well that the last year you have given up so much of your own inclination and desires, but it will have its reward, I am sure. Lately, when I have felt so handicapped and doing my work so slowly and not being able to bustle about, *you* have been such a huge help and I have felt you at times tugging me along. I am so interested in the sketch of Mother's hat and know she looked very nice in it, and now I wait to know what yours was like. I know the dress from the photograph. I think you have done splendidly about Amelia and think you have been very economical. I expect the shopping was trying to the patience as well as amusing (very) in part, I take it. Does she strike you as being fairly sensible and of some use as a baby-minder and a washer-up of plates and dishes and suchlike jobs? Jack has visions of her feeding chickens! Aunt Mary Wall writes and says she does not think she will be of much use, but she does not know our limitations or realize what a second pair of hands means, I am sure! We shall make arrangements for her to come on from Golden, but I hope we shall know the name of her boat. I take it she arrives about the 10th of September. I have written her a letter of instructions and told her to go to Golden Post Office to find further instructions on arriving, but I don't expect she will get excited. How about her outfit? Perhaps you were expecting further instructions from me, but I thought her coming was uncertain and our letters might cross. You know how worried I was when letters crossed from Gibraltar, so it was fairest and kindest to leave it to you to do your best. Don't worry about every penny of accounts. We are both so grateful to you and trust you utterly. I only hope I did not hinder instead of help you by not sending more instructions.

I am so glad you had Dollie and Winnie down to lunch and I take it their Mother's huff has blown over by leaving it alone—"silence is golden"![2] The fur toque sounds very "magnifique" but just the thing, I should say, and Amelia will fancy herself no end. I can always order things that will do for her from Eaton's or Pryce-Jones, but their baby things are very common. It is good of you to make the "trousers" but, mind you, I will pay you for all the work you do for E. J.[3] Jack woke this morning and said, "I like Sheila for a name." This is the latest, but I expect it will change again. Don't think I am slighting family names, but I want them all! M. G. is just off to Church with the Youngs to the monthly service, but my "good man" stays at home with his missus. . . . I think the photo will amuse and interest you.[4] Taken by Mr. Tazen, the Bank Manager when he came to lunch on Sunday, just after M. G. arrived. Jack looks terrible and so cross, the result of Miss Colebrook's presence! He absolutely hated her. She had just ridden up. M. G.'s hat is my old mushroom with a green band I had trimmed for the occasion,

2. Dollie and Winnie were Jack's cousins, daughters of Aunt Alice Ruston who had been particularly annoyed about his secret wedding.
3. Elizabeth John, possible names for the baby.
4. See fifth page of photo section. M. G. is on the left; Miss Colebrook on the right.

and she has on one of my blouses. The green curtain shows on the door, but you cannot see the curtains. The white is reflected light only. I am sorry the doors and windows were shut but it was a windy day. I think Amelia ought to have £2 to come from Golden here, to be quite safe.

Much love, dear old girl, to you and Mother.

Your affectionate sister,

Daisy

HESTON,
ATHALMER, B.C.
SUNDAY, JUNE 8TH, 1913

My dear Girl,

Sunday morning, 10:30. Have just finished work, dusted, cleared up the kitchen, put up clean towels and kitchen cloths, and all looks in apple-pie order for one day only, but that makes Sunday so nice and I really feel proud of my little house! M. G. is sitting outside the kitchen door cleaning the knives! This job is only done once a week. I have just been cutting Jack's hair and now, while he writes to Stewart, I am starting a line to you. I am afraid lately letters have been rather irregular but it all depends when Jack can go down to the post and I very often have short notice, so please excuse if they are scrappy. My thoughts are constantly with you and you are woven into so much that I am doing as your fingers seem everywhere, in all the little things I have about me. I had not undone the two parcels inside "Elizabeth John's" basket until yesterday and there I found the little blue windmill, so now that is on the dresser shelf among the brass. I am constantly finding things like this and cannot think how you thought of it all. The carpet binding is just what I wanted and cannot get here for odd matting for the kitchen. All the many little things of this kind mean far more than things that cost heaps of money. I expect a further account will come later as I have not had the bill for heaps of things. I think all the baby things are lovely and in such splendid condition. I never should have had time to make them, and all new ones would have cost such an immense deal.

You will hear from M. G. some day what a busy life mine is, continually getting up to tend the kitchen fire or put something on to boil. The only real time for straightforward sewing is from 7:30 to 9:00 in the evening when the day's work is done. I always rest from 2:00 to 3:15, and so does M. G. I believe, entre nous, that she gets quite as tired as I do, and she does not work any harder. I am usually up in the morning five or ten minutes before her if I can be, and begin to set breakfast. For the last month I have felt that I can give in a little and she will not feel I am under-paying her. I heard the other day that what she is having here is the same as the nurse has in the hospital, and *she* has all the work to do, cooking, tending patients, and cleaning. Do tell me what you think her impressions really are from her letters. She has no expenses, anyway, and I feel she ought to make £50 quite clear. She has not told me anything about expenses on the journey. She hides herself behind that funny manner of hers and "fences"! Jack asked her what her meals cost on the train and she said she did not know, but from what I gather she was in with "a party" of folk and a good many men, and she was "treated," so I should be interested to know. I like her and she is very willing to try and cook. She saves me, of course, doing all the heavy washing and she irons very nicely. I keep on thinking I could not have managed without somebody. The water is in the ditch not many hundred yards away. She and Jack fetch the day's supply every morning in baths and pails, and it is hot, heavy work. The men are now "tinkering" with the cistern and are going to line it with tar paper! The fact is they are experimenting on us poor settlers and nobody knows much about it all, but I hope we shall have water stored somehow before next winter. In summer it does not matter and everything runs along much more easily.

On Wednesday M. G. and I went to call on the Popes of "Pope and Sinclair", the people (Scottish) who have bought such a large tract of land (Lots 50, 51, 52, 25, and 26 on the map). They are not very far off, only thirty minutes' walk. I wore my blue alpaca and it is very cool and comfortable. Certainly, the coat is on the large side but it hangs well so I shall not alter it and I look quite respectable in it. My black hat with royal blue bow and sunshade made me look "toute complete." Mr. Pope has lived in India many years, he told us. He has one son, a soldier out there, and here one boy about fifteen, by his second wife. She is much younger than he is, very quiet but very nice, I think, with black wavy hair and blue eyes, butcher blue crepe blouse and linen skirt. Her sister (Miss Phillips), who is living with them, evidently does all the hard work and looks much stronger than Mrs. Pope. The house is quite large, a big drawing room, a small dining room (only for meals), entrance hall, passages, all with linoleum. Drawing room, polished floor and rugs. A staircase, quite broad and pretty, five bedrooms, a bathroom upstairs and lots of cupboards. But the stairs and passages and landings I am sure will make a lot of extra work. I think they are already overwhelmed with the work, the washing and baking. But they have been preparing to come out for two years, going to domestic schools and all sorts of things. They have moved straight into a comfortable house with hot and cold water supply and baths and conveniences all there, so they are not pioneers. I expect their income for a month would keep us for a year, but I would rather have our house any day. They have rough plaster walls, which I love. They do not like them as they brought wallpaper and it will not stick on the walls. I believe they are very musical, but certainly *not* artistic, and they have a lovely piano. They are coming back to tea with us next Thursday! I told them we live in a box compared to them. I must go and call on the Sinclairs next week while I can, I think. There is a Mr. and Mrs., and a Miss who is going in largely for poultry. I hope "Miss" is a nice girl as I don't want always to meet married women, though I expect they all think me a horrible "kid."

On Thursday M. G. walked down to Athalmer with Jack for the first time and they came back in a "rig." Jack has bought one! A frightful extravagance this year, I feel, but he has got tired already of going about alone and does not like my being shut up here, he says. I am too tired to walk far after my day's work and I must sit and sew. A rig is like an American trotting buggy, a seat for two, and on four wheels, very wide apart so very safe. As the roads are narrow we often have to drive onto the side and make room for wagons. I went for a drive with Jack from 7:15 to 9:00 last night and, my dear girl, it was lovely to sit and rest in the air. We drove round by Captain White's, and I had not been there since there was deep snow. There are several new settlers in that part and we spoke to one man sitting at his tent door mending his socks, a Mr. Edgell.[1] His wife and five children come out in July! He said he had lived in the Transvaal a good many years.

The baby chicks grow and thrive. Mother hen trots them round the verandah for inspection and puts them up there in the afternoon, out of the sun and out of the way of hawks! We have had several about this week, and the hens run to cover and squeak and squawk long before we notice the hawk. Yesterday morning, about 5:30, the old hen in the coop was frightfully distressed, clucking away and nearly pushing her body through the bars. Jack rushed out and I followed in night attire. No chicks to be seen. I finally found them, very frightened, huddled up together *under the kitchen table,* having lost Mother. The hens are always coming round the kitchen door for water and crumbs. Tarboosh[2] [the horse] is always hanging round the door too, trying to drink out of our waterbarrels instead of the ditch! Jack spoils all the animals. He found a toad outside the kitchen door this morning and wasted some time over that! I am getting on famously with the basket and hope to finish it this week, when I will describe it to you. The doctor arrived on Thursday afternoon on his motorbike and made M. G.'s acquaintance. He is going to England in the autumn to take his English degree so will be glad if "E. J." does not keep him waiting long, I expect. He stayed and had tea and made a very few enquiries. I suppose he thought I was in good hands! Don't worry about

1. The Edgells, an English family, had two girls and four boys. The two younger boys would long remain in the Windermere Valley.
2. The name "tarboosh" refers to the fez-type headgear worn by officers and men of the King's African Rifles.

Amelia. I am so sorry Jack wrote to you about it. Just now you must have so much to do, old girl, and don't be out of pocket, whatever you do. Just let me know railway fares expended for me in any way.

No time for more. So sorry.

Goodbye until next week.

> Much love,
>
> *Daisy*

ATHALMER, B.C.

14 JUNE 13

Dear Freda,

Daisy and I entirely agree with all you have done and suggest doing towards Amelia's coming out here. It is a busy time for you and Amelia's arrangements don't lighten your work so I am very much obliged to you for all the trouble you are taking for us. I'm sure I shall agree with all you do and offer only a couple of ideas (1) That Amelia should spend the evening before her departure at the Wembley Hostel to be under the B.W.E.A.[1] from the earliest time. (2) You will give her what money they say she needs for the journey with a little over. The only difficulty is from Golden here. The railway may be running a part of the way then so I cannot say for certain that she will change to a boat there. My idea, if you would let me know the date of arrival at Golden, would be to ask some woman there to meet and look after Amelia and to put her onto the boat. At that particular time my presence here is imperative. But unless I hear from you that the B.W.E.A. make all arrangements even at Golden, I shall consider that that point is where I make and continue the arrangements for her journey. We met a girl yesterday who had come out by the B.W.E.A. and who was very pleased with all they had done. With such complete arrangements it is useless for me to suggest anything. I am enclosing a cheque for twenty-five pounds (£25) for her passage and expenses. Daisy will be writing to you about Amelia's outfit and also writing to Amelia herself about it.

> Yours sincerely,
>
> *J. N. Phillips*

---

1. British Women's Emigration Association.

HESTON,
ATHALMER, B.C.
JUNE 25TH, 1913

My dearest Freda,

You are so awfully good and kind to your little sister, I hardly know where to begin, but Oh! the sweet little vests were simply perfect and lovely in my eyes, and I do thank you ever so much for them. M. G. says four will be plenty to begin with. Also the Weldon baby fashions are most interesting, and I can write for any patterns I need. . . . I think Trebalco, the soft white cotton, mercerised with pin spot, that one gets at D. H. Evans, would be splendid for first plain dresses with yokes, and smock collars with French knots on. They would be soft and easy to wash, and perhaps have one best frock. Elsie said she would send me two petticoats for "short coating," and I have all I shall want of "long" in every way, and these will be very acceptable. I feel over and over again I cannot thank you and Mother enough for all your thought and trouble. I could never have made the things myself. I will send you a cheque soon for a small amount to buy any small things and when you go to Painswick I shall write and worry Nelly for a bit, or Daisy Mac. I feel so much time you could otherwise spend on your work has been taken up by me and "us," but I do want you so badly to take up your work again and prosper. It will be a *real* grief to me if you don't and I shall save every penny I can to help you to come out here some day. Such a lot seems to have come all at once but it is much easier to do without than ever I thought, and with Jack here and you and Mother at home, I feel I am more than rich.

I do feel it is a big task just now for you to tackle Amelia, and I feel it is most unselfish of you and that you are doing it to help me. I feel I shall never be able to do anything to repay you but if ever the opportunity comes you know you can count on me. I think you have carried it all through *splendidly* and I feel the only way is to leave it to you to make the arrangements. It means giving you a lot of worry, but suggesting too many things from this side would complicate things and make it more difficult. Amelia's wardrobe seems tidy, and she had better bring these things with her to start with. I can buy things in Canada suitable for her at Eaton's, and she can make some things here too. A woollen hood, something like mine to come over the ears, will be necessary. A small felt hat and a burnt straw of some sort for the summer too. A cheap motor veil for the boat too, and, if you have not already suggested these, snow boots and felt slippers. I can get them at Eaton's—don't alter if you have bought those already! Amelia's luggage must be limited, but Jack is willing to pay excess for necessary things. He says a lot extra can come for ten shillings, he thinks, but anything I want had better be posted, I think, longcloth can always be posted in 3 or 4 yard lengths without duty! Let Amelia bring her own. She asks about her sewing machine (says it is not bulky). If not too heavy Jack says he will pay half. She also asks if she can bring her spirit lamp to make early tea! Yes, if she likes. Perhaps Mrs. P. will then get a cup too! You book her passage and arrange for her to go to the Hostel the night before, and I take it they will see her through to Golden and we must arrange from there. I will send her a letter to pin in her corsets, I think, in case she gets lost! Does she strike you as fairly clear and level-headed? I am only expecting her to be a "baby-minder," and then I shall only have to work as hard as I do now or have done up to now. M. G. and I keep on the go pretty well all day. I do hope she is happy. At times it is difficult to say but I think she is worried about her future. There is no work going for her about here, I fear. The nurse at Wilmer Hospital gets the same money as we are paying M. G. She has all the nursing, cooking, and cleaning to do, but M. G. says she got $80 when out here before! I don't believe it, and gradually it comes out what a really rough time she had at the Hansens — only I suppose "the man" gilded things for her then.[1] She is going to stay with friends near Calgary on her way back home.

I am so sorry to hear about Jennie's engagement being off. Dorrie Durant wrote the other day and sent me such a social letter and her photo. She is a kind little soul. Also, so sorry to hear about the vicar. My letters are always a rush so have not much time to touch on home letter news but am so deeply interested in all. Things look a bit more cheerful for old Stewart. Will you please thank Jack Dainty ever so much. I will write and thank him as soon as I have a second. I have nearly finished the washing basket, an ordinary size one like we use at home — $1.15 = 7/6d. — isn't it wicked? I have lined it with the blue (drawn up). The muslin looks splendid now it is got up, double frill all round and a double frill of muslin edged with lace on the edge, pale blue handles and little bows of blue ribbon along the edge. I am sure you would approve. The basket is finished too, so now I must rearrange drawers and packing cases, and turn six garments!

Jack and I drove over to the Poetts on Sunday. M. G. walked and met us halfway and we had open-air lunch. En route we called on Captain White as I heard the Chinaman had departed, and took him a large cake for which he seemed very grateful. Also, we hear that the Colebrook-Bennett engagement is "off." I think it must be true, and I am afraid it is her fault if so. She was not content with one man. Jack can't bear her anyway and gives her no pity! Mrs. Poett and the General were as usual very kind. They have not sold Westlake yet, though there is someone after it. Mr. Robinson and two boys turned up before we left. Miss Kitchener is staying with him for the summer. They had mislaid the wedding snapshots so we did not see what *I*

---

1. Molly Gleave had worked on a farm near High River, Alberta. The social details of her time there are unknown.

looked like! Today the Sinclairs have been to tea, very nice—very rich, I presume—but quite Scottish and homely, and very kind. I went to call last week. I have not seen their adopted daughter yet. She is going in for chickens and was too busy to come. She has had a nervous breakdown and been ordered an open-air life. Mr. Sinclair is a lawyer from Edinburgh, I think I told you. Middle-aged. The Poetts lent us a side-saddle so M. G. went for a ride on Tarboosh last night in her proper habit. She has been several times but has had to wear knickers, puttees, and my burberry. It looks quite nice but she does not care to go on the road in this costume. I have been thinning turnips this afternoon sitting on the ground on a sack! This is for the second time of asking, and boiled they are most delicious, our first green vegetable since Christmas Day! I do not think M. G. is really fond of gardening, but she is just splendid at washing and ironing and it is there I need the most help.

I wondered if Gilbert would be best man. He *will* feel important. I am glad I know the church and always thought it looked rather pretty and almost countrified for London.

Much love, dear old girl, from

Your affectionate sister,

Daisy

HESTON,
ATHALMER, B.C.
MONDAY, AUGUST 11TH, 1913

My dear Girl,

Awfully late with my letter this week. I seem to have been hindered all the week from writing so this really will be a short letter. I am simply delighted with the "trouserettes." You must have worked hard to get them done and they are awfully nice. Thank you ever so much. Also for the robe, which I treasure and admire very much indeed, tell Mother, and I heave a sigh when I see the amount of work she put into it and wonder however she managed to find time in the days when she only kept one servant and Stanley was a baby too. I was so interested in hearing all about *the* wedding. It must have gone off very well indeed, I think. Daisy Mac wrote me such a nice letter and told me all about it from her point of view. *You* looked very nice indeed and so did Mother, Connie very sweet, and Nellie she specially mentioned as looking very striking, and Daisy evidently admired her. The happy pair really must have had some very nice presents and the presentations must be very gratifying to Stanley and Connie. I am sure they will be happy, and after a little I expect you and Mother will feel you have done the right thing in not taking a house straight away. I am sure you will both enjoy the freedom after your busy time. I have tried to picture that last week at "4 High" with all the rooms turned upside down, and cannot possibly imagine it!

Last Sunday, I think I told you, we were to tea with Captain and Mrs. Houlgrave. She is quite a girl and a very nice little thing, but too far off for me to see much of her. Then did I tell you Mr. Moore came to see us—the C.P.R. man who brought out our "land" party last year? He saw your photo on the mantlepiece and said he had seen you at the London office with Mother (see what comes of having a telling face!), and if ever you come out he has promised to look after you! A most amusing letter from Amelia this week. She is looking forward to coming, full of your kindness to her, says her teeth look lovely, so perhaps she will "get off" [be married off] after all and we shall then regret the teeth!! She says her health is better, she is very fond of children, but the baby must not be born on a Thursday or a Saturday if I can possibly help it![1] On Thursday evening Madeline Turnor rode over and brought me some celery plants from Mr. Harley. We have put them in but their survival all depends on how soon the winter comes. The same evening while we were on "the patch" planting them, Mrs. and Miss Sinclair walked over. The first time Miss had been here. She admired your lithograph of Mother and the Japanese prints. She evidently does portrait painting herself, though just now it is given up for chicken farming. It takes all her time as she is getting new houses started before winter. She is very chic, and had on a pepper-coloured tweed skirt with bone buttons all the way down, back and front, the bottom three or four undone to show a very swagger plaid silk underskirt. The skirt was not tight, cut rather to spring out at the bottom, and the effect was quite charming—the very latest, I suppose. She always wears drab and browns, and tussore. She is fair, has lovely fair hair, and is "drab" all over but the effect is charming! They brought some lovely Scotch shortbread and a quart bottle of milk. People are most awfully kind. Mr. and Mrs. Marples and Miss Le Mere drove over to here yesterday afternoon. They had been to a little dance at Mrs. Poett's on Saturday night, given in honour of Mrs. Jefferson (Phyllis) who is here on a visit, and were rather tired in consequence. They admired Mother's basket very much and asked to see my various treasures. I am sure Mrs. Marples will be the one to advise me on baby matters. Molly is not very old, and she has *lent* me three lovely flannels that were Molly's so as to save the washing,

---

1. Monday's child is fair of face,
   Tuesday's child is full of grace,
   Wednesday's child is full of woe,
   Thursday's child has far to go,
   Friday's child is loving and giving,
   Saturday's child works hard for a living,
   But the child that is born on the Sabbath Day
   Is bonny and bright and good and gay.

she says. She is going to lend me her box bed for Amelia too, which will be splendid as M. G. can then keep her room quite to herself, and she told me if I worry about the house while I am ill, she admired it so much that she will come over and clean it herself before I get up! She will not have to, I am sure, as I know Jack will do it for me. M. G. was out as she had an appointment with Dr. Hannington at Wilmer. Mrs. Marples and her sister I can see don't like M. G. They always say, "Very nice but *very* hard, isn't she?" And other folks have made the same remark! I am sorry, but of course she has been everywhere with us and I think people have been very kind to her. She cannot be more anxious for the "event" to take place than I am, I tell her, but she has not many more weeks to wait now. I think her talk with the doctor has decided her not to take Wilmer Hospital for six months until his return. Invermere Hospital will be ready in the spring, but at present it will be run with a cook and a nurse, and the doctor thinks $50 very good pay. M. G. will not take less than $80, but I think nurses are not so highly paid in B.C. as in Alberta in the wilds, where they are more scarce. I felt I could not advise her, as if she stayed it would save us £30 but if it turned out badly she might blame us. So I expect she will come home after two visits near High River, and she talks of going home via Chicago to see friends, which I think will soon swallow up her savings! She has not said anything to Jack about Mother's money at present, but we will wait until she draws her next payment.

We actually sold some vegetables the other day, 5 cents each for some big lettuces, 2 lbs. of wax-pod beans (like yellow French beans) for 50 cents, and 1½ lbs. peas for 30 cents, turnips, too, for 5 cents per lb. — I think about $2 worth altogether. Jack hates selling. He likes to give, but Mrs. P. did it. Everyone else does. We have given away a lot to the Popes, and I have put this in a box to buy materials for "Elizabeth John"! We called to see Mr. Parham at the Experimental Farm. I went in and he recognized me at once. I should not have known him. He is just married and he and his missus are camping out, so I have asked them up to tea next Sunday. He says it is nine years ago and I have not altered the slightest little bit. He kept on saying this, which very much amused Jack! He has been fruit farming and poultry farming out here for eight years, and now has this Government job, which will be a well-paid one, I expect.

Our winter supplies have just come from Eaton's, so I have got them put away in good time. With regard to Jack's Uganda box, he says the plush curtain is not worth keeping so it can be given away to some poor person, also the cartridges. Jack says they are no good now, but do not give them to Price! The only safe thing is to take them down to the river and throw them in yourself. I am glad you are sending the daggers by Amelia![2] Of course,

---

2. Jack's collection of African daggers.

the curtain and cartridges will wait until your next visit to Windsor but I may as well give you instructions now while I remember. The portrait we should certainly like to have out some day, so be sure you keep it to remind Jack of the days when his hair was not so gray and thin on top! . . . Your portrait, my dear girl, gives me a shock. I really shall not know you when we meet. If you only knew how many times your brother-in-law says, "When Freda comes"! I know it would please you as it does me. Do not comment on what I say of M. G. but you will be interested to know that at present, 8 P.M., she is crotcheting a teacloth that I think is going to High River with her! Jack is itching to read *Brer Rabbit* aloud — he is now reading it to himself. I have finished the mattress for the "washing-basket" today, and I am using an old pillowcase of Jack's as its cover. I shall be so glad when these next few weeks are over. The days seem so long but I am thankful I have kept so well. I shall never have a fuss made of me again until you come, I can see. M. G. has no sympathy with small complaints, she says, so they are kept in the background. A good thing too, as when Mrs. Marples made me sit in the easy chair on Sunday and put a cushion at my back, the tears came and I really felt homesick for five minutes. Everyone is awfully sweet and kind to me and I know will help me after, so the winter will not be a thing to dread.

Ever so much love to you both.

Your affectionate sister,

Daisy

[The letters sent between 25 June 1913 and February 1914 have not been preserved. During this time Elizabeth was born, Molly Gleave returned to England, and Amelia Harris came out to replace her.]

HESTON,
ATHALMER, B.C.
FEBRUARY 3RD, 1914

My dear Girl,

It was good of you to write re your little sister's clothes. I did not intend to have anything, but you set the ball rolling and so the enclosed list will please you. Jack thinks Burberry is *the* place for a rough hat and says anything up to £2.10.0. as I shall not have another hat for at least a year, so will you go and prospect for me? Then Jack says I *must* have a "skiing" skirt and knickers. Dickens & Jones advertise them in the *Pictorial,* but of course I have given away all the numbers with that special advertisement. Jack thinks in greenish lovat tweed; anyhow, not plain colour. And I want a *very* short skirt, well cut for walking, and knickers of a sort they recommend to match. It seems extravagant, but we now have 6 or 8 inches of snow and I went for a short walk yesterday across the estate in "shoe-packs" (like moccasins only in strong oiled leather, no heels) and the tops were filled with snow. Jack has to sweep little paths to walk to the barn and "summerhouse" and so he finds my clothes are not short enough. I am using up my grey silk Apsey, and my Caley green for evenings as Elizababy spoils clothes (*not* by her misdeeds—she usually only has five bockers a day), my black velvet for Sundays at home, and my weddng coat and shirt with *your* velvet hat on the Sabbath if we go calling. My wedding garment fits me perfectly so you see I am as thin as ever I was again. We sent Frederick a wee pair of mocassins this week as I think he could wear them in the garden. I think they are lovely on kids I see out here, but wonder if Nellie will think them too "arty"!

We went to tea at the Marples on Sunday. "Nan" took Elizababy from me and even gave her her bottle and she was angelic all the time, so I went to the other end of the room and sat on the sofa and relaxed and rested, and it was perfectly lovely as I knew she would be managed and not spoilt. Entre nous, I have such dreadful fights with Amelia as if I ever go outside for two seconds and leave Elizabeth (asleep very often) she is always up in Amelia's arms when I come back. I have to go outside sometimes to fetch in washing or feed chickens, and today Jack had to tackle her again and say they were his *orders*. You see, it means I have such battles with her afterwards and it takes up so much valuable time. Like all babies, I suppose, happy in her cot kicking and cooing she is prettier and happier than anywhere else. I always have her up at odd minutes when I am free and every afternoon before dinner we have an hour's play. She clutches at her bottle now with both hands and has an enamel cup at teatime from which she drinks with furious energy! But plates and cups and saucers are pushed about so quickly I expect we shall soon begin to get smashes. She was five months last Monday and weighs one stone [14 lbs.]. She has a tremendous voice and shouts with joy or temper. She does nothing by halves. I bless the pram every day of my life as I push her up and down the verandah for half an hour, and usually I am rewarded by one or two hours' sleep. This between one o'clock and four in the afternoon if the sun shines. Twice this week it has been too cold and then she kicks in bed and I have to be on guard. The other day she had her baptism of fire as she fell or rolled off the bed! She howled, of course, but it did her no harm. Mother's drab shawl saved her and she was on my fur coat too, but somehow she fell face downwards! Jack only called me out of the room for a few minutes, but she kicks and rolls about and I suppose she was not quite in the middle of the bed. I wish you could see her with nothing on running round the table with Jack holding her, and looking round all smiles for admiration. She does this before going to bed. She sleeps lightly from

6:30 until ten, but from ten until 6:30 or 6:45 she is no trouble and we have never had a bad night.

I had a short line from M. G. this week saying she had arrived in England but she does not mention coming out to Canada again. Many thanks for the paper and cutting of the Bruce wedding.[1] It *is* a great excitement and I expect they will only live at Invermere for a few months each summer. *He* has something wrong with his eyes and has been under a specialist in Germany, so he told me last summer. I suppose I shall have to go and call on "Lady Elizabeth"! Will you please put a five shilling postal order in the enclosed letter to Jacky and send it off. Jack thought a money order too complicated for a small boy. I will send you another cheque soon.

Much love, dear old girl. Don't worry about my orders. I trust your judgment *entirely.*

Much love from us both and a kiss from E. baby,

Daisy

ATHALMER
18 FEB 14

Dear Freda,

Daisy is writing to Mrs. Oxley about the case of goods to come out to us so I will give you the details of my things at Ada's. There is an elephant's foot and two rhinocerous horns. The elephant's foot has been badly mounted and before coming out here I should like it to be sent to Rowland Ward's to be properly done up to act as a palm pot to stand on a table. The rhino horns are all right. I wrote to Ada about it some time ago and she was then unable to get at them, and if there is any difficulty about getting them now I do not wish her to be worried about them under any circumstances. . . . If it is convenient you could have them sent to Rowland Ward (paying the piper) and ask him to send them to the address of our crate. If it were not convenient you need say nothing about it. The things you send from my crate at Windsor I leave entirely to your excellent discretion. They are I think nearly all native curios which are interesting to me but if there is any rubbish — and I would not stoutly deny that there is none — it had better be burnt.

Mrs. Oxley asked about the infant's vaccination and as Daisy has so much to write about I will answer to you for her. The infant in its early months was as you know somewhat fractious and I broached the subject of vaccination to the doctor — a new one, Dr. Shaw. His answer was that if we

---

1. Robert Randolph Bruce married Lady Elizabeth Northcott in a sumptuous wedding attended by many of the nobility.

did not intend to leave our perfectly healthy home and did not intend to allow the infant to mix with other children vaccination was quite unnecessary. If we intended travelling and mixing with other children it was necessary. This seemed to me so sound that I thought the postponement of the operation to a time when the infant could stand a set-back more easily (and Daisy, too, for the troubles of the infant reflect on her) was by far the better policy.

The infant is quite fit now and we are trying to have her photo taken again to send you both a copy, but events move slowly.

You remarked that Daisy's head had been cut out of one of the photos we sent. That was my doing as it made her look so thin. I thought if it made her look ugly everyone would say, "Daisy doesn't look like that," if it made her look thin everyone would say, "Poor Daisy, she's dreadfully ill and worn out." No amount of words would contradict the second opinion which would remain forever corroborated by the photo. I decided that decapitation was the only remedy, and the slight disappointment could be remedied by the other photos.

Excuse armchair scrawl.

Best love to all.

Yours

Jack

HESTON,
ATHALMER, B.C.
FEBRUARY 25TH, 1914

My dearest Freda,

As I write this I cannot picture you anywhere in particular. I have been able to let fly my imagination all the time you have been in Cornwall, and am sure you loved every moment and all your quaint friends! I only wish I could see some of the work you have done, but I shall have to wait for that. I am glad you liked the picture of the two men looking "beyond." Yes, I think I can promise you some of the lumbermen I have seen or did see when we first came were just as picturesque and interesting as those, and of course the scenery too. I do not know if the men would relish posing as models, but we will see what we can do when you come. You may have to content yourself with snapshots of E. B.! The other day Jack said, "I suppose the 'infant' will sleep with Auntie Freda when she comes?", but I am afraid E. B. will not be an infant then. I now try to picture her out for a walk along Mount Hermon Road with Grannie. Jack wondered the other day if we could send her home later on for a visit by Parcel Post! This will be a short letter as a sty on my eye has made Jack issue orders that I go to bed at eight o'clock for a few weeks and this takes away my playtime, you see. Fellows Syrup has done me worlds of good and my nerves are quite steady again. Now I must try and grow fat. I am not thinner than when I came out here but I had "plumped up" a good bit, and I must and will do so again but up to the present I have never had a moment to rest. E. B.'s clothes are all ready now and I shall only have mending to do the next few weeks until the snow goes and we have to begin the garden. We are going to plant strawberries, a few more apple trees, more clover and more small fruits to replace some that died last year.

Last Sunday we went up to the Sinclairs to tea. Mrs. Sinclair is simply lovely to me and gives me good and motherly advice. Though not *very* old, she is so good and sweet, and I feel she has become a real friend. She has found it too much work alone, although they have a small but very pretty white cottage, and so a Miss Stuart, an old friend, has come from New Zealand to help her. They will come here next Sunday to introduce her to Heston. She is tall and Scottish, about 45, but has known Mrs. Sinclair when they both lived in New Zealand. While I think of it, my dear girl, I have given you lots of commissions, but if you and Mother find a house just let my things go. *There is no hurry for any of them, honest truth!* Buy the cotton things first and the others can wait until the autumn. No hurry for any of mine but send E. B.'s if you possibly can. I write on the verandah waiting for visitors to come to tea. Jack is splitting wood. E. B. asleep in the pram. Amelia in the kitchen with her false teeth out while she sips and eats her tea! I have just been in to make up the fire. The water is pouring off the roof and we are catching it at every point, a Chinook is blowing, and the sun is shining. It is nice to see green roofs again and the snow not quite so deep. Jack thinks the idea of a small house in Woking cannot be beaten, but it should certainly have *five* stories, with a nursery comfortably tucked away on the *fifth* floor. He is quite sure Job never lived in a five-roomed bungalow! I shall anxiously await your letters with all your future doings and plans. Mail days are always best. Last week Miss Sinclair and Mrs. Bennett, the engineer's wife, came to call together. Mrs. Bennett was calling around, went to Sinclair's first and brought Miss Sinclair (Winifred) over here with her. Mrs. Bennett was in grey corderoy velveteen coat and skirt, grey furs, and white lace veil, and Miss Sinclair in a sealskin coat with sable revers, a black velour hat with a big pheasant mount, and a rough tweed skirt of dark green and brown mixture. The colour scheme was very fine. I only tell you this to make you feel that people really do look nice out here—though, of course, when working overalls and aprons are the order of the day.

The hens have just begun to lay and we have had six eggs. It is nice to feel they will repay a *little* of the feeding. We have also sold some potatoes and think we shall sell more—only a few dollars, but it will be useful to keep E. B. in candy! She is still a very good little girl but when her will is crossed she has taken to *shrieking* most horribly—it is wonderful that so small a thing can produce such a volume of sound without apparently any discomfort. Last night Jack really had to shake her and say "No, no," very strongly. She dissolved into tears, but she is so knowing that I think we shall have to take stern measures with her or she will be a terrible handful by and by. Amelia is irate at much of our treatment. "The Master always had *his* bottle *full.* The Master was taken out in the brougham with the windows *shut!*" Poor Amelia. It was 60° in the verandah this afternoon. Jack begged her to go and sit out and enjoy the sun, but she gets quite angry as with snow on the ground she will not believe it is warm and will not try it. I go out without a hat or gloves and wheel E. B. and today she had her gloves off and played with her rattle. I told you, I think, I had a long letter from Stanley with flower seeds. Please thank Mother for buying me the stockings. They seem very nice ones and I shall be glad to have them by me. Mr. Cuthbert came up yesterday afternoon and brought me a pot of hyacinths, one pink and one white one out and two more to come. I gave him a few bulbs last year and they have grown a few themselves this year and I know these are their best. People are most awfully kind. I asked Mrs. Cuthbert to come to lunch next Wednesday, as she is a bit run down. We are both very much alike in temperament and always get on so well. She is a sweet little soul, and thought the bulbs would be a bit over if she waited until Wednesday. Jack has just ordered me off to bed so I must go. I think I shall stack some of my ironing tomorrow and continue if I can. . . .

HESTON,
ATHALMER, B.C.
MARCH 10TH, 1914

My dearest Mother,

I am writing this line on the verandah, four o'clock. E. B. is playing with my tape measure, and in her blue bonnet on the yellow pillow and the tussore pram cover the effect is most artistic. She has just had her bottle out here. It was so hot at three o'clock I had to take off her little bonnet. I have on a flannel shirt but no jersey even. This morning early it was brisk and cold and a very sharp frost, but midday on our sheltered verandah (due south) it is like mid-summer. All the same, we cannot persuade Amelia to come out here for a few minutes. She is so pigheaded at times and so unreasonable, I find the best thing for peace is just to leave her alone. She is a great help but will not do things my way, so I just have to swallow things down. She stays in the kitchen. It is small and she is warm and she just potters about all day and never will rest or sew. She says all her thoughts make her sad. Some days there is very little work but she always spins it out. Everything is kept very clean but she has no idea of order. You will understand, Jack occasionally gives her a pulling up. I tried to treat her in a friendly way but I suppose it never pays. The only thing is to give my orders, and more or less give her her head! When we had the five days cold she said she must go home before next winter, she could not describe what she endured! Now she has a little cold in her nose and makes just as much fuss so I just take no notice. Miss Farmer[1] wrote to her, and she wrote to me this mail and I will reply as soon as I can. Amelia is like other people. She forgets how long she had had little food, ill health, and not much comfort, and wrote such pitiable letters to Jack about lack of work. At times she is very pleasant and happy and I don't know what we should do without her, but why won't people be a little grateful? Don't comment in your letters.

I am feeling much better and E. B. is so strong and well and has such rosy cheeks I have much to be thankful for. Mrs. Parham has just had a miscarriage, poor thing—too much work, but she has a big house. She is up and about again now. The dear little bunny E. B. loves because she can eat him all up! Jack says, "Poor thing, he wants a Burberry and an umbrella!" Thank you so much, dear Mother. The cushion is just the thing for the pram. She uses *your* white pillow in her cot always as well as her own little one. The blue eiderdown is still like new, as the muslin case I keep washed (soft) and it hides the now rather dirty cot. Mrs. Young has lent us their baby cot. It is in fair condition—lacking the brass knobs, but I think four blue bows or rosettes will take their place and look nice. I shall have to order some ticking at Eaton's and recover the mattress as it is rather soiled and I do not like E. B. to use it as it is. I can honestly say, she has never had on dirty clothes or smelled at all stuffy. I suppose all babies are damp in the morning!

The Sinclairs and Miss Stuart (from New Zealand) came to tea on Sunday afternoon. Coconut cakes and gingerbread for tea. They walked and complained of the mud. The snow is still lying about but gets thinner each day. It thaws from the bottom and not from the top, if you can understand. I had a nice letter from Connie this week, saying she would like the christening robe and will return it. Also that the Dainty baby is rather a beauty but was never taken out the first five weeks of its life. I fear E. B. is being brought up very hard. At eight weeks she was out in a snow shower! Connie also says M. G. described E. B. as the "sweetest thing that ever happened!" Distance lends enchantment, I expect. Jack does not know I have told you about her, so if you comment do so privately. I always read *your* letters to him and usually extract from Auntie Freda's, bless her. I wish she could see E. B.

---

1. One of Amelia's former employers.

kicking on the bed in her woolly trousers! I had a letter from Mrs. Young.[2] They are near Salisbury, looking for a small farmhouse for a year. She says her heart is in the Valley, poor thing. I do hope she will get on alright.

Now about E. B.'s nightwear. If you find at 4 High there are one or two nighties, a little bigger even if old, I should be able to manage for this summer and she could have her warm ones in September next when she is twelve months old. Things too big are a good fault. At present her chest measurement with nothing on is 17 inches and her length 28 inches. I do not know from Jaeger's list what size the infant's nightgown @ 5/11d. is (picture enclosed). I see children's night suits (smallest) are chest 28 inches; length, without frill, 29 inches. This would be about 12 months old, I expect. The London Glove Company catalogue has *Wincey* suits, 2/11d. each. I wonder if it is extravagant to have Jaeger while E. B. is so small and growing so quickly. What do you think? Jack says she had better have woollen or woven nightwear. We never have very hot nights. I have been hoping to see Mrs. Marples to ask what Molly wore, but it may be weeks before we meet. Anyway, I do not want them immediately. I think "creepers" will come in for the summer. She can wear these over a vest and petticoat. Can you buy me a pattern and some material? I think khaki casement cloth would be nice and I could hem them with bands of material embroidered in blue flax thread. I think most of the necks are "Dutch" shape, and I should want a transfer border. Or you can get "nursery rhyme" galen, but I don't know where. What a lot for poor Auntie Freda. The creepers, the pattern of piqué coats, and a bonnet are what I should like fairly soon if possible. She has the little satin bonnet to go on with. The sleeping suits or nighties can wait for a month or so, and as I have lots of flannel I can make her some suits in advance, say, in an 18-month size. What I want are two nighties or suits ready for when she suddenly cannot wear her cotton ones a moment more.

I had a letter from Lily Thruscott this week, to tell me she is engaged to a man whose mother and grandmother live at Newquay. He has just come home from South America and she had not known him long. I am glad as she seems very happy. I enclose her photo, also a Liberty book to show you the style of clothes Jack likes for E. B. when buying material and paper patterns. I think a little embroidery on the things, plain in style, will be just as quick as inserting embroidery and lace, and any time when near a fancywork shop or Libertys think of transfers and flax threads or silks in blues. Jack says this style will go with mocassins which he wants E. B. to have,

2. Mrs. Young and her three small children came out with the Phillips on the *Empress of Ireland*. During the gap in the letters the two Young boys, Clement Arthur (7 years) and George Frederick (5 years), and Vivian Marples (8 years) were drowned when they fell through ice on a pond. Captain and Mrs. Young returned to England: after the war they returned to the Windermere where Mrs. Young could be near her sons.

though I think white socks and muslin will be nice for Sunday—but she is to be quaint.

Many thanks for the madapolam[1] and cake papers. What told you I was running short? You are a wonder—simply! A nice letter from old Stewart too. He seems more happy and content, I am glad to see, in spite of hard work. He says to me, "Old Gilbert would not be so critical if he had knocked about like you and I have now. It makes one jolly appreciative, doesn't it?" I quite agree. It does, I have to write to Aunt Mary Wall and Kittie this mail. They both have written me details of Ida's wedding. How I wish I could send you a photo of Babs. The one sitting up in her cot may be just a little like her. Still, the others are not. Everyone tells me she is so muscularly strong for six months. I always have too much to say and always write at top speed. I do hope I make my *orders* clear! When in doubt, just use your own ideas. I promise you I shall be quite satisfied. And buy E. B.'s things for 9 or 10 months old, I suppose.

Much love from us both to you both, and a sloppy kiss and a grin from Elizabeth. She licks the glass of your photo.

Daisy

HESTON,
ATHALMER, B.C.
SUNDAY, MARCH 29TH, 1914

My dearest Freda,

I will try and start a line today as I have twenty minutes quiet. You have the photos by now. I am so glad as I know they will bring us closer. Though they are not good they show Miss E. Baby in her happy but subdued mood. You must imagine a very vigorous person, and one who shrieks and howls when being dressed and even hits her poor mother now! The pelisse has come. My dear girl, it is just the very thing and she wore it yesterday with her two-in-one bonnet and looked no end of a swell. I put her legs into a bag made from Mrs. Poett's knitted blanket sewn up (as it is thin) and tie it under her arms. This prevents shoes dropping off. Jack always has to hold her and he always tucks her under his arm face downward much to the amusement of everyone! "Come along, Bubbles, you are a confounded nuisance," but he likes his wife's company and so has to put up with his daughter's as well. I had to shorten the sleeves a little from the cuff, and I have put a tuck in each, high up under the cape. Then the piqué and pattern of the little coat are both what I like and shall start on them this coming week and they will be ready in plenty of time. Also many thanks for the overall pat-

---

3. An Indian woven cotton.

tern, excellent too. Also ribbons, beading and insertion. I am well set up now, and am so grateful to you and Mother for all you do, especially now when you are house-hunting and must get tired and have much business on hand. When you get *the* house, don't worry about any of my things. They can come by degrees and I shall not mind the least little bit. I am glad you have seen Toussa, and I expect some day she will hear news of us via Mrs. Sedgwick from Mrs. Poett. I only wish *you* could meet Mrs. Poett. In an hour you would know so much, but I wonder if the opportunity will come for you to suggest such a thing. . . . I think E. B. has plenty for this summer. The great thing is to keep ahead in size, I can see, so if anyone makes any more let them be for next winter. I must make another white petticoat and I have made one pair of "first" drawers like the enclosed pattern from Weldons "short clothing" number. Mother says I am anxious about drawers. Well, at present all is well as she always wears your woolly trousers and they keep up the "bockers" but in the hot weather I thought these would take the place of over-garments. Jack's face is *such* a sight if they fall off. In the early morning her flannel smells a little fuggy sometimes, and in that case he will not touch his daughter! The great game is pulling herself up by his fingers as he carries her round, sits her on top of the wardrobe or on the mantelpiece, and in fact experiments. But the moment she cries down she goes in the cot and Mother comes back to find her howling. . . .

It has been the mildest winter the Valley has had for years, and I can honestly say the house has always been warm and I have not felt the cold indoors. Amelia has made a terrible fuss. I find she *has* to get out of bed a good many times during the night and it is always coldest here in the early morning, and she finds it cold for her fingers when dressing because she has not great vitality in the morning. Jack gets up and lights the kitchen fire and we have had the thermometer in to show here it is 60° but I think it is her morale. As long as she *sees* the snow she will not go out on the verandah even when Babs is asleep and she is too hot in her woolly bonnet and I can take her gloves off! Miss Farmer wrote to me the other day and sent Amelia more warm underclothes! She has more than enough and although I have asked her to wear a golf jersey first thing, she says she would die of suffocation! She always goes to extremes. This is entre nous. She is a great, great help. The only thing is to give her her own department and not interfere. I don't feel I am entirely the missus but as Jack says, anything for the sake of peace! In the cold she said she must go back before next winter. She has visions of Miss Farmer's house with central heating and her breakfast in bed, quite forgetting, as Jack says, that she cannot live there if she returns. Poor old soul. She brought her sewing machine but she says now it is out of order. It was because she didn't want her half-sister to have it, I believe. I don't think she will ever do needlework again if she can help it except to keep her stockings and clothes in repairs. She does not help me in this way. We find we must treat her as a servant. When she first came we were apt to treat her in a friendly way. But it was the old story. She took advantage and was rude and cheeky, and Jack said we must begin to give orders and not make requests or she would be "missus" entirely! This is entre nous but you may be interested. She is devoted to E. Baby but is so stupid and indulgent I find I must take entire charge and only let her go to Amelia for five or ten minutes at a time to be danced about. I have never been out and left her and I think I really must on Thursday as a dentist is coming to Athalmer. Jack says I must see him and I cannot have teeth stopped with E. B. in my arms! . . .

Mrs. Stewart started for New York on Friday. They filled the bottom of the motor with hay and she lay on that, wearing my fur-lined coat and white woolly hood and warm gloves. They had to start at eight o'clock in the morning to catch the train at Spillamachine. I met Mr. Stringer yesterday and he returned the coat, said it was rather a jolty journey and she was very tired. The mud and ruts in the road when it thaws here are awful, the mud halfway up the axles of the wheels!

By the way, I never thanked Mother for the *Pears* book.[1] It is the most useful thing we have in the house. Jack reads it at breakfast instead of a morning paper and we usually refer to it several times a day. For instance, the "size of Woking," the meaning of the word "classical," and the "School of Medicine at Greenwich" where Dr. Hannington went for five weeks.

March 31st, 1914. Elizabeth has cut her first tooth, at the bottom! She was restless in the night and had to be turned five or six times as she cried. While I was dressing I discovered the tooth through, so opened the window and called out to Jack. He remarked, "Did you hear it pop?"! I have cut out a piqué coat and have begun the scalloping round the sailor collar. I quite enjoyed myself last night as I did not go to bed at eight and it was so nice to do some fancy-work again. We have had eleven eggs today — a record — so I think we can take two dozen down to Town on Thursday. They are only 40 cents a dozen now. The time they pay is in winter. They were then 75 cents but you must have very early chicks for this. They have never been 40 cents before. They were always 50 cents but as more are put on the market of course the price is reduced. I have seen my first train after two years and felt quite giddy. It was a construction train, a small engine with trucks of ballast. A roughly laid line now runs through Athalmer. I should not trust myself in the train running on the lines but it is there and the embankment is being made. They are working both ways now, from here to Spillamachine and from there to here. Last Friday after dinner a knock came at the kitchen door. "Would Mrs. Phillips lend Mrs. Sinclair her feeding cup." Miss Stewart was very ill, they thought appendicitis. I sent over the cup, also bedpan as I thought perhaps they had not one. Jack rode over to enquire, and she is

1. An encyclopaedia of general knowledge.

going to be alright—not appendicitis but peritonitis, and we hope to go up there tomorrow to enquire again.

Now I will turn to your letter, very torn. E. Baby always will tear your letters. While I read she shakes the paper. I think the crêpe for the dress I shall like very much indeed. The white crêpe blouse is always washed so quickly and no ironing required. I like the sound of your "Liza" dress. I am so glad you are near shops again and London too. I like to hear of Caleys and the girl at the Stores. It stirs my brain. I wonder if I am turning into a turnip! The ornament is sure to suit me even if the colours are crude. I suppose I must be in the fashion too, so send me crude colours! . . . I was very interested in the account of Gladys Trail's wedding. What picture did Stanley and Connie give, and what house are they living in? I cannot make out from Connie's letter. Tell her when you write. I do so deeply sympathize with the pain in her "tail." I had it very badly indeed and I longed for a sofa to lie down on very often, as sitting down it used to hurt very badly sometimes. It

Portrait of J. N. P. after gazing on crude colours for 23½ hours out of the 24.

has quite gone now and I never feel anything of it. I feel I am going to enjoy my summer this year. I hope I shall not be disappointed. How funny to think of Mr. and Mrs. Frank Buckland dining at "4 High." I know I always think of it as it *was,* not as it *is!* I like the sound of the Byfleet house so much.[2] I do hope you will get it. I feel it is my home overseas as well. I am so interested in every detail though I always give our news first and never seem to have much time to touch on your news very much. The weekly mail still means so very much to me. You cannot realize, I am sure, unless you are in a strange land. I am so glad you are in touch with Toussa again. Give her my love. We often talk of her. Tell her the Thermos flask is in constant use for E. baby and is so useful. Jack liked Mr. Rough so much, *the* [Army] bond, I suppose. It goes through all. Jack likes everyone, but gets on with the Service much better than the others except Dr. Turnor (and his father was a soldier and served in the Crimea, and Dr. Turnor was a Wellington[3] boy, he told us the other day). I must stop now—eight o'clock and I must stir the flour into the butter as the bread stands to rise all night. I am wearing my grey silk with cream fichu collar (grass lawn) to freshen it up.

Heaps of love to you both from us both,

Daisy

---

2. Freda and her mother eventually moved here.
3. Wellington College, an English private school for boys whose families intended that they become army officers.

My dear Girl,

I am so awfully glad to hear that you and Mother are safely housed at Merton and, although very tired, are happy and content. I suppose by now you are another Aunt, though at present I cannot realize that I am one too. I do hope all goes well with Connie. How different for her than me.

I have prepared four chickens for the Show, helping to wash them and vaseline their combs. Miss Sinclair came over and gave us a lesson, and then on the Sunday morning I sat on the floor of the barn on some straw and arranged the vegetables in trays for the Fair, and in the evening walked down to the patch and held the wheat while Jack cut out specimen pieces to make a sheaf. On the way back heavy rain came on and I was so wet I had to change my clothes when I got in, but it is all over now. With a doctor at your call on the other end of the telephone you must feel very different inside; I feel I can enjoy every moment of my life this summer and be so thankful for all my mercies and in having such a happy, healthy, strong little baby. I do hope Mother is better and that the doctor, bed, and the feeling of having a home once more will soon put her right. I think you really are a wonder and I am very proud of you in your new role! Well done is all I can say when I hear what you have done in so short a time. I like *all* the wallpapers and so does Jack. He likes your bedroom and the staircase, so you see how well I have educated him. We are going to beat you and have *rough* dirty white plaster on our walls *when* we come home. The hall and staircase sound so cosy, and now in Mother's letter of yesterday she speaks of curtains being up so I hope the photo can soon be taken.

I am so glad you like our photos, but already E. baby has changed very much. She is growing so fast, and she can now sit up by herself on the floor or in bed. She sleeps in her pram at present as she is too long for her basket, but I keep that about still as she can sit in it and play while we have meals. Her chief amusement, when she goes in to Amelia to play for twenty minutes in the evening while I change, is to sit on the floor with a mackintosh apron on and feel her hand in a pail of water, and have a ramekin case to sail as a boat. Of course, Amelia allows her to do whatever she likes, even to soaking herself to the skin if she wishes, "little dear," so she does not go to her for long! She loves to drink water out of a glass and to blow bubbles. The other day Jack was suspicious as he saw Amelia always giving her a drink out of a ramekin case, and as this was standing on the kitchen table he put his fingers in and found it had so much sugar in it it was like the syrup of fruit salad! So I had to speak up. We cannot trust her where E. baby is concerned, but in anything else she is trustworthy! This is entre nous. I know it is only in the kindness of her heart. All the same, if I do not stop it she will feed E. baby all day long! The little mob cap is very sweet and gives shade to the eyes. I shall make another from the Bourne and Hollingsworth Valencia lace and a Dutch bonnet out of the embroidery, so tell Mother not to worry as she has plenty to go on with. A sunbonnet shape would give a little shade. She still wears her cashmere pelisse for driving, and a little wool jacket when she is out in the pram on the "estate." On the verandah it is 70° so she needs nothing extra. The corsets do very nicely indeed and are comfy. When dresses are so sloppy, why are tight ones necessary? I like the blue dress very much, the buttons are so chic. The material is so awfully nice. The skirt strikes me as funny, but I suppose is quite normal. Your black velvet bow I like and find most becoming, and it makes the dresses. Thank you so much for all. The little blue "tunic" dress takes Jack's fancy. It is just fine, he says, and I can easily copy it and do embroidery in different ways. Thank you so much, you seem to understand so well what I want and like. I think this sort of tunic and knickers to match, made in drab casement cloth and worked in colours, or in blue worked in red or white, don't you? You mustn't go spending *your* pennies, but *do* buy anything similar if you like it as long as the money comes out of my advance box. This is the style of garment I fancy will be best out here for every day and easy to make, and E. baby can have white muslin for Sundays. I hope to cut out two sleeping suits in flannel I have some time this week. She can have bought merino ones next year, which could be big and last two winters. I am advised to make the legs long without the feet, and for her to wear sleeping socks. I then can make the trouser legs wider and quite long. Jack has not had to pay much duty, so we are lucky so far.

I am glad the seedlings are coming on. I have planted Stanley's flower seeds this week. I have been so busy helping Jack with all the vegetables, but they are all in now except the beans as we often get late frosts which kill the young sprouts. We grow dwarf peas and beans to save the sticks or strings, but this year we have a few scarlet runners. Tonight we have had rhubarb from our own garden, baked custard from our own eggs, and milk "cribbed" from our own baby, as Jack says! We have 1½ pints of fresh milk every day. Baby food takes most and have a little drop over. Otherwise we use milk from the "tin cow." The tulips I planted last year have all come up and flowered. We have four yellow ones in the brass bowl on the table now. The narcissus have died. I took four more up to Mrs. Sinclair last week so I must get you to send me a dozen in the autumn, just the plain small variety. I have yellow, pink and red. I have a box of mustard and cress on the verandah nearly ready to cut. Oh for some green food! It seems such a long time to wait for lettuce. I hope to put many more beans in salt this year. I do like the new brass fender. Have you still got the same bed? You speak of a ladybird. I had never seen one but was weeding on the patch the day after your letter came and found a large one on a small plant. Our clover crop is coming on splendidly and our peas are just shooting. Our chickens come off [hatching] this week. I hope we have luck, lots of pullets and few cockerels. The hens have been so good. We take one off each day and let her have a dust bath. I wonder what the neighbours will be like? And who will be your first visitor?

I have been trying to tidy up a bit round the house. It takes so long to do this on bushland. All the odd sticks and stones seem to increase and we have made bonfires of many old dead trees lying about. Don't worry about my account, *that* can wait, and don't overwork yourself, there's a good girl. I know what it is to be most awfully tired, but you mustn't. I am wondering if you have enough cash. Don't be afraid to speak. I always like you to have some in hand. E. baby is so funny with Cupi, she is still half afraid. I put him in her bath this morning, and she says "Oh, Oh, Oh!" and won't touch him, but she loves the soap!

Much love from us both, dear girl. Don't work too hard.

Love to Mother. I hope she is better. I know when she is tired by her writing! I never mind a p.c. — you both are so good,

Daisy

HESTON,
ATHALMER, B.C.
MAY 19TH, 1914

My dearest Freda,

I do think it awfully good of you to send me the weekly letter in the midst of all your work but you know I am most interested in every detail even to each seed that comes up in the garden, and I try and picture you and Mother very often — I expect I do it all wrong! All our planting was finished yesterday, so I am writing this on the verandah at 2:30 while E. baby sleeps. Lately I have wheeled her down to the patch directly after her two o'clock bottle and put her under a tree to sleep while I helped Jack plant seeds, and lately potatoes. I take tea down with me in the Thermos so that we can go right on — everything comes with such a rush and the growing season is so short. I felt very tired at 7:30 when I felt I *could* sit down but now I am going to sit and sew from 2:00 until 3:00, and start work after tea as it is pretty hot in the afternoon. I have been wearing my "topi" and find it lovely and cool on the head. It gives shade and is not so hot as a sunbonnet, though I wear that for washing.

I am so glad you have got a garden to work in and interest you. It is the best cure for many things — and as for being a "grub," I wish you could see me when I have been planting potatoes in dirty soil! My shoes, for instance, and I have to beat the dust from my skirt! We have to keep a dust "mulch" on top to preserve the moisture from evaporating after irrigation, so you never see the nice wet-looking soil as at home, except after rain and then you must cultivate at once. Our rhubarb has done well and it is very nice when green vegetable is scarce. I am eagerly watching the lettuce and spinach grow. They are only just showing. I am glad "the temporary" is the right sort as that must be a great help. I hope too that Mother is better. I am glad the doctor is a nice man, but I expect bed was all that Mother wanted—reaction after all her wanderings and it is nice she can be in bed "at home." I like to hear about the trees by the canal and the gorse bushes. I sometimes shut my eyes and look at the Long Walk [in Windsor Great Park] but never see anything but firs and larches in the damp hollows. The grass is bright green on our land and looks so nice, and the Saskatoon bushes are all white with flowers like wild cherry and I have it in all the vases. Of course, do not picture meadow grass with daisies and buttercups. It is tall thin grass (pine grass), more like what one sees on sand dunes only greener.

I do not think the man opens the letter rate parcels very often, but all parcels go to the Customs Office. I do not think you need worry about small things. This week Auntie Louie sent me a woollen jacket and a rattle for E. baby in a *very* big blue linen envelope and that was not questioned. She is a wonder! The jacket is a splendid shape and so firmly made. The rattle has a bone ring to *bite* and three bells (blue, pink, and white, and ribbons to match) so we keep it for best as she sucks all her toys, and is so strong with her fingers she pulls things to pieces! I think Fellows Syrup is splendid stuff. I am feeling quite my old self again and if I lived an English life I should be bursting with energy and wanting to take long walks, but I am on the go all day, from 7:00 until 7:00 as a rule before I feel I am really free. But I am very happy and so is Jack. Sometimes he says, "What should I do all day in England, on our small income I could not afford to keep a horse or hunt or play golf!" Living as we do all the time very carefully and economically cost us £240.0.0 last year, nearly all our income, but that was the cost of everything—sleigh, chicken feed, chickens, implements, etc.—this is entre nous. If only food was the same price as at home we could have so many more things but everything is so expensive. Butter is 45 cents per lb., you cannot buy cooking butter! Lard is in tins, but that is 19 cents per lb. I have a little bed of flower seeds near where we are standing in the photo and I have planted sunflowers at the corner and nasturtiums under the rails of the verandah. All the other flowers are on "the patch" on the outer edge just inside the fence as they are easy to irrigate with the other things. The strawberries are coming on well. I only wish we could have planted them last year, but that was owing to "Miss E. baby"!

I have two broods of chicks a week old, 13 in one and 9 in the other. I have the coops near the kitchen door as they are fed every two hours. They all seem nice vigorous little beggars, no weaklings! One hen hatched out her fifteen but they came out during the night. Fifteen in the nest were too many and two were suffocated. The other hen hatched out six. She had not sat so well and then she became impatient so I had to bring the eggs into the kitchen and wrap them up in flannel in a basin. Three hatched out. I am afraid the others were over hot, but while we had dinner Amelia was supposed to keep an eye on the thermometer in the basin and it went up to 110°, and 101° is the highest. Still, it is all experience.

E. baby loves to sit and watch the chicks and yesterday grabbed one in her little fat hands and nearly squeezed it to death. Her favourite game is to have a long wooden spoon and to rake about in a tub of water with the mackintosh apron round her. Needless to say, this is Amelia's idea. She goes to Amelia while I am busy in the house and cooking in the morning and does just what she likes, but it is the only way I can get my work done. When she is in my charge it is strict discipline, either in her chair or pram! She sits up to lunch now in her chair (lent by Mrs. Bennett). It is quite plain oak with a little tray in front, that is all. The chair has no tricks but it will serve its purpose. Then she has a crust to bite but she is so vigorous she gets large pieces off and nearly chokes. A drink of water out of a big glass is her chief delight because she can shout down it and make a noise! She can sit up on the floor by herself and is beginning to crawl quite well, so it is no longer safe to put her on the bed. We have written to Eaton's for one of those children's "pens" but our stores have not yet arrived. We expect them every day. We have also ordered a little baby hammock covered with mosquito netting. I hope she will like it. I have been wearing my brown dress and like it very much and my Jay hat looks very nice with it. The hat with the blue and green rûche goes with the blue one. I like the crêpe material so much. I think E. baby's jumper dresses will look nice in that material, in light butcher blue or white worked in red and white. I have finished her first crawlers, in blue (my old overall), worked with the shamrock transfer on a round Dutch neck, and French knots on cuffs and band. Now I am starting on two more in the Liberty stuff.

Lady Elizabeth has arrived in the Valley, but I do not think she will get a very cordial welcome from the settlers as we are all fighting Bruce and the C.V.I. Company for compensation because our cisterns leak and we have paid too high a price for our land. There is now a Settlers' Association to try to fight and right matters. Jack has gone to a meeting again tonight. He has to ride, and the other night he did not get back until past eleven o'clock.

Last Sunday we drove over to Windermere. It is the other side of the Lake, very pretty, near the water, but only a handful of houses. It is not so wild as this side and reminded me in places of "Old England." We took the luncheon basket with us—sardines, hard-boiled eggs, and cake—but a picnic with a baby is rather difficult from Mother's point of view. She was very good most of the time. We started at ten o'clock and got home at 5:30, a good day out for a baby of eight months! Jack wants to do things and make expeditions just the same as if there were no baby and if I say, "Let us wait until next year," he says, "Bother Elizabeth," so I just do my best. But she is so heavy in my arms when we are out all those hours and of course she *must* be good all the time. We had a cup of tea at Mrs. Bell's in Windermere. I had met her at Mrs. Cornwall's (the Bank Manager's mother in Athalmer) and that was good enough out here as she is English. A very sweet little woman with three kiddies, Peter, Francis and Janet (7, 5, 2½). Her husband is Canadian and is the engineer in charge on the Banff motor road which is being made. They are birds of passage as he moves about. She had not had a servant for three weeks. She always keeps one and pays £50.0.0. a year for a lady's help and hired girl. Her last was a Swede who found it dull. She is now expecting a nursery governess just coming out with a party from England. She had heard of her through a Colonial Agency. E. baby saw a teddy bear and did not cry at all. I think she was interested in the other children. They all stood round and stared at her and brought her picture books, and she drank out of a mug! We have ordered a china mug and nursery plate from the Stores—cannot buy them here. I am wondering what E. baby will eat when she leaves off bottles, as Amelia suggests wonderful things! I shall be sorry to leave off Allenbury[1] as she has never been sick or seedy and is regular in her habits and never has medicine. Mum-ma, ba-ba, gee-gee, is all she will say at present.

I went to the cemetery at Windermere and put some flowers on the little Youngs' graves and straightened things up. It is a field by the Lake just fenced in and all the graves, three with a headstone, are fenced as cattle break in. All the other mounds are just earth and a stick of wood at the head, no name or anything. It seemed so terribly sad to me, strangers in a strange land. On our way home we saw a figure walking (we only met two people going and two coming all the way to Windermere!) on the road, blue and white shirt, red tie and big black sombrero hat. It turned its face and it was Mr. Metz, a very nice fellow, a friend of the Poetts who lived with them all last winter and spring to help the General. He is an Austrian Count and his mother was a friend of the Poetts. He had been at the Coast all winter, had a very rough time, work is very hard to get. There is a slump all over B.C. just at present. He had worked in railway gangs, milked thirty cows a day on a dairy farm and had a really rough time, so returned to the Valley on Saturday night to look for a job. He had been up to see us in the morning and was then on his way up again. He *did* enjoy his dinner, I can tell you. He was best man at the Poett wedding and is about 22. He returns to Austria for military training in two months time. I gave him a free invite for any meal and am sure he will come again.

1. Powdered milk for babies.

Have no more time and it is getting dark. We have nearly run out of lamp oil and there is no more in the Valley at present. There is a block of goods at Spillamachine. The railway is not much good at hastening things at present.

Much love, dear old Girl. God bless you.

Love from us both and E. baby to dear Grannie,

Daisy

HESTON,

ATHALMER, B.C.

JUNE 3RD, 1914

My dearest Freda,

By this mail I send some snaps of E. baby taken by "Nan" Marples. They were taken on Good Friday so you will be able to judge how she has grown since the other sitting. She is very round now and has tight bracelets, and draws herself up straight and stiff directly her will is crossed! The photo with Molly Marples has not the faintest likeness to E. baby but it is so amusing I send it for you and Mother to see, not to be passed on, I think! Mrs. Marples says I look as if I had been dead and buried a hundred years and then dug up! But it is only the heavy shadow and looks alright with the magnifying glass. I had just been hard at work in the barn putting out potatoes to sprout, hence the turned-up sleeve. I have on a matt skirt I believe I made myself. Do you print your own photos? If so, will you buy a packet of papers and print me three each of the two good photos enclosed and keep the rest of the paper as a present? I should like to send old Stewart a couple, and Fanny, and keep two for ourselves. You can have these prints and keep the films. I was surprised to see the drawn-thread bib. I suppose *I* did it years ago, did I? Anyway, I was telling Jack one evening about the drawn-thread bibs I made for the MacGregors and wondering what quick way I could make some "going out to tea" ones for E. baby, and the very next day this came! She took it out with her on Sunday as wherever we go a biscuit goes too now! She drinks quite nicely and holds the cup by the handle if you please. She sits up to tea now and has a sip of milk, and at lunch she has her biscuit. Her great excitement is "Gaggey," her Daddy. She shouts out directly she sees him and looks to him to play with her when he comes in. I see Jack's heart is gradually softening. She can crawl all over the place and I am thankful her "playpen" has come from Eaton's. It is not a square fence like the English ones but collapsible and opens out like the things you wind wool on, and makes a big round fence. She always wears her crawlers in the morning and I put on her clean clothes at two o'clock when she has her bottle and afternoon nap. We have also got a little baby hammock from Eaton's. It is blue and yellow, so carries out E. baby's and the colour scheme of the verandah. It makes a change to put her in and give her a swing, and is cool on these hot afternoons. It was 90° on the verandah yesterday. We sling the hammock across the verandah in the shade and the higher it goes the more she chuckles! Did I tell you she has a very deep laugh and voice at present, and of course a shriek when she is naughty.

I look at the Merton photos so often and I am beginning to think of you and Mother there. I had a letter from Dorrie Durant and Daisy Mac this week. The latter quite approves of E. baby and hopes to see you and Mother soon. I am sorry to hear May is going. I liked her so much in the photo, in fact, I loved to look at her, and hope for better luck next time! I am so glad Mother is feeling a little better, slow and sure progress is best for her, I am sure. It is blowing a gale, so excuse as I am outside on the verandah. I am glad to hear my niece wears woolly boots as after what M. G. told me I thought I was committing a crime to let E. baby wear them! Now it is warm she only wears shoes and socks on Sunday, bless her, and loves the buttons and pom-poms. The parcel from Herberts Stores has not come yet but we have a card to say it is at the Customs. I am glad the Windsor news is good. Tell Connie to lie low, there is no need for her to start working *very* hard too soon. I cannot picture Stanley with a screaming infant, but perhaps she never cries!

I am afraid my last mail's letter may not arrive, as we have heard the *Empress of Ireland* has gone down,[1] so you will understand if anything seems missed out. We have heard no details, only a telephone message has come through. Our garden is coming on well, we had our first radishes yesterday, with Dutch cheese we had ordered from Eaton's. Our small fruits, apples, and clover are all fair, we shall not make a fortune just yet! I wonder if the doctor's wife has called and if she is *nice*. I do hope you will get to know one or two folk that you really like by and by. You shall make us a front garden when you come as in the summer there is plenty of water if you have the energy to carry it in buckets from the flume at the top of the fence. I have a little bed by the side of the house, and mignonette, sunflowers and sweetpeas are coming up there. The watering you would love is the irrigation on "the patch." Jack does this on the contour system. The ground is not level but the ditches have to be to keep the water running. The fruit trees are so dry, and the water flows about in the clover patch and gradually soaks through. The vegetable garden is done in straight lines and you block up and open the channels with a hoe as they are irrigated. The sun is so hot it bakes the surface, and directly after irrigation (this goes on for 24 or 48 hours, say) you cultivate, and so on.

Last evening at five I was just coming up to put E. baby to bed when Cap-

1. On May 28, 1914 the *Empress of Ireland,* the C.P.R. passenger liner, collided with a collier in the Gulf of St. Lawrence and sank in fifteen minutes. More than a thousand lives were lost.

tain and Mrs. Houlgrave[2] came. We had killed a chicken as she was leaving off laying, and so said stay to "pot-luck" which they did. The chicken was tough and the bread sauce poor, custard and rhubarb to follow, but I must help Jack and keep out all I can just now for E. baby's sake and my own as I want to get quite fit again this summer and I know at any time I can take up the cooking. Amelia does that part as she can take her time but I must not interfere and show her how to do things. However, I wrote to Miss Farmer about her and she has written me a very nice letter and has written to Amelia as well and given her good advice so for the present she is more amenable. Pro tem we live *very* plainly and Jack does not mind. I had to show her how to make curry, she will not fry anything (it makes the stove in a mess), but there, what matters! As long as she will stay until E. baby is two years old I do not mind swallowing a great deal, so say no more about it. We have a lovely view of the Rocky Mountains from "the patch." It is awfully pretty. As I write this under the smoking room window I can see the Rocky foothills through the trees on my left and Mount Hammond covered in snow on my right. I have been hoeing all afternoon to make a patch from the barn to the house and outlining it with stones — it is a great improvement! But a baby is such an uncertain creature! I have asked the Parhams up to lunch on Sunday. Cold roast beef and Russian and potato salad, fruit tart and custard and a jelly I think will have to be the menu. Now I have had a message to say all the Turnor family are coming to tea so I shall have a busy day. Never mind, we do not have any other excitement except to see somebody else about once a week.

Much love to you and Mother from us both and a kiss from E. baby.

Always your affectionate sister,

Daisy

My dearest Freda,

I hope by this mail to send off the net yoke and sleeves. I do not mind how the bodice is made but a similar style to this or the picture I sent. The collar can be improved upon as you will see it does not sit well, and the opening I leave to you, "as they are now being worn," I suppose. The other dress in either an Oxford shirting or blue and white stripe galatea (a thin make), and I like big buttons. I want them to be neat and trim but just working dresses,

---

2. Houlgrave was a naval captain who tried to raise horses in the Windermere. His wife was frail and pregnant (see letters of 15 November and 21 November 1914).

cool and loose so that I can roll up the sleeves as I get so hot when working around. The "middy" blouse is for you to *garden* in — a Canadian product. It is rubbishy material but I saw it advertised in a Toronto catalogue and if you find it comfy you could have it copied in white piqué. We cannot get anything here in decent quality though things seem often very stylish. The Canadians' motto is "wear and throw away"! They never keep stores of house linen or things of that sort. They have no accommodation in their houses and of course everything is to save labour.

Many thanks for sending off the scrap book and the carved bracket. E. baby will love the scrap book as her greatest treat is to have her animal picture book and turn it from back to front over and over again as a treat, of course, when I can play with her for a little. She loves tearing up paper but I have not encouraged it as it will make her destructive. She always has your envelopes. Today she snatched a vinegar bottle on the table and because I took it away she was so angry she turned and bit my arm! I turned up my dress as it really hurt and found the marks of her little teeth — so you see, I *have* got a daughter and no mistake! Many thanks for the Weldon children's fashions. Sitting here looking at the mountains it takes me back to the busy world, or rather to Smiths at the top of Peascod Street, and funnily enough I quite enjoy it. I think I shall get ideas so buy me a copy every month — I think I can afford that luxury — until further orders! I am wondering how cream casement cloth would be with red and blue embroidery? I can make these in the winter, I am sure, as they are small and really do not take very long. If this is a success, she could have some in tussore. If ever you come across "nursery rhyme" galon[1] for trimming overalls buy me some too. I hope you can sort all this out but you can always be on the look out for transfer designs suitable for frocks if you are at Liberty's or anywhere likely, and buy them for me.

It seems to take me a whole evening to write you this furious scribble. Jack has gone to a Settlers' meeting so I am alone. It is hot and E. baby is restless and does a good bit of screaming without tears so I am up and down and presently I have all the young chicks to drive to bed. The mignonette is out and looks and smells lovely and the clover looks fine after the rain. I hope it can be cut this week.

Lots of love,

Daisy

P.S. A maple leaf, picked on Sunday. A clover leaf, from crop!
    N.B. There are smaller leaves!
    We have had six raspberries!!!

---

1. Galloon: a narrow, close woven ribbon, often of silk, used for trimming clothing.

ATHALMER, B.C.
JULY 13TH, 1914

My dearest Freda,

First of all I must compliment you on your bookbinding. The dear old scrap book looks quite smart and I think you have managed it very cleverly. What a fund of hidden genius lies behind your glasses. Have you taken to a thimble yet? I often try and picture you with your knitting needles, but a paintbrush or a pencil always comes instead. What a pretty piece of stuff you found for the cover. I told Jack it was the other piece of ribbon off his chocolate box before I opened Mother's letter, and of course *he* had to open the parcel *at once!* E. baby loves the scrap book or, rather, turning over the leaves by herself, lying on the ground flat on her tummy. But her thumb and first finger with which she holds most things, quickly found the edges and she began to tear, so this afternoon (it was wet) after a cup of tea Jack and I pasted down all the unstuck pictures. I found one card from Grandpa Oxley to me, 1880! and Jack is most interested in the whole book. "Judy," or "Judy, gaiter," as Jack calls her, is a fine thing for E. baby to have. She does not scold her, but looks at her hard and then bursts into a laugh and tries to pick out her eyes, and today at breakfast she turned up her clothes and found her legs, which gave her great delight! The arm is quite well now and I think the scab will come off tomorrow and E. baby is as fit and boisterous as ever. Her hair is beginning to curl. After her bath it is just lovely, so I rub it round with my fingers and I hope the curls will come to stay.

As I write all the vases are filled with mignonette (the result of Stanley's present) and here and there Californian poppies, deep orange yellow. It is so lovely to have garden flowers. Godetia, Shirley poppies and Sweet Sultanas will all be out tomorrow. Do you know the latter? I think they are most charming. Larkspur, summer chrysanthemums are all coming on. Of course, the season is later and shorter than at home as the ground is cold until the middle of May, but they all seem to do well. I have planted wallflower seed and shall leave it out all winter just as an experiment. All my flowers are in the patch, just on the edge of the small fruits so they do not make extra work for me irrigating. I have put them in a long line, or rather, two lines with irrigation trench between, just to see which flowers do well and I can repeat next year. So far all are good except the asters. Perhaps they do not like great heat and sun. I also have a small bed near the verandah, African marigolds, cornflowers and sunflowers are there, but the chickens are rather a nuisance and will scratch about. We have a long row of sunflowers on the patch too, as the seeds are awfully good for chickens in the cold weather. All our vegetables are doing well and the marrows will soon be in flower. I have my eye on them for *jam* as Jack likes it. I think we shall have peas on Saturday. The spinach is nearly over and we had young cabbage this evening with mince. Jam tarts and cheese straws to follow. I expect you will be interested in these homely details of our menu. Do you know that the thinnings of beetroot (the green tops) make excellent spinach, you can hardly tell the difference? We are also planting Sea-Kale and beetroot, and shall leave it in all winter ready for early spring. I recommend it to you. You can get it at Suttons. It is as easy to grow as beet and you eat the stalks. My parsley too is quite large, two long rows. I pick it in September and dry it slowly in the kitchen and then break it up and put it in tins for winter use and it makes dishes look nice when I cannot garnish with greenstuff.

We had it very hot last week, 100° or thereabouts on the verandah every afternoon! White is the only thing to wear then for comfort, and from two until four it is too hot to work much. Now we have had lots of thunder and rain, which for us is sad as the clover should have been cut last Friday. It is a lovely thick crop now but Mr. Sinclair has bought it and of course will not cut until all chance of rain has gone. I send some leaves. We hope the second crop will be enough for the horse and chickens all winter, but it will not be such a large crop as the first. The rest of the land is down in clover and alfalfa now, but we do not get a crop until next year. However it will be less work for Jack as he will only have to irrigate. Of course, weeds grow quickly here, the same as other things. You can really see peas and beans grow in a night. We put notches on the scarlet runner sticks (we are trying these this year). I shall try and put lots down in salt and also I am going to try and dry some peas, scalding them in salt and alum to keep the colour. Then drying them in the sun and put them in muslin bags—like Farrows peas. I only hope it will act; anyway, they will make soup! This last week I made rhubarb chutney! Don't laugh, it is really *nearly* as good as tomato chutney. Not quite, of course, but quite cheap as we grow the rhubarb. I made three jars to try and as it is a success shall make three more. I should like the recipe of our home piccalilli some day. I might not be able to get all the spices here but I could roughly take the quantities of vinegar and sugar and see what I can do. As the time goes on, the more of this kind of thing I can do the better to save housekeeping expenses. Jam, pickles, etc. are all expensive and yet we use more than at home because we cannot get the variety in foods. I shall try marmalade of sweet oranges this winter for I think it would be cheaper as Jack eats such a large quantity. Oranges are 2½ cents each so E. baby is the only member of the household who can indulge. I have started her on a little custard pudding or sponge cake beaten up in milk at mid-day now and she evidently likes it as she scolds if I do not keep her mouth filled quick enough! She tries to imitate the noise her Teddy Bear makes. It makes my throat feel sore to *hear* her but it evidently does not hurt her. Not a pretty noise for a little girl!

Jack has just been off to fetch the horse in. He is grazing outside our fence and I have just been into the kitchen to mix tomorrow's bread. I have on my brown Apsey dress. I wonder if it will wash? Remember, I shall want a very nice winter hat of the frieze, pheasant wing order, but Christmas will be time enough to get it out here. Such crowds of things are in my head when I write to you but I never have time to put them nicely together. Jack has been repainting the white window frames outside today so we look very smart. I think it will help to preserve the wood when we get drips from melting snow. We are going to have a porch put over the kitchen door and the plat-form enlarged outside, as when Amelia goes E. baby will have to be handy where I can keep an eye on her as already she can pull herself right up in the pram and loves to throw things out and then lean over to see where they are! I am glad you like Nan Marples' photos. E. baby has altered so much even since then and they are not her at her best. And it is really *not* like me. My dear girl, I shall never grow fat out here! I am on my feet nearly all day long but I feel a tower of strength now compared to last year and this winter when I used to feel as if I should break in half, but you see I didn't! I feel so deeply thankful to feel as well as I do now and I hope if E. baby stays well I shall too. My feet do get tired and next time I must have size 5, not 4½. My arms and legs have grown, and I suppose my feet too, but when I am on them so much I must have comfort above everything. I shall get on quite well when Amelia goes as I know Jack will help me more. I do not mind the cooking, cleaning the knives and pots and pans and kitchen stove is the only hard part. But there, things might be worse, and we shall be saving £20 a year and have no disagreeable element in the house. What a great help to other people good temper is, to be sure. Amelia has many more words than deeds and Jack says she will be sorry.

I do not get up until seven o'clock now and am taking things as easily as I can. On Sunday we went up towards Mount Hammond, about 13 miles. It was most lovely. We followed Toby Creek nearly all the way. For a few miles up it was visible in the gorge and as we rose came nearly level. It is a rushing cateract, about twenty yards broad in places. The road is just used by wagons going to Paradise Mine, and that very seldom. In places the road is sheer on the edge of the precipice and I do not think it would suit Mother very well! On the left the creek and on the right fairly dense bush. We saw and ate wild raspberries, wild gooseberries, and there is lots of wild vine—besides lovely butterflies and flowers—also maple trees and bushes which we do not see about here at all. We never met another soul the whole way, but saw a recent wagon track that had come down recently. There is a camp up there now and Dr. Hannington goes up once a month! They talk of the mine opening again when the railway comes so I think they have gone up and are putting the road in order on the way. We drove over little streams and bridges made of tree trunks as in Switzerland. E. baby was very good, but 22 lbs. sitting on your lap is a good weight and it was a hot day. We stopped for lunch at one o'clock by the roadside and put E. baby to sleep with the drab shawl wrapped round the air pillow for her head, a brown army blanket for her couch, the drab cotton "buggy duster" for her top cover, and the ever-useful drab cotton sunshade over her head! The roaring torrent quite close did not disturb her and as we watched her wake up she began to chatter to herself and was not the least perturbed. I said to Jack, "I wonder what Mother and Freda would say if they could see her now." We started at ten o'clock sharp and that meant getting up early as we had to do nearly a day's work before we started—leaving the house in Sunday order, bathing the infant, making the food, as well as getting all the provisions, bottles, nappies, etc. for the day, space and weight being a great object. When we were within forty minutes of home a thunderstorm came on so E. baby you see can stand anything! I wonder what cousin Brenda or her mother would say to it all? It is no good for me to be nervous or worried about E. baby. Jack expects me to do things with her that three years ago I should not have dreamed of doing without her, bless him. Jack said on Sunday, "That umbrella is dangerous with lightning about." So down it had to come, and E. baby had my Burberry right round her head tucked under her chin, the only thing visible a little hand holding Cupi aloft, she saying, "Oh, eh, ah!" as the thunder rolled about.

E. baby yells and stiffens herself now when I attend to her so she has to be spanked, though she is a very good little soul on the whole. As you say, "Keep your temper. Be kind and just." but it is not always easy when Mother is tired. I could go on for ages but it is time to clear up. I have finished one flannel sleeping suit. It looks a fascinating garment and I have cut out No. 2. I suppose she had better have three. There is enough flannel, but I have made them *very* large.

Much love,

Daisy

ATHALMER, B.C.
8 AUG 14

Dear Freda,

The beautifully packed vest arrived last week, so completely disguised as a letter that it passed safely through. I'm very much obliged to you for it and hope you will not think the returned sample of the stores is a typical example of my garb out here. Daisy agrees a house flannel is now its proper role.

This war will I'm afraid modify our plans very much. At any moment I may be called up, either back to England or to any part of the globe and during the uncertainty it is useless to go on developing so have cut down all our expenditure. Unless we are extremely lucky we shall, in the event of my being called on, lose most of the money we have put in here. Still, we both realize we have duties to perform, and if that is the only sacrifice we have to make for our share in a successful war we cannot complain.

It means too that Amelia cannot yet go home and the fact that she is at our mercy has already made her much more amendable and life in the house much more pleasant. We have had many rumours but no reliable news so we can only await events.

Your suggestion of Barnardo Boy or the like has occurred to us before but we have rejected it for two reasons. Our house is too small to entertain one who is not one of the family and there is a Canadian Act called the "Master and Man Act" which says that any contract entered into outside Canada between master and man is not binding in Canada. So that when a boy arrives here on small wages and associates with other boys earning higher wages he at once becomes discontented and goes when no legal power can hold him. It sounds—and is—unjust on the master but there was a great deal of abuse which in the first place caused the act to be passed.

You talk of your garden soil caking. In this very dry atmosphere our soil cakes immediately after rain or irrigation so perhaps our methods may not be out of place for you. To overcome this caking we plant *everything* in rows from one to two feet apart and the space between the rows is always kept constantly raked (technically called cultivated); after every shower of rain and every irrigation the ground is thoroughly cultivated until a coating of dust about two inches deep lies on the surface. This dust is quite dry but it has two effects. It prevents the sun's rays from drying up the roots and it prevents almost any moisture in the soil from escaping. The dust becomes as dry as a bone and the soil looks hopeless but two inches down it is moist and the effect on the vegetation is wonderful. When we irrigate we never water the surface, that encourages a crust. We dig a deep channel with a hoe—say three inches deep between the rows of vegetables or flowers—and allow the water to run slowly for a night or so, then we turn the water off and rake again. This economizes the water and moistens the roots, though of course it means a good deal of time is needed. I expect our rows are longer than yours need be and our atmosphere is drier, so a night might be a good deal more than is necessary to irrigate your garden rows. We have a "cultivator" with a wheel and three broad teeth which does the raking easily and quickly. I expect you would only have to do this in dry summers but in almost every summer there are dry spells when you might with advantage try our

side view   *back*

system. Never water your surface with a watering can, the hoeing of your trenches between the rows is a much easier job than it sounds. Have your trenches deep and narrow.

Yours

Jack

HESTON,
ATHALMER, B.C.
AUGUST 26TH, 1914

My dearest Freda,

Here we are still you see and waiting still. We know not if orders will come tomorrow, Thursday, by the English mail or if they will come in a month or two so I cannot get on very far with packing or anything of that sort. It is very unsettling and makes my poor old Jack so restless he finds it hard to do anything on "the patch." We are going through all our things, stores, clothes, etc., and more or less sorting out and making plans, but these are difficult. We must shut up the house and board up the doors and windows, but wooden things soon go to pieces if not well looked after and herds of cows and horses will break through the fence at times in spite of a strand of barbed wire, and now we wait for two rolls more to put up a second row. It ought to be here this or next week as it comes from Eaton's. I saw Mrs. Houlgrave the other day and she said she would be glad to have Amelia if we go—that is if Amelia will go, of course! I do not think it will be possible or advisable for her to return to England just yet. I may not be able to cross with Jack but hope to go with him to St. John's. With regard to money we have plenty for present needs. I think we have about £200 out here as we have kept on transferring some all the time from London and only quite recently I had £60 transferred from my account as the Savings Bank department of the Bank gives 3 per cent interest and I thought that would help keep Elizababy in clothes! I sent you a cheque and wonder if it came while you could cash it. I feel at a time like this you must hoard every penny so please charge all postage to me.

We had the *Overseas Mail* yesterday. It was such a relief to get an English paper and see all that is going on. The Mother Country is just magnificent, I think, in the way she is facing things and an example to the world at a time of crisis. I am sure the Colonies can supply her with food and men to fight as well. All the corps at Calgary are full up I heard yesterday from Mr. Stringer, a young lawyer in Athalmer. All the youth of the Valley has enlisted, Mr. Pope's son, Mr. Lunn, Acheson—all nice English boys—and various reservists called up. I daresay you have learned by now that the reserve of officers are not called up with the reservists, but as they are required. Jack is anxiously waiting for tomorrow's mail. If I come home I propose that E. baby and I come to Merton anyway to start with. I know you will be pleased to see us. Living will be high, I know. I see it has gone up 50 per cent but if Jack is on Service he will have pay and I can throw in my little with your little. If need be and you have to cut down wages (which I hope you will not do if possible), I am sure I could manage the work with you with, say, a charwoman occasionally to keep things going. I feel old Stanley will have a heavy burden and great responsibility but he is sharing it with hundreds of others. I think the *Express* this week is lovely and the leaders splendid. May you all be given strength to go on as you have begun. I was so interested in reading all the local names on the roll. There is no *authentic* news coming through and I expect you get very little either. We have heard about brave little Liège and that a Naval battle by this time I expect has been fought.[1] *Pears Annual* has come in so useful in looking up things and for maps, comparing numbers engaged in the Napoleonic wars, etc. Mr. and Mrs. Marples came to tea on Sunday and they had had a lot of letters on Saturday from friends in different parts of England—Folkstone, Dover, London, etc. —and were full of news about the state of things at home. Mrs. Marples' people are all on the Stock Exchange, her uncle on the Committee, and it will hit some of them very badly. But if bad for England what must it be for France and ten thousand times worse for Germany. Fancy all the men having to go at a moment's notice without time to make arrangements but I suppose the women will just carry on as best they can. I think the *Express* is quite right, that it is our duty if we cannot fight. So many things go through my head. I do hope Auntie Kate will be able to keep her post and keep fit and well. How will it affect Gilbert? I know it must be very bad for old Stanley. While I think of it, if you can, sow all the vegetables you can at once. I think lots of things will stand the winter, and your gardener will tell you what is best, but spinach and onions are some of the things, I think. All your "shoppings" have come. The mail comes more or less as usual but letters only once a week.

Now, my dear girl, I must thank you for your lovely birthday gift to E. baby. It is a real beauty, so cosy and soft, and I love the colour, quite one I should have chosen to look nice on her pram. I think you have knitted it aw-fully well. I am sure you are more critical than I am nowadays. Tell Mother I think the sleeping socks are splendid and a very good shape indeed, and her little legs look so sweet in the gaiters. The woolly coat by the pattern I should say is Auntie Kate's handiwork and it is very sweet of her to do it.

---

1. The defence of Liège, in the opening days of the war, slowed the German advance in Bel-gium. The city was eventually taken after a bombardment by German heavy howitzers, the first of what were to be many examples of their destructive power. To assist the Belgians, British troops were landed at Ostend near the end of August. The associated concentration of British warships led to the naval battle of Heligoland Bight, the first major naval engage-ment of the war, in which three German light cruisers and a destroyer were sunk.

Thank you both ever so much for everything. I feel it means very much work time and thought given to us, but I do appreciate it all very deeply. My jersey is ripping and I like the open neck as it will look nice if worn over another blouse if necessary. The colour is right and Jack quite approves. Your Liberty purchases are quite to my liking too. The galens look very nice and I do not mind the red and black. The cross-stitch piece I shall put on a white frock and the other will look well on blue overalls. The transfers are very pretty, also the flax threads, the paper pattern, too, and the thimble is right for size. You are a dear old girl to do it all so well and your parcels always come in such good condition. Quite right to hold back Jack's vest for the present. I feel you have already given us too much. I only hope I can repay you some day. Jack shot a hawk yesterday and we have the wings, tail and claw drying. I am glad you bought the length of blue crepe, it is such a nice colour. The brown dress has had hard wear, but I have kept the blue in reserve.

My dear love, and God bless and keep and help you all.

Your affectionate sister,

Daisy

HESTON,
ATHALMER, B.C.
SEPTEMBER 28TH, 1914

My dearest Freda,

I am afraid from the tone of your last letters that both you and Mother were rather counting on our coming home, but you see we are still here and the best thing to do is *not* to expect it! Every Monday I wonder if this is our last washing day, and every Thursday we look for a letter from the War Office. Otherwise we do not say much and try to go on much as usual but both feeling unsettled inside. Jack has now written to the War Office as he saw in a Canadian paper that all retired officers were called to the Colours (not that Canadian paper information counts for much in our opinion). We shall doubtless hear soon, and Jack wants to go badly, very badly, and chafes and frets. At the same time he feels he is not justified to volunteer, having sunk his capital here and worked so hard. If he is called up he can make claims on the War Office after the War and may get a job of sorts. If he volunteers, after the War they say, "Thank you very much for giving up all, now you can go," and of course if we leave here it means giving up all and unfortunately in this country it is almost impossible to find an honest man to look after things. Honour is a thing that is little known or practised in any business dealings. This is all entre nous and Mother to let you know how we are placed. If we do return I expect Jack would go straight to his

Regiment in Belgium, so do not picture him on home service in Kitchener's Army. For my own part, I am ready and willing to come if Jack has orders but I do not let myself think too much about it. It would be so lovely to see you all again and at times I quite look forward to having a rest at Merton. There is no chance of a holiday out here. We keep going continuously even when we feel tired. If you leave things they accumulate so quickly and then it makes such hard work. Each day brings quite enough of its own to send us to bed tired every night. Still, I should soon grow tired of a rest, and I would far rather be with Jack dead licked than as fresh as paint without him!

Our troops are doing so magnificently and showing up so well although they are such a tiny speck. We have heard rumours of a Naval disaster and a big advance by the Allies,[1] but must wait for definite news until Thursday. Dear old Gilbert, he will find it hard and trying at times. As Jack says, the life of a private, especially under canvas, is not all lavender, but he is doing his country work and his regiment is one that has a magnificent record for keeping going. Will you please send him some tobacco from me? I do not mind if it is all in one packet, although I would suggest a small amount every two or three weeks. Doubtless you are sending something, but send this from me unless there is anything else he really wants. I think the Canadian troops are very largely represented by the Englishmen in Canada. I do not say there are no Canadians, but a very large percentage of English boys and men out here have set the example. They have their own Canadian officers, I would say, not English. After all, Canada is not England and Canadian ways and people are totally different in nearly every way. I see from my Red Cross information that the Red Cross in London do not forbid flannelette but they *prefer* flannel. Here they ask for flannelette, so part of our work is to be *flannelette* pillow slips, and scarlet flannel bedjackets. They have sent a small pattern on paper to be enlarged. Then we are making towels of various sizes with tapes, and some flannel foot bags to go over bandages, and knitted socks and stockings. I have ordered 24 lbs. of wool from Spencers at the Coast but it takes so long to come, and is so difficult to work out how much I need as I do not want to run short or have materials over. But we can only do our best. I find folk are not so particular out here as I am. They ask me to order buttonhole tapes for the pillowslips! They are a slack lot, and it is only the Englishwomen in most cases who are good at sewing, but there are lots of Scotch and Irish women in Wilmer and

1. On September 17th three British cruisers were sunk in the North Sea by a German submarine. The second and third were hit as they tried to pick up survivors from the first. Some 1400 lives were lost, and as a result heavy ships were ordered not to pick up survivors from torpedoed ships. On land the German advance through Belgium and into France was stalled in early September at the Battle of the Marne, one of the decisive early engagements of the war.

Athalmer and they are all good with knitting pins. We had a committee meeting at Mrs. Bennett's last Thursday to call in the money and we have just over $150, which is very good as times are bad out here and money short. All the folks have it, but in "real estate" a thing we don't know much about at home.

E. baby was very good at the meeting, but having to look after her and keep my thoughts on business and getting folks to settle what they *would* make just kept me going. I never dare leave her with Amelia for an hour or so to go out with Jack. It would be such a rest if I could. "If you please, will you come. Baby's standing up in her pram and won't sit down," (meaning Amelia won't make her cry). "Oh, baby's got something in her mouth," when Amelia has been asked to look after her for a few minutes while I go and bring in the washing. Still, Amelia does wash up and is a help, but in her own way not in mine. With regard to sending her home, the fares have all gone up considerably and also the freight rates. If we stay here, I think Jack intends making her stay the winter and she still thinks the Atlantic is unsafe and will *not* realize when you talk to her that there will be want or distress in England. She always argues or says, "the poor live on tinned food." If we come I expect we shall bring all our treasures, linen and silver, as we never know how long it will be before we come back. Anyway, it will be an expensive business. How thankful I am we have been so economical all the time we have been out here. I think this last year we have lived on under £200 for everything, including horse feed and chicken feed! Not so bad, is it? But this, of course, is *quite* private. E. baby grows such a big girl and is becoming a little child, I feel, and not a baby. She now stands up in her cot when put to bed at six or for her nap after her dinner at two o'clock, and it means going in several times and arguments as a rule before she lies down and goes to sleep. We hear chuckles and laughter going on, all to herself and "the baby in the glass," as she slowly moves a step or two holding onto the rails. The grip hurts her hands and when she tumbles and collapses she usually looks at the palms of her hands and scolds! She never attempts to pull herself up when crawling on the floor, or hardly ever, but will stand up in her pram in spite of being strapped and tied. She is so heavy I begin to think it will be nice to put her on the floor and see her stand instead of collapsing. Still, "she is rather stout," as someone remarked the other day so it is all for the best she still prefers her tummy to get about on! She loves the big scrap book and lies on the floor and turns over the pages and chatters and I am afraid nearly always her little fingers tear off a tiny piece somewhere. I value the book, but it leaves me free to run around for twenty minutes or so before she tires and I know she is safe. She picked up Jack's gloves and carried them one by one to the grate the other day and carefully put them on the hearth and patted them down, and she always makes a dead set for the poker! But sitting in the clothes basket with the peg bag and pulling them out and putting them back is a safe amusement for a rainy day. I wonder if she recognizes her cot and its trimmings.

I have found that green tomatoes ripen in the warm kitchen. We keep some on the dresser and often have them cooked for lunch, so I shall only make the small ones into pickles. They are such a nice change. We had two lovely cauliflowers for dinner tonight. We have had about a dozen already and many more are coming on. We have been eating our cockerels and saving a butcher's bill and I certainly find I like young chicken when you cannot recognize old favourites. The carrots, turnips, beets, and onions are all in the root-cellar and Jack is busy now on the potatoes. I have begun to embroider the light blue zephyr in red and blue ready for a frock for E. baby *if* we come home. Jack is out and will not be back until late.

Much love to you both from us both.

Your affectionate sister,

Daisy

HESTON,
ATHALMER, B.C.,
THURSDAY, [? 1914]

My dearest Freda,

Here we are again, mail day, and not a line put to my home letters! You must put it down to Red Cross work for that has taken up so much of our time, the material (red and white flannel) came and had to be cut out. There has been delay enough in getting materials so the only thing was to set to at once. On Wednesday we had to drive round to all the towns and arrange a meeting of the Committee or district collectors at our house yesterday (Thursday). Before that, Jack and I were busy cutting out lengths for pillowcases, surgical socks, and nightingales, and yesterday the various ladies took away bundles to distribute in their districts. We had to order needles, linen buttons, etc., and all this has to be worked out. They even demanded buttonhole tape to put on pillow cases! No time or too lazy to work buttonholes! Now we have to order more red flannel for more nightingales, but we have collected £30 for the funds and we are sending off $80 of it for a start to headquarters today. There are other collections going on for the Patriotic Fund, etc., so we feel as money is so short in the Valley we have done pretty well. We have met with very little opposition in the work. Mrs. Parham has been away for a three weeks' holiday and come home with pamphlets and red hot to start Red Cross work! Mr. Bennett, the Invermere district collector, explained we had started but no, she *must* do something herself. She has called a meeting at the schoolroom in Invermere this evening, so we settled that Jack must go down and make a statement of what we are already doing and explain matters. Dr. Hannington came up to fetch his wife yesterday and swelled our tea party. He is quite willing to carry on if we go—and keep up the accounts—and Mrs. MacKay in Athalmer will have the receiving depot at her house so that is fixed up. The bank manager has promised to audit our accounts and we shall post them in each town so all can see we are honest.

On Sunday the bank manager's mother (Mrs. Cornwall) and a little grandson who is staying with her came to lunch. Jack drove down to fetch her and I think the old lady enjoyed herself, also the small boy of seven, who is a vegetarian! We had tea at four and just as she left Mrs. Barber (the nice woman who has a ranch beyond the Poetts) rode up to see us with three little boys. Then shortly after came Captain and Mrs. Houlgrave and a man who is staying with them, and the cakes and scones only just held out. I think people are getting wind we are likely to go soon. On Monday afternoon (Washing Day) the whole Turnor family arrived to say goodbye! They had heard we were off at once, so rumour gets around. Jack gets quite annoyed at times and says there is as much excitement as if he were off to a convict settlement! Mr. Cornwall wants to buy the length of cretonne and likes our curtains and the Madras muslin too, I think. If we cannot sell the carpet and rugs they must go in the packing case. I sometimes feel it is all a dream when we talk so lightly of selling things, which are of no great value but all so precious as this has been our first home. Mrs. Houlgrave says she would like the pram as she is likely to have use for it soon.

I expect Jack will have news next week. N.C.O.'s are what they are very short of in training all these new men. The rumour of news yesterday which came through on the phone was bad all round, but I suppose we cannot expect to go straight ahead. Right must conquer in the end and the day of reckoning for Germany must come, as Jack says. In the meantime we must steel our hearts and try to be brave.

Thanks so much for the vest and gloves. It was quite "a bright" to send them as E. baby wanted the gloves for present use. She is so proud of them and holds up her hand and shows people. They are quite a nice shape, tell Mother. She does so object to anything on her feet but does not mind her hands being covered. All her words have disappeared now. She talks rubbish all the time, and has a little old diary from which she reads aloud. This is her present chief amusement. She stands in her cot the moment she is put in to lie down and we have many battles, but there is no sign of walking at present. I believe passages are quite easy to book now, and I suppose Amelia has to be carted home too. We have had a lovely little Indian Summer with glorious tints everywhere, but we have fires now. Am glad there is good news from Gilbert and that he has had his reward. I am trying to get a few

minutes to write old Stewart, but I keep everything washed up ready in case
we go and so I do not have much spare time. There is always mending or
sewing for Jack and E. baby in the evenings.

Much love to you and Mother from us all, and a big kiss from E. baby.
Your affectionate sister,

Daisy

HOTEL WINDERMERE
J. E. Stoddart, Proprietor

WINDERMERE, B.C.
SUNDAY, NOVEMBER 15TH, 1914

My dearest Freda,

I am not sure if it is your turn or Mother's but think it is yours. I am writing this letter chez nous *not* at Windermere, but Jack sneaked some notepaper as we thought you would be interested in seeing the Hotel. Well, on
Wednesday at 11:30 Nan and Molly arrived. We had everything ready for
them as we worked hard on Monday and Tuesday, with washing, ironing,
and cleaning up, leaving drawer and cupboard space in our room for their
things. We wrote out directions for E. baby's food, daily routine, and hours
for feeding chickens for Nan and a daily programme for Amelia, as they had
mid-day dinner and a sit-down tea. Nan is round and jolly and wears
glasses, knows all about babies, adores them, and is a very experienced
nurse so I had not the slightest fear in leaving her. They brought over a musical box and books and playthings of various kinds and I am quite sure
E. B. had the time of her life.

We left about noon, drove to Athalmer and called for the mail, and then
had a picnic lunch by the roadside. We then drove on to Windermere,
reaching there about three o'clock. We went straight to the little cemetery
and I tidied up the little graves[1] and put two wreathes that Nan had brought
over from Mrs. Marples (of course, home-made). Then we went to the
Hotel on the notepaper and booked our bedroom. It is very like a little
country inn at home only a wooden building, of course. The low building
was the original part, I think, and that is now the bar. Where they produced
three motorcars from, I cannot imagine. I guess that such a thing could only
happen about once a year! There are only about twelve houses—or wooden
cottages or bungalows, I should say—in the whole place and one made of
stone. But it is a lovely situation and from the Hotel one looks right onto the

1. The graves of the Young children.

lake. The parlour is the bow window on the right, and there we sat on the first evening. We had dinner at six: soup, beef, steak, cauliflower, potatoes, crab-apple jelly and sponge cake, and tea. Of course, we always drink tea with lunch and dinner. They had a piano in the parlour and on the piano the song "It's a long way to Tipperary," so we do not feel quite so out of it after all! We read the papers and talked to the village school-mistress (there are fourteen children at the school but many come from distant farms) and the proprietor's sister and then to bed. Such a relief not to have to change Elizabeth and get her bottle, and I felt two years younger by next morning when we started at ten. We bought apples, biscuits and chocolate at the store, and the man there told us it was rumoured that the *Emden* had been sunk![2] We drove on until 12:30, meeting one wagon and the mail coming in from Cranbrook, and stopped at a place called Fairmont which is really a big ranch owned by a Mr. Holland, a reported millionaire from Manchester! He is not here but has a manager, who came out and asked us in. But we ate our lunch sitting on some logs and then walked about. There is a hot spring and we saw its steam from quite a long way off. The spring rises on a small hill and leaves a greenish deposit. A bath has been made by an excavation, 4 feet by 3 feet deep, and over this an arbour is made of twisted fir branches and a small bench is provided. As it comes up the water is too hot to sit in, but an inlet of cold water is arranged. I quite wished we had some towels — a real bath with water all over would be such a treat. We had a drink of the water. It has only a very slight taste but I believe cures everything! It seems such a pity it is so far away from everybody but I suppose some day a syndicate will come and develop it. It is all on the opposite side of the lake to us. We then trotted on until five o'clock passing one other ranch called Thunder Hill. The owner's wife was drowned in the *Empress of Ireland* and the poor husband was so terribly upset he nearly went out of his mind. He went to England for a trip and is now in France or Belgium fighting and some cousins are looking after the farm. We then reached a place called Canal Flats, very impressive (28 miles from Windermere). We passed the upper Columbia Lake which is very pretty. It empties itself there and is all sandy marsh. However, the railway from Cranbrook has reached here (they are working from both ends) and there is a railway camp, and *one* house as well as the Hotel! We thought we might have a rough crew at dinner, but it was the middle of the week and the landlord gave us his own private sitting room for the evening and was most kind. He took us out to show us his two Ayrshire cows, and Berkshire sow and little pigs, also his turkeys and chickens which he had brought there from Toronto. Everything was beautifully clean here as at Windermere, and a Chinaman cook is the

2. The rumour was incorrect. The *Emden* was then operating in the Bay of Bengal as a successful raider of merchant shipping. She was sunk in 1915 in the South Pacific.

order of the day. We had soup, beef and boiled onions, slaw, and shallow apple pie and tea for dinner. The big gramophone was going all the evening to entertain the company in the bar and I very much enjoyed it too!

Next morning we woke to find nine inches of snow on the ground and it snowing hard. Nothing for it, we had to make a start and started at 8:30, Jack walking behind and I driving the horse at walking pace too. Your fur coat was indeed a blessing. I put on Jack's Burberry on top, and of course there were several men of the lumber or teamster order to see us off. One man came and hooked up the Burberry tight round my neck, saying "A new experience for you, but *not* for me!" It was slow going and the wheels clogged with snow but Jack never grumbled. He got in at all the downhill parts of the road and when I could I drove on and waited for him. At last we reached Fairmont again and Mr. Crawford (the manager) asked us in. He has a Chinaman who soon produced stewed chicken and vegetables, fig pudding and coffee (I think Mr. Crawford had just finished lunch) and this soon bucked us up and made us warm. From there on the snow was not so deep and we reached Windermere at five o'clock, quite happy and smiling. By this time I felt about ten years younger and had almost forgotten that Elizabeth belonged to us. We had dinner and then went to see Mr. and Mrs. Kingston. They have the *big* house and ranch at Windermere and are Canadians. Jack had met Mr. Kingston and he asked if we would go in and see them. I took my white Apsey voile for evenings. We had a very pleasant evening, Mrs. Kingston very chatty and Mr. Kingston somewhat like a ponderous pork butcher, though the biggest and best farmer here. A large house with underground heating and gratings in all the rooms. Jack says, "A very superior apartment look about everything," but *that* is Canadian! Linoleum-covered floors with plenty of rugs on top, a double sitting room divided by curtains—both large. A son of about 23, quite a nice youth, who owns a motorcar, but they have no such things as good pictures or silver. We talked war, and Mrs. Kingston was busy making helmets and body belts. Mr. Kingston wondered if it was possible to collect money for a motor ambulance from the East Kootenay District, so you see the Empire does exist! Neither he nor she had ever been to England. They gave us apples and (barley) maple sugar when we came away, and a pressing invitation for a weekend visit, but that is Canadian too! They are more than hospitable. We came home the next morning to find all very happy here, E. baby and Molly huge friends. Mr. Marples came to fetch them after tea. I feel it was awfully good of Mrs. Marples to have spared Nan, who is her right hand and so strong, and is devoted to them all.

Today we have been to see Mrs. Houlgrave. Her cousin left this week for the War and she is expecting the baby about the 21st of this month, poor little thing! She lives so far away, and as it means she would be left for two or three hours while her husband goes for the nurse and doctor, Jack suggested E. baby and I should go and stay with her on Thursday for a few days and we can leave directly the nurse comes. They live so far away, I am afraid she will have the "funks" if she is all alone. I have lent her my mackintosh sheet, binders and bed-pan, for which she is very grateful. Her washing basket is just as pretty as mine, only it is pink and white spotted muslin. Poor little baby being born in the snow, and last night it was only 2° above zero. E. baby has on all her woollies now and wore her white teddy-bear coat and bonnet today.

I wonder when we shall hear news of Nellie? I had a long letter from Daisy Mac this week and the short one from you, which I expected. We are not coming yet and you must not prepare. . . .

SATURDAY,
NOVEMBER 21ST, 1914

My dearest Freda,

Excuse pencil and a short letter but E. baby and I are staying with Captain and Mrs. Houlgrave for a few days. The new baby is expected today but has not come yet! They live a long way from the doctor and had a cousin living with them until last week but now he has gone home to join a corps and so there would be nobody here with Mrs. Houlgrave while *he* goes for doctor and nurse. Jack said he would spare us for a few days and is coming to see us tomorrow. Mrs. Houlgrave is quite young, dark hair and rosy cheeks and is *very* fit and well. They send all their washing to the Chinaman, and we are just keeping going with simple fare (brawn and fried pork chops as they have just killed a pig). I help with the housework and washing up all I can but it is really quite a holiday and not half such hard work as at home. I suppose I am too particular in the way things are kept, but I can't help that and Jack likes it too, also punctuality! Here they are very happy-go-lucky and I do not get up until 8:15 and then have time to wash E. baby before breakfast. She sleeps in the big bed with me and has not tumbled out yet! She looks such a sweet thing in her little sleeping suits and her curly head when she goes to bed, Captain Houlgrave spoils her and is always giving her "tit-bits" of sugar and strawberry jam so E. baby is in a constant state of saying "ta-ta" for everything she sees on the table. She and a small kitten have great games on the floor. We have not got her high chair here, so she is tied onto the rails of a sort of carving chair where she has plenty of room to move about. The snow is deep on the ground so Jack put some runners on a sugar box (as the pram can only be used on the verandah) and we brought that with us and I drag it about with a long rope. It is very deep and E. B. seems very comfy in it, though it is slow work pounding along.

While I think of it, will you send me some more "back and front" hair nets when you can get them and a pair of brown leather strap shoes, *size 5,* for E. baby. The red ones are very nice but I had better have a pair in reserve. Declare them below value! The Marples have asked us to go there on Christmas Day if we are here. I saw a letter from Mrs. Poett this week. The General has a Brigade in Kitchener's Army and is down at Purfleet. His son-in-law has gone home with Phyllis (from Vancouver) and has been made his Aide-de-camp, and Phyllis is living with Mrs. Poett in London. This all makes Jack wonder why he has not been called. Mrs. Poett says there is a shortage of officers. Edie Bird says they are eating their hearts out to be employed. Captain (now Major) F. B. Young is missing in the last casualty list. I hope he is only a prisoner.[1] I have just finished one pair of drawers, two year size, for E. baby from that set of patterns you ordered. I shall make three, also three of the princess-shaped petticoats. Will you buy me 6 yards embroidery edging, about ½"–¾" wide, and 6 yards insertion about ½" suitable for knickers, petticoats, etc. Also 6 yards Valencia lace for the neck and arms, about ½" wide. I shall need them whether we stay or come, so buy when convenient.

We packed and sent off our crate of Red Cross things this week, 166 articles: 43 pairs of socks, 31 nightingales, 12 pairs of cuffs, and the rest were pillowcases and towels. We have collected $185 all told, so that is not so bad, I think, and I am glad they have gone. No more time as Jack must take this.

Much love to you both,

Your affectionate sister,

Daisy

HESTON,
ATHALMER, B.C.
DECEMBER 7TH, 1914

My dearest Freda,

Directly we got the cable I sent you a pencil line and almost wish I had not as I am sure you will go rushing around and thinking we are coming "tomorrow," but here we are a week later and we have heard no more and do not expect to for another week. Jack wrote at once to the military authorities at Ottawa for instructions as it did not say in the cable. Canadian or British dealings with the War Office are always like this. It may mean they want Jack to come over with some of the Canadian troops. If so, then E. baby and I will come alone and I don't know what arrangements we shall make. Anyway, if alone I know I can write to Elsie and Walter to meet me

1. He was.

at Liverpool. You see, I have just to wait and see myself. It is no good supposing as we are sure to suppose the wrong thing! If Jack comes I expect he will not be at Merton more than a couple of days for shopping in London. We shall bring the cot, or rather it will be sent by freight with the silver straight to the Army and Navy Stores, also blankets, linen, etc. They unpack and air things for you, and I then can store what I do not want at Merton. I think *when* you hear we are coming you had better hire a cot for the first week or two. If you cannot get one at Woking, would Connie get one sent over from Willis at Windsor with option of buying—a second-hand one, of course. I wish we could bring the pretty pram but it would cost too much and our expenses will be very great as it is. I hope to sell the pram to Mrs. Houlgrave but shall not get much for it—but beggars cannot be choosers. We have packed our books and re-stencilled our luggage and packing cases. It is no good doing more until we know. We have made a list of all our grocery stores and shall try and sell them to other settlers. Jack will have to take them round on the wagon!

Jack rode out to see the good Mr. and Mrs. Newton,[1] about twenty miles away, to see if they were still quite willing to come and they are. They gave Jack a nice joint of venison, also a buck's head. There are plenty of deer near them. Jack has cured the skin and it is now drying, and the horns are quite good ones. Jack is now sitting opposite me skinning a squirrel, the third one, and I hope they will make E. baby a little muff. Captain Houlgrave came to dinner the night we had the venison and it was very good, crabapple jelly taking the place of redcurrant. I am letting him have bread while his wife is away. She was very bad and nearly died but she is coming on very well now and the baby is very healthy, a boy, Gerald Patrick. We hope to go and see him tomorrow, and as our hens and pullets are now giving us eggs I can take her some. It is great to have them at this time of year and we feel for once our luck is in. Yesterday (Sunday) we went to see the Edgehills and E. baby had a great time. Keith (aged 10), Frank (12), and Peggy (4) played with her all the time, giving her everything she asked for [or] demanded. However, finally she pushed Peggy out of it altogether and had the two boys to herself! I was helping Mrs. Edgehill, buttering scones for her in the kitchen, when a very forlorn little Peggy came in and said "Elwirbus would only play with Keith and Frankie." Joan, the elder daughter, whispered to her mother, then disappeared, afterwards bringing a most lovely "ugly" doll she had made and designed herself for E. baby for Christmas, but on seeing her she could not wait! She had made a head in linen, painted the face and hair herself. It has a brown, stockinette body and brown cloak with a red bow at the neck. It is awfully clever, as she has nowhere to gather her ideas. They are inside her, and she must be full of

1. Mr. Newton had agreed to look after their land and would eventually buy it.

them. She is only thirteen, writes fairy stories and poetry and draws figures and faces. "Did you copy his head, Joan?" I asked. "Oh, no. I just looked at Peggy's eyes to see how they were and drew the face." Her Christmas cards are all figures of children, all out of her head. I thought how you would enjoy helping her. She was very pleased when I explained how much cast shadows would improve one or two figures. Her mother paints very well and has nice broadwash sketches she did at St. Rhémy, Italy, and in Canterbury. She says sadly, "I have no time, Mrs. Phillips, to help my little Joany! I feel so sad." She also plays the piano charmingly though she has not had lessons for two years.

Joan and Peggy are coming to spend next Saturday with E. baby. I had made a big batch of Turkish Delight for Jack so took some over with us, and before we left they gave us a brace of grouse as their boys had shot eight. The two eldest boys were camping for a week after deer, as when the first snow comes the deer come down and it is easy to track them. Jack is disappointed he cannot go out, but with all the uncertainty and to save expense he did not take out a shooting licence. E. baby wore the woolly bonnet yesterday and it was much admired. She looks fine in it and carries it off well! She wears my little sable tie round her neck when driving, so this too found a place. Yes, her second jersey has come but not Jack's second vest. We also shall get $2 back on things you have sent E. baby the last few months. Jack wrote to the Commissioner of Customs and complained of charges, and this is the result. The good man here had been overreaching himself. Of course, he did not like it, but occasional presents of small value *are* allowed in free.

I am so glad to hear of the arrival of the puppy and am sure he will be a great pal. I think Tipperary is *the* right name—that is the name of E. B.'s ugly doll! We are not giving presents this year except to E. B. and to Stewart. It is very good of Mother to send us a pudding. I don't know if we shall be here for the 25th or not but I can make arrangements if you have been able to do my small commissions. I am so glad Stanley went to see old Gilbert, and that he is off to France and not to Egypt. I feel so very, very sorry for Nellie and Arthur but I did not mention it in my letter. I hoped to make Jean something, but under the circumstances I hope Nellie will understand if the small gift comes later. I am trying to keep everything mended right up so as to have nothing in my work bag, and the same with washing and ironing. Though whenever the time comes there must be soiled linen—table linen and underclothes—and washing bills in England quite alarm me!

I do so hope above all that our advent will not upset Bessie. Tell Mother not to worry about menus:

Breakfast   — Sausages

Dinner   — *Mutton*, not beef. Artichokes (we have not tasted them since we left), fruit tart of sorts,
and if fish — fried fish (we have not seen since we left).

You have mid-day dinner now so the fish can wait for the second day! E. baby loves bread and butter so *she* is quite easy, though I can't say if she will fall out with baker's bread after Mother's. If we come, I shall enjoy going to church so much and singing hymns. I am glad you have not done the cards. In so many cases they would not be appropriate. Jack's great friends in the Regiment, King and Johnson, the former killed and the latter wounded in the last list, both retired and called up. We only heard from King about five weeks ago. He was then so excited at the prospect of going and now Jack is sending his sympathies to Mrs. King. But you know what Jack is. He just shuts up about anything he feels. My income, like yours, is now so small. I shall only be able to afford a new hat, boots and shoes, though Jack talks of buying me a new evening dress. It is to be black with his lace on, I believe. He is now looking through *Punch* for a picture of a dress he *knows* he likes. I wore my black velvet on Sunday with your black velvet hat, and now have on my green silk. I live in my blue jersey for work. It is a boon and a blessing. I hope I shall not have to come without Jack, but if I must — well, I must.

Much love from us *all* to you both,

Your affectionate sister,

Daisy

ATHALMER, B.C.

[UNDATED]

Dear Freda,

I have just washed my fountain pen so you can watch this aenemic scrawl grow into a full blooded letter.

I thank you very much for the mitts which will prove most useful and comforting but I thank you far more for the family of swans. I have played with them then Daisy and I have played with them then Elizabubbles and I have played with them.

I expect a fortnight after you receive this we shall be putting in an appearance but you must not let Mrs. Oxley upset the house or herself on our account for our three years stay here have made us easily satisfied, and we shall give her ample notice by wire. Our only need which you might previously arrange if you would is the visit of the washerwoman the day after our arrival to take our fortnight or three weeks washing.

Of course though we talk of coming home we may be sent anywhere — we only presume I shall go home and not to India, Egypt or elsewhere. Then if we do come home our stay or the length of it will be very uncertain. I wish we could give you some definite news but it is most upsetting all round — most of all to us that we cannot [sentence unfinished]

Thanking you both once more for all the lovely presents to us.

I am (leaving Daisy to give you all the news).

John N. Phillips.

HESTON,
ATHALMER, B.C.
DECEMBER 22ND, 1914

My dear Mother and Freda,

This is only a line to let you know we are very busy packing up. No pictures left on the walls, no ornaments, no silver — all packed in the box which locks! We do not know how long notice we shall have, but Jack must be ready long before and it all helps to keep him going, he is so restless. It is sorting out clothing or stores which bothers me as there are so many things I know will be useless to store in England and yet I cannot bear parting with them. Jack is for throwing away everything about which there is a question, and I am giving various hats and blouses, also my white coat and skirt and my grey snowstorm tweed coat and skirt, to the Turnor children. These clothes are five years old and Jack keeps impressing on me that an officer's wife *must* be well dressed at all costs and I think of my banking account reduced to £9 per annum!

Your letters have always been a great joy. They were specially so at first and now at the last they will be too. These are rather trying days. Jack is so good and helps me along but I know I love every possession and corner of this place and there is no knowing when we shall see it again. I had a heavy day yesterday, washing up toilet covers and table linen to put away clean as I shall not have time to starch and iron. Jack was out and came back about five with a large mail. I was tempted and fell! — parcels for December 25th had the string cut quickly and soon E. baby and Jack were busy on the floor with a pie dish and the baby ducks while I opened the Union Jacks, lavender, calendar, and mitts, and the lovely purple duck on wheels which takes my fancy very much! Also, many papers as they have not come through for ten days — the *Queen, Lady's Pictorial,* etc. They all gave very, very great pleasure. The calendar is the only picture on the walls, so is in its glory! E. baby sat quiet, waving her flag for ages this morning. It quite takes her fancy, and tonight she and Jack had another "go" at the ducks, *each* lying full length on the floor! I have sent a flag to Peggy Edgehill as I made a big batch of almond toffee for them this morning. Gerald Turnor has one too as we were sending him some bon-bons we ordered from Eaton's, and I shall give the other to various small friends. I made lemon curd for Mrs. Sinclair and Mrs. Marples for Christmas gifts. I told you, we go to Paul Bennett's Christmas tree on Christmas Eve and to the Marples on Christmas Day. I intended E. baby to have a little tree of her own this year but it cannot be. The pudding, horse, etc., have not come yet but tell Mother *her* present and the horse shall be in E. baby's stocking in orthodox fashion. Will you see if you can match the ribbon enclosed for E. baby's bonnet strings, and buy a length as I cannot match it here. We hear that Whitby, Scarborough, and West Hartlepool have been bombarded with great loss of life. Why? is all we ask, but we may have authentic news soon. All Jack says is, "The act of a defeated nation! A fine thing for recruiting!"

Thank you both so much for the woollies for E. baby. The petticoat is lovely and the jersey just charming. I hope you will see her in them soon. The little shoes are just what I wanted, and the size is right as I like things big and can put wool in the toes. She wears her red ones and they please her much. I have washed the white shoes and put on little blue ribbon rosettes for her party and she will wear a silk dress that is still new! She can now say "please" and "tea" and sits for hours with a shawl or towel trying to dress herself up. I hope Miss Hall can lengthen my Harrods skirt and perhaps make me a silk skirt. I also hope our advent will not upset Bessie! I shall be really glad when the wrench of leaving is over and I have been able to put all I want in boxes and packing cases.

Much love to you both from us both and kisses from E. baby,

Daisy

INDEX